# THE VIKING IMMIGRANTS

Icelandic North Americans

STUDIES IN GENDER AND HISTORY

General Editors: Franca Iacovetta and Karen Dubinsky

# The Viking Immigrants
*Icelandic North Americans*

L.K. BERTRAM

UNIVERSITY OF TORONTO PRESS
Toronto Buffalo London

© University of Toronto Press 2020
Toronto Buffalo London
utorontopress.com

ISBN 978-1-4426-4551-6 (cloth)
ISBN 978-1-4426-1366-9 (paper)
ISBN 978-1-4426-6301-5 (EPUB)
ISBN 978-1-4426-6300-8 (PDF)

Studies in Gender and History

___

**Library and Archives Canada Cataloguing in Publication**

Title: The Viking immigrants : Icelandic North Americans / L.K. Bertram.
Names: Bertram, L.K., author.
Series: Studies in gender and history ; 49.
Description: Series statement: Studies in gender and history ; 49 | Includes bibliographical references and index.
Identifiers: Canadiana (print) 20190209801 | Canadiana (ebook) 2019020981X | ISBN 9781442645516 (cloth) | ISBN 9781442613669 (paper) | ISBN 9781442663008 (PDF) | ISBN 9781442663015 (EPUB)
Subjects: LCSH: Icelandic Americans – History. | LCSH: Icelandic Americans – Social life and customs. | LCSH: Icelanders – Canada – History. | LCSH: Icelanders – United States – History. | LCSH: Immigrants – Canada – History. | LCSH: Immigrants – United States – History. | CSH: Icelandic Canadians – History. | CSH: Icelandic Canadians – Social life and customs.
Classification: LCC FC106.I3 B47 2020 | DDC 971/.0043961–dc23

___

University of Toronto Press acknowledges the financial assistance to its publishing program of the Canada Council for the Arts and the Ontario Arts Council, an agency of the Government of Ontario.

 Canada Council for the Arts    Conseil des Arts du Canada

Funded by the Government of Canada    Financé par le gouvernement du Canada

*For my family*

# Contents

*List of Illustrations*  ix

*Acknowledgments*  xi

Introduction  3

1  Dressing Up: Clothing and Upward Mobility in the Early Immigrant Community, 1870–1900  24

2  The Coffee Pot and King Bacchus: Icelandic Immigrant Drinking Cultures  54

3  Unsettling Apparitions: Power, Ghost Stories, and Superstitious Belief  76

4  Main Street Vikings: Anglicization, Spectacle, and the Two World Wars  101

5  Icelandic Cake Fight: A Brief History of *Vínarterta*  135

Conclusion  161

*Appendix: Historical* **Vínarterta** *Recipes*  167

*Notes*  175

*Bibliography*  211

*Index*  229

# Illustrations

A    Sigfús Eymundsson, *Hópmynd, Vesturfari*, 1886. Group of Icelandic emigrants aboard the *Camoens*, departing from Langanes, Norður Þingeyjarsýsla, Iceland  4
B    Guðleif Stefánsdóttir and Kristján Stefánsson  9
C    Helgi Einarsson and his three sons, Henry, William, and John, March 1946  15
1.1    Friðjón and Guðný Friðriksson with their daughter Aurora, ca. 1880  25
1.2    Woman wearing *peysuföt* and *skotthúfa*  29
1.3    W.E. Bowman, *"The Little Esquimaux Lady," Miss Olof Krarer*, 1889  34
1.4    L.B. Foote, *Thordur G. Thordarson in Winter Clothing*, ca. 1915  41
1.5    L.B. Foote, *Fishermen Posing with Catch Taken through the Ice of Lake Winnipeg near Riverton, Manitoba*  42
1.6    Sigtryggur Jónasson and Rannveig Briem  45
1.7    G.W. Searle, portrait of Sigríður Jónsdóttir, Winnipeg, ca. 1885  46
1.8    Portrait of Aðalbjörg and Sigríður Jóakimsdóttir from Árbót in Aðaldalur, Þingeyjarsýsla, Iceland, after their arrival in Milwaukee, ca. 1874  48
1.9    The Icelandic Women's Society, Winnipeg, mid-1880s  51
2.1    *"Kaffi fært raktstrakonum um 1910"* [Coffee being served to women raking hay around 1910]  58
2.2    Coffee in a turn-of-the-twentieth-century Icelandic farmhouse in Brownbyggð, MB  63
2.3    Guðrún Búason, 1913  67
2.4    Long-haired Jóhannes ("long-haired Joe") Stefánsson and unknown companion  70

3.1   Guttormur Guttormsson visiting Betsey
      and John Ramsay's graves near Riverton, MB   91
3.2   Graftarnes, MB, and surrounding farms   95
3.3   Bergljót Sigurdsson   98
4.1   John David Eaton and Signy Stephenson
      on their wedding day, Winnipeg, 1933   102
4.2   Viking ship float featuring costumed Icelanders during
      Winnipeg's Diamond Jubilee celebrations, 18 June 1924   105
4.3   Enlistment advertisement for the 223rd
      Canadian Scandinavians   112
4.4   Badge from the 223rd Canadian Scandinavians   113
4.5   J.B. Zwecker, *The Fjallkona*   119
4.6   The "bald" *Fjallkona*, Sigrún Lindal, 1924   120
4.7   Norwegian SS poster, 1943   123
4.8   *Last Day as Neighbours.* Japanese internment
      at the Osland settlement, 1942   127
4.9   Promotional photograph of Sonja Henie and John Payne
      in *Iceland*, 1942   131
4.10  Unveiling of the Gimli Viking statue, 1967   133
4.11  Signy Eaton as the *Fjallkona,* with Wilhelm
      Kristjansson, 1967   133
5.1   Nelson Gerrard, photograph of *vínarterta* prepared
      by Arden Jackson, 2016   136
5.2   Jóna Goodman (Mrs. Svein Peterson)   148
5.3   Step-by-step *vínarterta* preparation instructions   149
A.1   Aðalbjörg Benediktsdóttir Brandson's Icelandic Cake,
      from her 1936 recipe   170
A.2   Jóna Peterson's recipe for her seven-layer *vínarterta*, 1949   172
A.3   Helen Josephson's 1962 recipe for her famous six-layer
      *vínarterta*, known as *the* Winnipeg *vínarterta*   173

# Acknowledgments

This is a long acknowledgments section. Fifteen years have passed since research on the earliest components of this book began, and over this stretch of time I have travelled thousands of miles, learned a difficult but beautiful language, and benefited from the help, insight, and support of a very large number of people. First and foremost, I must thank my doctoral supervisor, Franca Iacovetta. I first encountered her amazing work as an undergrad, and I often pinched myself at how lucky I was to be able to work with such a brilliant scholar of gender and migration history. I cannot thank her enough for her time, her support, and her generosity. The members of my doctoral committee, Elspeth Brown and Steve Penfold, in addition to Adrienne Hood and Ian Radforth, formed a wonderful network of intellectual guidance and support that was critical to the creation of this book. My excellent postdoctoral supervisors, Adele Perry, Gísli Pálsson, and Frances Swyripa, also helped me explore critical parts of this book that emerged after my defence.

A large network of friends, scholars, and supporters welcomed me to Iceland to do research and helped me tackle the rich collections there. This included Atli Ásmundsson, Consul General for Iceland in Winnipeg; and Þrúður Helgadóttir, who I must make special mention of for their incredible support. In 2006, Atli helped arrange for me to travel to Iceland for the first time to present my research, and the trip opened up a whole new universe. His support, personal insights, and encouragement over the following decade were sincerely appreciated. So, too, were my dear friends Sigurjón Baldur Hafsteinsson and Tinna Gréttarsdóttir, essential to the process of researching and writing. Their beautiful kitchen on Blómvallagata hosted many engaging and challenging discussions and warm, welcoming evenings, while their critical insights and innovative research pushed me to consider new dimensions in my theoretical approach to this history. Their advocacy and generosity over the years were essential to accessing the rich, varied, and enormous archives and collections in Iceland. My launch into Icelandic archives would not have been possible without the support of excellent language teachers like Haraldur Bessason, Margrét Björgvinsdóttir, and Helga Hilmisdóttir. Dear friends, including Lovísa Arnardóttir, Cameron Corbett, Bradley Sykes, Bergur Benediktsson, Rán Ingvarsdóttir, Atli Bollason, Egill Guðmundsson, Helga Þors, Ragnheiður Kjærnested, Steindor Grétar Jónsson, and many more, made time in Iceland very bright.

At home in the North American west, I found a warm welcome from Icelandic communities on both sides of the border. This included major original settlements like Gimli, Riverton, and Winnipeg in Manitoba and Mountain in North Dakota. There were also the "newer" (post-1885) settlements that I had never visited before, such as the fascinating town of Wynyard, Saskatchewan, and surrounding sites; the tight-knit communities in Alberta; and the beautiful landscape that surrounded the groups that had settled in British Columbia and Washington. Here I encountered countless community members who invited me into their homes; dug up old photographs, recipe books, and heirlooms; and/or generously offered their memories and important insights. These people include Margret Wishnowski; Lynne Johannesson-Bazilewich; Carol Hryhorchuk; Charlie and Connie Ostertag; the late Captain J.D. Clifford and his wife, Beverly Stevens; Ruth Christie; Barry Magnusson and family; the late Thomas Finnbogason; Malla Jeroski; Metta Johnson; Einar and Rosalind Vigfusson; Donald Gislason; the late Robert Ásgeirsson; Maxine Ingalls; Erla Jónasson; Elva Simundsson; the late Ken Melsted and family; Metta Johnson; Blair, Cliff, and Lilja Holm; Meredith MacFarquhar; the late Leona Morrow; the Honourable Janis Johnson; Bragi Simundsson; Dilla Narfason; Wanda Anderson; Janis Ólöf Magnusson; Ben Sigurdson; Jen Miller; Heather Ireland; Arden Jackson; Joe Martin; and Agnes Bardal Comack.

I am also indebted to a number of archivists, librarians, museum curators, and administrators, in both North America and Iceland, who helped me access and think about the large collections on both sides of the Atlantic. These include the staff at Landsbókasafn (National Library of Iceland) and Þjóðminjasafn (National Museum of Iceland), the late Sigrid Johnson at the University of Manitoba, Tammy Axelsson and Julianna Roberts (especially for her cookbook sleuthing) at the New Iceland Heritage Museum as well as the staff at the Manitoba Museum, the Provincial Archives of Manitoba, Rare Books and Special Collections at the University of British Columbia, the Western Canada Pictorial Index, and Library and Archives Canada. This research was made possible by generous funding from several agencies, to whom I am deeply grateful. These include doctoral and post-doctoral support from the Social Sciences and Humanities Research Council of Canada, the Icelandic Centre for Research, the Grant Notley Fellowship at the University of Alberta, and the University of Toronto. Kind thanks also to the editorial board at the journal *Gastronomica*, who published an earlier version of my vínarterta research as "Icelandic Cake Fight: History of a Recipe's Migration" (*Gastronomica* 19, no. 4, Winter 2019). Support from organizations like Núnanow, the Icelandic Canadian Club of Toronto, the Icelandic National League, and the *Lögberg-Heimskringla* community newspaper have made a meaningful contribution both to research and to community outreach.

My editor, Len Husband, has been more than patient, generous, and supportive, and I owe a major debt to him for all his time and quality advice. Thank you, Len, for the many productive and challenging meetings, which also managed to be tremendously enjoyable. UTP is a wonderful place to publish a monograph. I must also thank the anonymous reviewers who invested so much of their time in reviewing my manuscript, and provided such productive and very helpful feedback and guidance, as well as Stephanie Stone for her excellent work on the final stages of the book. Special thanks also to the brilliant artist, Charlene Kasdorf, who designed the image for the book's cover and was one of my very earliest collaborators.

Friends and colleagues also provided incredible encouragement and advice during various stages of this project, including my wonderful fellow faculty: Heidi Bohaker, Carol Chin, Sean Mills, Melanie Newton, Alison Smith, Nick Terpstra, Yiwen Wang, and Lori Loeb. Special mention goes to Camille Bégin, Nadia Jones-Gailani, Maggie McDonald, Jo Snyder, Robbie Richardson, and Ryan van Huijstee for their invaluable support in the earliest years of this project. I must also thank Maya Fontaine, Sarah Michaelson, Lorena Fontaine, Kegan McFadden, Ryan Eyford, Freya Olafson, Jón Olafson, and the late Donald Bailey (University of Winnipeg) for their insights, encouragement, and friendship. Emily Albertsen and Martin Albertsen provided excellent translations of rare, early recipes that were not only incredibly helpful for this study but that will also, I hope, be of great interest to the larger Icelandic community.

I gave birth to two very good babies during the production of this book, twins Siggi and Magnús, and I would like to thank them for making the last two years of work on this book so memorable. Although they are *exceptionally* good babies, I learned first-hand why so many mothers are not able to publish their work – both now and a century and a half ago. A network of strong individuals and close friends came together to help out at home and make sure that my work was not totally derailed during the dangerous traverse across Diaper Mountain. I owe them tremendous gratitude. To my family and the genius and hard work of Kem Campbell, Wendy Johnson, and Kristen Brown, as well as Kate Sjoberg, Mylee Nordin, Sayla Nordin, Hilary Nordin, Sula Johnson, Dave Lucas, Brenda Johnson, Steph Guthrie, Tom Dorey, Cheryl Gudz, Caroline Young, Denis Brown, April Aandal, Latisha Thomas, Nat Cooper, Peter Carrington, Laura Day, James Lourenco, Heidi Ackerman, Lindsay Sinclair, and Bryna Johnson, I say thank you so much.

I also owe special mention to *móðirbroðir minn* (my uncle) Nelson Gerrard, genealogist and historian, for his extensive support and access to the Eyrarbakki Icelandic Heritage Centre archives. Many of the images in this book come from this large collection, while Nelson's attention to detail was essential to recovering the stories of so many people who scattered across the continent and might otherwise be totally lost from the collective record. It is through Nelson that I have been able to access many rare and valuable accounts left by the community outside major institutional archives – both in print and in oral narratives. In a sheep-feed shed equipped with a coffeemaker at Viðivellir, his farm on the outskirts of Riverton, or by the fireplace at his house at Eyrarbakki, Nelson's countless early stories from the community – some dating back over two centuries – enriched this book and the process of creating it.

Last, but certainly not least, I must reserve a special place for thanking my wonderful family for their support. Caitlin Brown, my partner in life, has provided almost a decade of innovative insight, constructive feedback, and Herculean co-parenting. For all her thoughtful and productive comments about structure and context, and for everything else, I say thank you so much. My parents, Christine and Laurence, have long supported my archive fever, with innumerable historical family road trips; long, prairie driving discussions and debates; car loans for oral history treks; and warm, irreplaceable support. To them and to my siblings, Stephen and Andrea, I say thank you very much for everything you have done to make this project come to life and your generosity over the years. My grandparents, Jean and Tom Bertram and George and Helga Gerrard, further fostered my inspiration for this book with their own dedication to community history.

Personal note: In a striking coincidence, I finished the copy edits on this book the same day that I drove up to Shoal Lake, Manitoba, to sit and have coffee for the last time with my 99-and-a-half-year-old Amma, Helga (Olafson) Gerrard. She left this world the next day as

I sat beside her, my mother, and my aunt. My Amma was a farm wife and self-taught curator, who inspired my approach to this book and its focus on everyday people, life, and labour. Growing up, I often watched my Amma manage huge family dinners and many sink-loads of dishes before sitting down to work on her own family history books or small exhibits for the local museum in Strathclair on topics like knitting machines or church hats. These projects and her many stories about Riverton, Winnipeg, and Iceland often took us late into the night. I look back fondly over these chapters as a reminder of the many conversations and cups of coffee that I had with her and others from the community who helped make this book possible.

# THE VIKING IMMIGRANTS

Icelandic North Americans

# Introduction

I grew up in an Icelandic and Scottish family in Manitoba, home to the largest concentration of Icelandic people outside that far-northern country. It is relatively easy to spot Icelandic immigrant culture in this part of North America, including Icelandic food traditions, Icelandic flags, and the Viking-ship parade floats that appear in the summer, "sailing" along the main streets of Icelandic towns like Mountain, North Dakota; and Gimli, Manitoba, the capital of New Iceland. Icelandic identity remains strong among many of the descendants of those who arrived in Canada and the United States between 1870 and 1914 (Figure A). Despite numerous predictions of the "impending death of the community" over the years, signs of growth and continued cultural production among North Americans of Icelandic descent endure. Indeed, the number of Canadians who identify as Icelandic has actually increased, from roughly 70,000 in 1996 to over 100,000 in 2016, although respondents are now third-, fourth-, fifth-, and sixth-generation descendants of the immigrant generation.[1]

How can we account for this continued identification? From the 1870s onward, Icelanders were accepted by the Canadian and American governments based on claims that they would be loyal "Viking" citizens in anglophone North America and ultimately blend into the dominant settler population. How has their sense of identity and cultural continuity persisted after a century and a half of dramatic change, anglicization, and conflict?

Arjun Appadurai and Matthew Frye Jacobson argue that immigrant cultures have a texture – they are three-dimensional and "profoundly interactive."[2] From what they eat to what they wear, community members' sense of touch, smell, and taste all contribute to identity formation. I grew up steeped in this kind of three-dimensional culture, surrounded by what I thought were quintessentially Icelandic habits,

Figure A. Sigfús Eymundsson, *Hópmynd, Vesturfari*, 1886. Group of Icelandic emigrants aboard the *Camoens*, departing from Langanes, Norður Þingeyjarsýsla, Iceland. Þjóðminjasafn/National Museum of Iceland (ÞMS), Reykjavík.

customs, and material culture or objects. These included Viking-themed tea towels and Scotch glasses, a penchant for all-night coffee-drinking, the preservation of exceptionally terrifying ghost stories, and the consumption of Icelandic foods like the striped torte, *vínarterta*. Although I, and many others like me, grew up surrounded by these kinds of traditions and habits, most of us had never been to Iceland itself. In 2006, I began to act as an informal tour guide to numerous Icelandic artists and performers from Reykjavík through Núnanow, an art and music festival designed to build bridges between modern Icelanders and the descendants of Icelandic immigrants. Imagine my surprise when group after group of these Icelandic visitors looked around at the cultural landscape and traditions of the immigrant community that were so familiar to me – so "Icelandic" – and said, "I've never seen this before."

In 2006, I also travelled to Iceland for the first time, and I realized the differences between the evolution of modern Icelandic culture and society and the evolution of the Icelandic North American culture I knew so well. The nineteenth-century rural society that had produced the immigrant generation was a distant memory to modern Icelanders, whose society had been transformed by the modernization and urbanization that accompanied the occupation of their country by the Allies and NATO, beginning in 1940. I was fascinated by the differences I observed in Iceland and the confusion of the Icelandic artists and musicians I met in Canada about how antiquated and unusual Icelandic North American culture and identity seemed to them. In school, they had learned almost nothing about the immigration of roughly 20 to 25 per cent of the population of Iceland to North America and the distinctive culture that had emerged here. They questioned me about the many differences they observed as we visited old Icelandic sites and centres like Winnipeg's West End, Gimli, Riverton, and Arborg. Their questions revealed much about the divergent paths taken by our ancestors more than a century ago: Why do so few people speak Icelandic anymore? Why do most Icelandic people here have English names? Why are people so obsessed with *vínarterta* (people don't really make it in Iceland any more)? What is with the Viking statues? What is a *goolie* (ethnic slang for an Icelander)?[3]

Similar questions about food and popular practices could be asked of a range of North American immigrant communities, whose traditions and culture now differ so widely from the countries their families left a century and a half ago. Of course, it is tempting to write a cultural history of an immigrant community that focuses on continuity with the homeland and the preservation of tradition, particularly given the enduring power of the image of the Viking immigrant so common in North American Icelandic and Scandinavian communities. However, this would ignore the vast history of change that Icelandic immigrants and their descendants have experienced since 1870. Instead, this book focuses on the unseen qualities – the *immigrant* habits, ideas, and traditions observed by so many Icelandic visitors and the distinctive, everyday popular culture that emerged in North American Icelandic communities.

Despite the frequent references to the Viking Age, this was a culture rooted in the nineteenth-century Icelandic society that produced the immigrant generations and was shaped by conditions in nineteenth- and twentieth-century North America. Here Icelanders crafted new

"Viking" and ethnic identities to gain acceptance, using the high regard for Viking Age history and literature and notions of "Scandinavian" racial compatibility in nineteenth-century anglophone North America in an attempt to deflect widespread anti-immigrant sentiment. Moving beyond ideas about cultural authenticity, cultural preservation (especially language retention), and assimilation, which continue to define the narrative of Icelandic migration, we begin to see a new world of complex immigrant cultural practices that did not and do not exist, at least in the same way, at home in Iceland. Instead, they were and are, to quote a popular novelty button from Gimli in the 1990s, "Made in Canada with Icelandic parts."

This book joins the ranks of works that seek to interpret and understand the cultural history of North American communities in new ways.[4] It also challenges popular existing portrayals of the Icelandic community and others as nation-building pioneers; a rustic, unscathed, nineteenth-century time capsule; or a fully assimilated, colourful, Viking-themed pageant that exists only in multicultural spectacles. Although this project began as an Icelandic offering to North American immigration-history scholarship,[5] it gradually became part of a response to the official silence that surrounds the emigration in Iceland – and so many other northern European countries that sent thousands of immigrants to North America, including Norway, Sweden, and Denmark. As with these Scandinavian countries that produced huge numbers of emigrants destined for North America in the nineteenth century, Iceland lacks a strong connection to its emigrant past. For decades, anti-emigration sentiment there meant that references to the departure of almost one-quarter of the country's population were muted or simply absent from national histories. As a result, many Icelanders and Scandinavians simply do not know how to explain, or totally ignore, the distinctive, alien-seeming cultures of their distant cousins in North America. A growing historiography and important initiatives in Iceland – including cultural exchanges, the establishment of heritage centres, television and radio programs, and even popular Icelandic emigration tours to North America – have attempted to resolve these omissions, but the gap endures.[6]

Despite the silence surrounding this migration in Icelandic official national histories, numerous scholars and journalists have studied the immigrant community, and many Icelanders have taken an interest in the subject.[7] But it is the Icelandic-language literary output of the immigrant community that has attracted the lion's share of that interest.[8] Much remains to be done to understand the larger, longer history of the migration, particularly the endurance of community identity after mass migration ended in 1914, as well as the experiences of everyday Icelandic North Americans beyond ethnic organizations.[9] In their work on ethnic heritage spectacles, memory, and commemoration, Anne Brydon, Jónas Thor, Frances Swyripa, and Tinna Gréttarsdóttir's groundbreaking works also point to the richness of community life after migration ended.[10] Together with a sizeable collection of community-authored texts and memoirs, these studies resist the idea of "cultural death" or the larger tendency to treat anglicization as the final chapter in the community's history.[11]

Such predictions about the death of the Icelandic North American community also fail to account for its stubborn endurance in the twentieth and twenty-first centuries and the compelling and distinctive alternative archives it has produced. From large collections of oral ghost stories to film, food culture, fashion, and Viking ephemera, much of which remains largely unexamined, Icelandic North American cultural production did not grind to a halt following anglicization. By analysing the roots of some of these popular and commonplace traditions – particularly those previously dismissed as trivial and taboo or linked to women or other marginalized historical characters – this study seeks to shed new light on cultural change in the community. More than documenting a history of community leaders or institutions, it reveals how everyday forms of cultural production, from making coffee to altering clothing, can shed new light on major generational shifts and cultural transformation.

## A Brief History of *Vestur Íslendingar*

Known in Icelandic as *Vestur Íslendingar*, or "Western Icelanders," the Icelandic North American community was founded in the late nineteenth century, when at least 14,268 Icelanders, or roughly 20 per cent of the population of Iceland, departed for Canada and the United States between 1870 and 1914.[12] This number accounts for only those whose departure was confirmed in Icelandic records; however, the "record is certainly far from complete and the number of those lacking may run into the thousands."[13] Volcanic activity and climatic pressures, including long periods of very poor weather, made life on the island difficult in the eighteenth and nineteenth centuries, and they have often been blamed for this exodus.[14] Indeed, areas of Iceland most severely affected by pack ice produced many of the emigrants who would travel to North America. In 1875, the year New Iceland was founded along the shores of Lake Winnipeg, the volcano Askja erupted, showering parts of eastern Iceland with ash and poisonous gas, and motivating departures from that part of the island.

Although geography and climate loom large in Icelandic history, scholars have also debated the role of human factors in the nineteenth-century mass emigration of Icelanders to the Americas. Icelandic nationalism, fanned by the movement for independence from Denmark, has dramatically shaped the depictions of the migration era and the forces that made migration desirable. Guðmundur Hálfdánarson argues that a tendency to only blame climate and Danish control in fostering poorer conditions on the island has deflected critiques from Iceland's home-grown, rigid socio-economic system. Many of the problems that helped fuel nineteenth-century emigration came from Icelandic society itself, he writes. This included "an almost religious adherence" to the country's "rigid system of socialization," which trapped labouring Icelanders in poverty, with little room for upward mobility.[15] A growing population placed additional strains on Icelandic society during this period, fostering frustration and desperation among the poor and the working class. Statistics Iceland reports that, between 1870 and 1914, Iceland's population increased from 69,463 to 87,137, in spite of the population drain created by emigration.[16] Few opportunities existed for developing new farms, thereby fuelling overcrowded housing and poverty on farms and in towns.[17]

In the late nineteenth century, poor and working-class Icelanders suffered most under the country's existing economic and social structures and so were doubly motivated to migrate.[18] Sometimes officials also paid to effectively deport struggling families and individuals – like the siblings Guðleif Stefánsdóttir and Kristján Stefánsson, who were sent in 1887 and 1888, respectively – to rid the community of the financial burden of care[19] (Figure B). Other officials, however, opposed large-scale emigration. The rigid control of Iceland's landless working class benefited the country's landholding class, who depended on large pools of cheap labour to turn a profit in the country's rural industries of farming and fishing. As a result, many Icelandic nationalists, public officials, clergymen, and landholders often staunchly opposed departures for *Amerîka*. They accused emigrants of betraying their homeland and attempted to disrupt emigration by spreading disturbing claims about life in the new land, including reports of cannibalism, and interrupting public information sessions about emigration.[20]

Figure B. Guðleif Stefánsdóttir and Kristján Stefánsson. Undated photograph. Eyrarbakki Icelandic Heritage Centre (EIHC), Hnausa, MB.

## The Migration Era

Those considering migration viewed the success of their nineteenth-century Norwegian, Swedish, and Danish counterparts in North America as an example of the possibilities that migration could offer. They also framed migration as an extension of the Viking Age travels of Icelanders and others to North America around the year 1000, embracing Leifur "the Lucky" Eiríksson as their unofficial patron saint.[21] As part of a society in which the medieval Icelandic sagas remained an important part of popular culture, they argued that Icelanders were seeking freedom and opportunity in the very land that their saga-era forebears once had.[22] Two earlier, smaller, international nineteenth-century migration schemes had preceded the major waves of emigrants in the 1870s. In 1855, a small group of Icelanders left for Utah after visits from Mormon missionaries ended in successful conversions, and over the next decades, more than 400 Icelandic emigrants followed this initial party, settling mainly alongside Danish converts at Spanish Fork, Utah.[23] In addition to religious conviction, promises of better wages, food security, and improved climate and health clearly influenced this early departure for North America.[24]

Other emigration schemes did not fare so well, including an ill-fated proposal for a renewed Icelandic colony in Greenland, where Leifur Eiríksson and others had lived between the tenth and fifteenth centuries.[25] In the 1860s, some Icelanders also examined the possibility of a colony in Brazil in response to a larger European Brazilian migration movement in the mid-nineteenth century, which promised migrant farmers lucrative shares in the country's coffee industry.[26] In 1863, a small party of Icelanders left for Brazil, but innumerable delays and complications hampered their actual travel. Of the hundreds of Icelanders who added their names to a list of those willing to make the journey, only thirty-four actually did so.[27]

Despite their relatively small numbers, these earlier settlements in Brazil and Utah were conceptually significant, reflecting growing dissatisfaction with conditions at home and a growing awareness of migration options – conceiving of life far beyond Iceland's borders. A much larger wave of Icelanders embraced renewed opportunities for emigration to North America in the 1870s, but often struggled with choosing between settlement in Canada and settlement in the United States. In 1870, a small group began the exodus to North America, settling on Washington Island in Lake Michigan after reading of good conditions in letters from William Wickmann, a Danish immigrant who had lived in Iceland.[28] Rather than staying in one place, migrants[29] often relocated numerous times after they arrived, including frequently moving across the 49th parallel in an attempt to secure better wages and homestead lands. Migrant leaders and agents wrestled with the difficult task of both attracting and securing permanent settlers for a range of settlement projects. Páll Thorláksson (Þorláksson) became the primary advocate and organizer for early immigration to the United States, while Sigtryggur Jónasson promoted and organized large-scale Icelandic settlement in Canada.

Conflicts between American and Canadian settlements signalled a larger political and spiritual divide in the early migrant community. Thorláksson encouraged Icelandic immigrants to the United States to follow the pattern of adaptation established by the Norwegian communities in Wisconsin by working as labourers on Norwegian farms until they were able to establish their own homesteads,[30] and he promoted the faith of the Norwegian Lutheran Synod. Two other Icelandic leaders in Wisconsin during this period, the Rev. Jón Bjarnason and editor Jón Ólafsson (who himself had fled Iceland to avoid charges of "a scathing attack he had printed against Danish officialdom"), eventually settled in Canada and accused Páll of promoting assimilation and subservience to the strict Norwegian Synod.[31] They argued that Icelanders should establish their own colony in North America, where the community would be, to some degree, sheltered – linguistically, spiritually, and culturally – from outside influence. Most immigrant leaders ultimately turned away from this protectionist view, as explained further in chapter 1. This original desire prompted Jón Ólafsson to develop an ill-fated plan for Icelandic settlement in America's newly purchased Alaskan Territory.[32] Dreams of a new Iceland in Alaska failed, but the ideological and spiritual divides among Jón Ólafsson, Jón Bjarnason, and Páll Thorláksson would shape the new Icelandic settlements in Canada and the United States.

## Towards a New Iceland

By the time Icelandic settlers began arriving in North America in the 1870s, a considerable amount of the prime land suited to settlement had already been appropriated by decades of mass migration from other parts of Europe. The Canadian government hoped to attract new arrivals farther north, into the vast territory it had purchased from the Hudson's Bay Company in 1869, without consulting with the territory's many inhabitants. The west also suited Icelandic settlers and their plans for their own colony, one that could offer some degree of cultural autonomy. The first two groups of Icelanders arrived in Ontario in 1873 and 1874 near

Rosseau and Kinmount. However, employment, accommodations, provisions, and homesteading prospects there proved insufficient, and the immigrants struggled with hunger, cold, hard labour, and disease in a heavily wooded and rocky area not suited to farming. About eighty of these early migrants also decided to try settling in Nova Scotia in 1875, establishing a community known as Markland, a reference to both the area's dense forests and the legendary settlement described in the Icelandic sagas. These settlers also found the area a poor fit, and, as news spread of better opportunities in the west, Markland had largely evaporated by 1882.[33]

Migrant leaders seeking alternatives to these early, ill-suited settlement locations then received favourable reports about possibilities in or beyond the newly founded province of Manitoba. Scouts representing Icelanders in Ontario and Wisconsin eventually selected land on the western shore of Lake Winnipeg, beginning seventy-five kilometres north of Winnipeg – at the northern border of Manitoba, as it then existed. Sigtryggur Jónasson and John Taylor then lobbied members of the federal government for funds to relocate the Ontario group and reportedly encountered some resistance until word of the request reached the governor general of Canada, Lord Dufferin.[34] Fortunately for the Icelandic delegation, Dufferin had a well-established interest in Icelandic history, culture, and geography.[35] He had visited the island as a young man in 1856, one of many early "gentleman travellers" who were drawn to its natural wonders and medieval "Viking" past.[36] Dufferin evidently intervened on the group's behalf and helped to secure support for the move west. Sigtryggur then returned to Iceland to promote the new settlement site, while Taylor accompanied the majority of the Kinmount group west in the late summer of 1875.

Winter was approaching when the Icelandic group arrived in Winnipeg on 11 October. Some stayed in Winnipeg and secured work, while the bulk of the group pressed on to the New Iceland settlement on Lake Winnipeg. On 21 October 1875, the settlers arrived at Willow Point, just south of present-day Gimli – a place that has since become a significant site of commemoration in the Icelandic community. Although the weather had been unseasonably warm, they were disappointed to find that few preparations had been made for their arrival. The Icelandic arrivals found the physical conditions along the shores of Lake Winnipeg incredibly different from those in Iceland. Accustomed to building houses out of turf in their treeless island home, they struggled to erect log cabins for themselves in a new townsite. They called the site Gimli, a name from the *Prose Edda* that described the place where the worthy went after *ragnarök*, the end of the world.

## "The Republic of New Iceland"

Historical debate surrounds the establishment of a unique form of local government in the Lake Winnipeg settlement, frequently and mistakenly represented in recent decades as "The Republic of New Iceland."[37] The primary focus of the governing council was municipal governance and civic administration. It is clear that the council did not intend to supplant the Canadian state, to which it was directly responsible, nor did it attempt to implement any laws in areas of federal jurisdiction, although it did reflect the desire of the Icelandic immigrants for a degree of political and cultural autonomy. The so-called republic has since become a popular topic for some twentieth- and twenty-first-century community members, who think of it as an autonomous migrant state created within a larger, imagined tradition of Icelandic freedom and independence. Rather than reflecting the political nature of the original settlement, the Republic of New Iceland represents the broader popularity of the idea of self-government imported by migrants who had left Iceland at the height of that country's movement for political autonomy from Denmark in the nineteenth century.

Although numerous Icelanders hoped to establish a new, linguistically and culturally cohesive colony capable of reviving and preserving their culture in North America, conflict, disease, poor weather, and poverty undermined this vision. In New Iceland, bad drainage, dense bush, inexperience, and relative isolation hampered early farming efforts, and settlers were forced to subsist on a diet composed almost entirely of fish and potatoes. Reports of the impressive success of Mennonite farmers south of Winnipeg discouraged them further.[38] During these early years, the community also endured a period of intense religious strife, and these divisions, along with dire poverty and disillusionment, prompted a large group of New Icelanders to head to Dakota Territory under the leadership of Páll Thorláksson.[39]

Disease also dramatically shaped the immigrant experience for years after the settlement was established, but the most devastating of these outbreaks was the 1876–7 smallpox epidemic. In 1876, a new group of immigrants arrived in New Iceland in the wake of the eruption of the aforementioned volcano, Askja. This wave of arrivals, known as "the big group," had passed through the immigration sheds in Quebec City, where – some later speculated – one or more of the group had been exposed to smallpox. This group brought the disease to New Iceland, where an epidemic erupted in the winter of 1876–7, spreading to many Indigenous communities around Lake Winnipeg.

## Relations with Indigenous Communities

The Icelanders' relations with local Indigenous people and technologies were complex and diverse, and they changed over time, but they are essential to understanding the history of the community. The Indigenous presence in North America is at least 24,000 years old and remarkably diverse, although this cultural diversity is often overlooked or given only a cursory mention in non-Indigenous histories. The Icelanders encountered many, many different Indigenous cultures from different language families across North America in the nineteenth century, from the eastern shores of the Markland settlement to communities in Alaska, Washington, and British Columbia. Indeed, there is no singular narrative of Icelandic-Indigenous exchange or encounter. Still, these relationships form part of a distinct history. Icelanders share the oldest confirmed history of trans-Atlantic contact with Indigenous North Americans, likely including the Dorset as well as the ancestors of the Inuit, Innu, Beothuk, Maliseet, and Mi'kmaq, starting in the tenth century.[40] Some of these contacts, in Greenland at least and possibly farther west, lasted as late as into the fifteenth century. Together with the stories from the Icelandic sagas, archaeological findings and Greenlandic oral narratives suggest that these relationships ranged from friendship and trade to war, kidnapping, and murder.[41]

Five hundred years later, the nineteenth-century Icelandic community seemingly recreated this dramatic range in their many different relationships with First Nations and Métis people. Some, like Helgi Einarsson and Rannveig Tómasdóttir, joined local Métis and First Nations families through marriage and adoption (Figure C). As the popularity of *vínarterta* there can attest, other Icelanders lived in or around Métis and First Nations communities, including Matheson Island, Sainte Rose du Lac, and Fisher River Cree Nation. Icelandic fishermen also frequently lived with or alongside Indigenous co-workers; a sizeable number learned the languages of the Nehiyawak (Cree) and Anishinaabe (Ojibwe) while working in the Lake Winnipeg fishery and other languages in the larger northwest during the nineteenth and twentieth centuries. Numerous oral histories reveal that local Indigenous people also learned to speak the immigrants' language, including John Ramsay, who, Magnús Eliasson reported, spoke "splendid Icelandic."[42]

Other Icelandic-Indigenous relationships, however, could be very negative, and some immigrants treated their neighbours with racism and disdain. Some embraced Indigenous in-laws and mixed-race children, while others refused to acknowledge them. Some sympathized with Indigenous grievances against the Canadian state, while others supported the government's policies. In 1885, for example, roughly

Figure C. Helgi Einarsson and his three sons, Henry, William, and John, March 1946. Reprinted from Helgi Einarsson, *Helgi Einarsson: A Manitoba Fisherman*, trans. George Houser (Winnipeg: Queenston House, 1982).

twenty Icelanders enlisted with the Canadian state forces during the North-West Resistance, taking up arms against Indigenous forces fighting the illegal appropriation of their land.[43] Collectively, the arrival of Icelanders in the Interlake region in the 1870s had a generally devastating effect on First Nations families. The 1876–7 smallpox epidemic was one of the most visible ways in which the arrival of Icelanders along the western shore of Lake Winnipeg affected local Cree, Ojibwe, and Métis populations, but the actual relationship between colonialism and immigration in the region was far more extensive.

Rupert's Land (which was partly composed of the areas that became modern-day Manitoba, Saskatchewan, and Alberta) had been under the jurisdiction of the Hudson's Bay Company before being purchased by the newly formed Dominion of Canada in 1869. The purchase ignited grievances for Métis and First Nations' inhabitants about rights to their land, self-governance, and economic activity, and this resulted in the Red River Resistance of 1869–70. Responding to demands set forth by provisional government head Louis Riel, the Dominion of Canada entrenched Métis land rights in the Manitoba Act of 1870, guaranteeing 1.4 million acres for Métis families and their descendants. These rights were quickly eroded and erased by lack of enforcement, while other negotiations with First Nations in Manitoba were hastily organized amid the arrival of European settlers.

Ryan Eyford's compelling research into the Dominion government's granting of land for an Icelandic reserve describes a similar pattern of overlapping treaty negotiations for First Nations and preferential treatment for European immigrants. Moreover, he argues, the Icelandic deputation who had visited the future site of New Iceland was aware of Norway House Cree claims to the same territory and had asked Lieutenant Governor Alexander Morris "to give [the Icelanders'] claim priority."[44] Even the land rights afforded to local First Nations who had signed treaties with the government were far from secure. If and when post-treaty populations encountered the erosion of land and/or fishing and hunting rights, the Indian Act, legislation imposed on treaty signatories by the Canadian federal government in 1876 (and amended over time), barred them from most civic rights and avenues of redress.

While Canadian officials may have focused on containing First Nations and Métis communities within a range of poorly implemented, ignored, or marginal settlements, they began to negotiate far more generous settlements for Icelanders and immigrant populations from Europe. Driven by business and railroad interests, the federal government pursued and signed land deals with a number of European groups, including large grants for Mennonites and Icelanders in areas still occupied by Métis and First Nations communities.[45] In the case of New Iceland, the "principal man of the [Sandy Bar] band,"[46] John Ramsay (often mistakenly referred to as the band's chief), asserted land claims both through official channels and through a confrontation with the first settlers on the Icelandic River. However, government agents rejected these claims to the land as well as official recognition of the band as an entity.[47]

Far from being innocent bystanders, the Icelanders had a relationship with the colonial project that was sometimes a very intimate and direct affair; this was evident in Ramsay's discovery that Icelandic settlers had moved onto the land surrounding his camp and garden plot while he was away on a hunting trip.[48] The skirmish between Ramsay and Ólafur Ólafsson at Ós, far from popular depictions of vacant prairies and noble pioneers, further illuminates the central role of migrant settlers in both armed and policy-based biopolitical (population management) displacement of First Nations people:

> Three settlers rowed across the creek to their work. Ramsay was awaiting them with an angry look, and when they attempted to land he pushed the boat out again, making it very clear by his actions that he was forbidding

them to step ashore ... the three put into shore a second time, and once again Ramsay shoved the boat away, but the third time Ólafur walked to the bow with an axe and instructed the others to row in. They succeeded in getting ashore.[49]

While this Icelandic account is intended to highlight settler bravado, or "pioneer spirit," it is a stark reminder that the Icelanders had arrived in the midst of unresolved conflicts over territorial expansion into often unceded Indigenous territory. South of the border, in the United States, Icelandic settlers in Dakota Territory arrived just two years after Custer's defeat at Little Big Horn in 1876, and they were afraid of renewed action against the American military and settlements by Sioux and allied forces.[50] Although individual Icelanders might have had positive personal relationships with their Cree, Ojibwe, and Métis neighbours at certain times, the Icelanders overall were very aware of and, in many respects, dependent on the appropriation of Indigenous land by the Canadian and American governments and the violent state repression of organized Indigenous resistance in the late nineteenth century.

### Settlement beyond New Iceland

Entanglement and participation in colonial policies were two of the many facets of North American life that shaped Icelandic immigrant culture and identity in a community that has always been shaped by fissures and fragmentation. Migration to North America created a myriad of opportunities for the formation and re-formation of new identities, and migrants did so in their own particular ways. Many Icelanders embraced the possibility of new lives, opting to change their names, learn English, intermarry, and blend into new, non-Icelandic communities. Some cut ties altogether and disappeared from community life. The immigrants were also profoundly mobile and formed numerous Icelandic communities in North America beyond the often-referenced Lake Winnipeg settlement. Indeed, by the 1880s, the idea of establishing a singular New Iceland had run its course. Although it had functioned as a symbolic headquarters for many Icelanders in North America, it did not blossom into their chief destination.

The difficult conditions in New Iceland and a series of crises, including the smallpox epidemic, religious strife, and a major flood in the fall of 1880, prompted the Icelanders to seek a range of new destinations. New Iceland recovered from this exodus, to some extent, but lost its status as an exclusively Icelandic "reserve" in 1897. New Iceland (and particularly the town of Gimli) has continued to symbolize the Icelandic community in North America, but by the end of the nineteenth century, it was neither the largest nor the most successful Icelandic settlement on the continent. To all outward appearances, by 1883, Winnipeg might have claimed that title. Icelandic migrants flocked to several neighbourhoods in the city, including Shanty Town, Point Douglas, and Ross Avenue, drawn by the promise of plentiful manual labour for men and a very strong demand for female domestics, seamstresses, and laundresses. By the turn of the twentieth century, the city's west end was becoming the nucleus of Icelandic boarding houses, cafés, and businesses around Sargent Avenue, also known as Icelandic Main Street, attracting new arrivals to Winnipeg rather than New Iceland.

By the 1880s, Icelanders were regularly exploring new locations for settlement on both sides of the Canadian-American border, beyond pre-existing settlements in Utah, Wisconsin, Dakota Territory, and Minnesota. Some settlers moved among four or five Canadian or American Icelandic districts in their lifetimes, crossing the border repeatedly if conditions seemed promising. The revered *skáld* (poet) Stephan G. Stephansson, for example, first settled in Shawano County in Wisconsin in 1873 before relocating in 1878 to the new settlement in Pembina County, Dakota Territory, where he joined many ex–New Icelanders who had fled the struggling colony. Ten years later, Stephansson left the United States altogether to settle near Markerville, Alberta, alongside a number of other Icelandic Americans in search of better land and opportunities.

Beyond New Iceland and Dakota Territory, Icelandic migrants increasingly moved west in search of homesteads throughout the 1880s and 1890s, to new settlements in the Argyle (Baldur-Glenboro) and Lake Manitoba districts in Manitoba and the Thingvellir, Lögberg, and Vatnabyggð districts in what would become Saskatchewan. Fishing, a milder climate, and skilled-labour opportunities also drew migrants to the Pacific Coast, resulting in the establishment of Icelandic settlements in such diverse places as Victoria, Seattle, Whatcom County (Blaine-Bellingham, Washington), Point Roberts, and Osland, near Prince Rupert. This pattern of movement among Icelandic settlements on both sides of the border illustrates the secondary role that Canadian or American nationalism and identity played for many early Icelandic immigrants as they decided on their final destinations, much to the dismay of immigrant leaders and agents, who devoted themselves to the settlement projects of particular states. It also complicates the identification of strict divisions between Canadian and American Icelandic communities until sustained, larger-scale immigration closed with the onset of the First World War in 1914.

## Understanding Immigrant Popular Culture

How should a history of an ethnic community be written? Scholars of Canadian and American migration have long searched for better scholarly models for understanding the immigrant experience, without binding their histories into singular stories of progress or assimilation. Works by older Icelandic scholars and authors, including Wilhelm Kristjanson and Walter J. Lindal, frequently relied on what Franca Iacovetta terms the "cohesive community" model, which focuses on "the gradual but successful adaptation to the new society" and "the institutional completeness of ethnic communities."[51] While these kinds of histories acknowledge hardship and strife, they fail to convey some of the more complicated, ambiguous, and less redemptive aspects of immigrant culture, including its relationship to the colonial project, gender and sexuality, anglicization, and political radicalism. By focusing on the great accomplishments of immigrant community members and their contributions to North American society, these kinds of histories create an image of community cohesion based on the values of the immigrant elite. In so doing, they cast other parts of the immigrant community, including the poor, working class, and women, as well as popular forms of cultural expression, as marginal, inauthentic, and trivial.[52]

A number of scholars have found that material culture, or the history of objects, offers a helpful alternative for understanding both everyday historical life and the complexity of historical populations. As Bruno Latour writes, "Things do not exist without being full of people,"[53] and so this book often intentionally turns its attention to objects commonly found in everyday immigrant life to help capture this diversity and complexity. Some objects, like the cherished coffee pot, Icelanders' "household god," reflect ways in which immigrants preserved Icelandic traditions they brought from the homeland. Others, like the practice of wearing moccasins with Icelandic woollen socks in the Lake Winnipeg ice fishery, reflect the changes they made to those traditions to meet the challenges of life in North America. By attending to the different forms of expression embraced by Icelandic immigrants, from culinary culture and fashion to oral narratives and commemorative practices, this book seeks to provide an alternative road map to immigrant community life and cultural formation. Along the way, the particular pressures and possibilities that have faced successive generations become clear, as does the lasting imprint they left on the distinctive culture that emerged in North America.

## Sources

The research in this book draws substantively from published memoirs, stories, and immigrant newspapers as well as archival collections in Canada, the United States, and Iceland. It has benefited significantly from the richness of immigrant print culture,[54] particularly the Icelandic autobiographical tradition, which has produced volumes by everyday people, regardless of class, including labourers, farmers, and fishermen. Also essential have been immigrant letters, newspapers, daybooks, store ledgers, and photographs in the exceptional collections at Landsbókasafn Íslands (National Library of Iceland), the Provincial Archives of Manitoba, Library and Archives Canada, and the Icelandic Collection at the University of Manitoba.

Since Icelandic women, in spite of producing a respectable literary output, remain under-represented in the written record,[55] this book also focuses on a range of non-printed sources, such as clothing, objects, photographs, and oral histories,[56] to better understand their *central* role in the formation of Icelandic North American popular culture. Thus, the findings presented here reflect the wealth of other physical imprints left by migrants and their descendants, including artefacts in the collection of Þjóðminjasafn Íslands (National Museum of Iceland); the Manitoba Museum in Winnipeg; the New Iceland Heritage Museum, Gimli; the extensive archive of Icelandic immigrant writing, artefacts, and photographs at the Eyrarbakki Icelandic Heritage Centre at Hnausa, Manitoba; and the Canadian Museum of History in Gatineau, Quebec; as well as the rich collections that can be found in a number of regional museums on both sides of the international border.[57]

## Overview of Chapters

This book uses everyday immigrant practices as signposts in a larger, general chronology. It begins with the clothing of the immigrant generation in nineteenth-century Iceland and moves on to explore popular practices among the first North American–born generations, including those who lived through the two world wars. It closes with a discussion of commemorative practices and baking among community members in the late twentieth and early twenty-first centuries. Chapter 1 argues that clothing can reveal the everyday processes of collective history and transformation of the immigrant generation. Using immigrant letters, newspapers, memoirs, and photographs, it uses cloth to retrace lived experiences of poverty, marginalization, disease, cold, and eventual access to North American commercial goods. It also uses textiles to investigate broader cultural change, particularly in relation to immigrant negotiation of class, gender, and racial identities in the nineteenth-century North American west. From the adoption of Métis and First Nations styles by Icelandic immigrant fishermen to the politics of fashionable working-class women in Winnipeg dressing beyond their station, this chapter shows how cloth helped establish distinctive new identities – and divisions – in late nineteenth-century Icelandic immigrant society.

The second chapter analyses the history of drink in Icelandic immigrant life. It begins with an investigation into the role of coffee and alcohol as luxuries in nineteenth-century Icelandic society and their association with Danish merchants and political notions of self-governance. Immigration created significant shifts and disruptions in beverage consumption due to a range of factors, including poverty, isolation, and the promotion of more economical tea as well as the temperance movement in anglophone North American culture; while these factors relegated some forms of beverage consumption to the fringes of migrant society, they did not eliminate them. Indeed, Icelanders rejected the sole reliance on tea and the often-poor quality of coffee in anglophone North American society by home-roasting their own beans and establishing coffee houses, while dedicated drinkers of stronger beverages also tried to escape anti-alcohol sentiment and legislation by maintaining all-male drinking spaces. Far from simply revealing consumption patterns, the discourse surrounding alcohol and *kaffi* reveals that drink was an important medium through which Icelanders mediated relations, experienced rupture, and pursued enjoyment in difficult and rapidly changing conditions in North America.

While the first two chapters reveal the intensity of Icelandic immigrant anxieties about collective image, respectability, and acceptance in anglophone North American society, the third chapter turns to forms of culture that were more often hidden from outside eyes (and ears). Examining the large archive of supernatural lore in the Icelandic language reveals several fascinating developments in the oral culture of the Icelandic immigrant community, including the adaptation of the *hjátrú* (superstition) narrative tradition to North American life. Although a sense of taboo pervades open discussion and admissions of belief in the supernatural, this chapter's examination of Icelandic-language oral archives reveals that Icelandic immigrants brought with them a rich narrative tradition and system of popular belief. These traditions offer a particularly valuable window for examining how immigrants understood trauma, colonialism, and power. As discussed further in the chapter, narratives involving a phenomenon known as the *fylgja* (fetch, or follower spirit) imbue children, young workers, the elderly, and other victims of violence and exploitation with tremendous physical and spiritual power in death, capable of haunting, harming, and even killing their abusers. Rather than signalling the fossilization of First Nations populations, hitherto untranslated *hjátrú* narratives featuring Indigenous figures also reveal a more diverse Icelandic understanding of colonial trauma as an unresolved, disruptive, and active force capable of harming those who ignored that history.

The fourth chapter examines another powerful – albeit more public – historical spectre that dominated Icelandic North American landscapes and spectacles: the image of the Viking. The anglicization of the Icelandic immigrant community and the proliferation of North Americanized Viking imagery, including roadside monuments, community murals, and parades, are often a source of consternation for native Icelanders who visit their cousins in Canada and the United States. These distinctive monuments and the anglicization of the community are arguably linked, shaped by the Icelandic community's navigation of several periods of volatile anti-immigrant sentiment in North America, including the xenophobia that accompanied the First and Second World Wars and the Great Depression. This chapter demonstrates that since the image of the medieval Norse was admired by anglophone North American society as an ancient symbol of Protestant whiteness, Icelanders frequently emphasized their historical Viking connections as a way of both acknowledging and neutralizing their difference during periods of anti-immigrant sentiment.

Chapter 5 focuses on a more literal relationship between identity and consumption by examining the community's *vínarterta* tradition in the post–Second World War era. Using the history of this particular fruit torte, considered essential to important Icelandic family and community gatherings, this chapter analyses the transformation of relatively commonplace, nineteenth-century-immigrant material traditions into almost sacred ethnic symbols. It also explores *vínarterta*'s unexpected Cold War political career, arguing that the torte, while popular with the immigrant generation, emerged as an ethnic symbol after onslaughts of North American spectacles that publicly promoted it as a symbol of Cold War hospitality and friendship in response to homeland protests against NATO's occupation of Iceland. This chapter also seeks to understand the reasons why *vínarterta* became so intensely and personally symbolic in many Icelandic North American families. Using oral testimony, recipe books, and familial commemorative practices, along with archival research, it argues that many Icelandic North American *vínarterta* producers and consumers saw the torte as a powerful intergenerational binding agent, representing the links between living community members and past generations of *vínarterta* makers.

## Conclusion

Since the first Icelandic mass migrants arrived in North America roughly a century and a half ago, a compelling sense of identity and culture has taken root in the communities and families they helped establish. In spite of numerous declarations about the so-called death of the Icelandic North American community, its stubborn endurance in the twentieth and twenty-first centuries speaks to the unexpected cultural afterlives of immigrant generations and the problematic nature of narratives of decline in immigrant history. It also asks pressing questions about what constitutes an immigrant culture. A continued emphasis on certain forms of cultural expression, particularly literature, has disguised the three-dimensional nature of immigrant culture and kept our attention focused mainly on Icelanders who produced written texts. Yet the rich oral history collections, material culture, and new traditions produced by the community reveal that Icelanders on the margins, including working-class domestics, bar patrons, immigrant fishermen, children, and elderly women, have played central roles in the formation of immigrant identity. Analysing the roots of some of these popular and commonplace traditions – particularly those previously dismissed as trivial and taboo – reveals an alternative road map of the historical evolution of Icelandic North American culture.

*Chapter One*

# Dressing Up: Clothing and Upward Mobility in the Early Immigrant Community, 1870–1900

When he saw a pair of homespun Icelandic underwear flapping in the breeze on a Milwaukee clothesline, Friðjón Friðriksson was deeply relieved.[1] It was 1873, and Friðjón and his wife, Guðný Sigurðardóttir, had just arrived in Wisconsin after leaving a failing settlement of Icelanders in Kinmount, Ontario. Unfortunately for the young couple, they had also misjudged their expenses and were suddenly alone in a strange city with only fifteen cents to their name. With no shelter and little money for food, the couple was desperate to find the other Icelanders they knew had settled in Milwaukee. Once Friðjón spotted this unofficial Icelandic flag, husband and wife secured much-needed shelter and employment for the winter. They lived and worked in Milwaukee before returning to Canada in 1874 and establishing a store in the fledgling colony of New Iceland the following year. Within a few years, the couple had moved into one of the nicest houses in the settlement and secured a comfortable life, selling moose meat, coffee, farm supplies, dress cloth, and footwear (Figure 1.1). Few would be able to tell from the 1880 portrait of the successful merchant couple, dressed in fine North American fashions, that a humble pair of homespun underwear had played such a memorable role in their survival and eventual success.

This chapter explores the essential role of clothing in Icelandic immigrants' invention of new identities, their building of new lives, and their navigation of the physical, cultural, and economic demands of life in North American society. It argues that the decline of "traditional" Icelandic fashions and the migrants' engagement with the North American garment and fashion economies offer important avenues for understanding the early immigrant community towards the end of the nineteenth century. By peeking into the migrant generation's wardrobes and examining the prolific information about dress in immigrant

Figure 1.1. Friðjón and Guðný Friðriksson with their daughter Auróra, ca. 1880. EIHC.

memoirs, letters, and store ledgers, this chapter uses clothing and fashion to understand the migrants' early experiences as well as their changing identities and ideas about class, race, gender, and sexuality in Icelandic immigrant society. In so doing, it argues that, rather than representing a sign of cultural decline, Icelanders' engagement with the new clothing economies and styles helped them craft new identities and navigate the pressures and possibilities of life in North America.

Few historians imagine immigrant communities without their clothing, yet this essential part of immigrant life, experience, survival, and adaptation has received limited historical attention. While the clothing of many North American immigrant communities has been the subject of ethnographic studies of so-called traditional ethnic folk costumes, these studies often avoided in-depth analyses of immigrants' engagement with North American fashions. Since the 1960s, however, numerous international and interdisciplinary scholars have recognized and begun to fruitfully explore the rich history of the wardrobe beyond the folk costume. As Sophie Woodward argues, human dress is "fundamental to social, cultural, and psychological existence," and the study of clothing practices and fashion offers a rich resource for a range of economic, cultural, and labour histories.[2]

Historical clothing should not be understood as a stable relic, but as an instrument of power through which people "fashioned" different identities and public images for themselves. As scholars like Peter Boag, Monica J. Miller, and Mariana Valverde document, changing clothing could publicly transform a male into a female, a sex worker into a respectable middle-class Englishwoman, or a former slave into a glamorous socialite.[3] It is the close relationship among fashion, power, and identity that make clothing histories an excellent resource for exploring how such identities are formed – and subverted – in immigrant communities.[4]

This chapter begins with an analysis of the clothing worn in Iceland at the time of migration. Garments mediated migrants' physical experiences. No cultural medium was as quickly affected by North American geographic, social, and economic pressure as immigrant dress. Initially, many emigrant women wore traditional Icelandic clothing to express their support for their homeland's independence movement, but these garments, when worn in public in North America, could attract unwanted attention, including xenophobia. Some North Americans ridiculed Icelandic garments as "peculiar," but still often demanded exotic displays of a far-northern people who many hoped would be clad in sealskin and polar bear fur. As the career of "Eskimo" impersonator Ólöf Sölvadóttir makes clear, late nineteenth-century North American audiences considered clothing and fibre a deeply symbolic extension of the body, one that acted as a prominent sign of racial and ethnic difference.

This discussion then turns to an analysis of the popular clothing practices and styles that emerged in the immigrant community. As the disastrous impact of inadequate winter clothing and bedding during the New Iceland smallpox epidemic of 1876–7 reminds us, clothing was *essential* to health, survival, and work in the west. As a result, some working-class New Icelanders embraced new clothing traditions more suited to the severe climate and even began to develop blended Icelandic and Indigenous clothing styles. While some immigrants turned to Indigenous people as arbiters of style and providers of good-quality clothing, their wardrobes stood in stark contrast to those of urban and middle-class immigrants. In Winnipeg, wages unheard of in Iceland encouraged many working Icelandic women to embrace Anglo-Victorian clothing and fashion to create an outwardly anglophone appearance – essential for employment and acceptance. The look of some single working women in expensive clothing also fuelled speculation about their potential relationship to the city's booming sex trade, but fashion spoke to much broader and more complex changes in the lives of Icelandic women. Far from the poverty and restrictions they faced at home, the fashionable dress of working-class Icelandic women represented the radical upward mobility that immigration could offer.

## Icelandic Clothing and Nineteenth-Century Mass Migration

Migration dramatically shaped the clothing that Icelanders wore. At home in nineteenth-century Iceland, clothing was a politically charged form of expression tied to the country's independence movement. This movement sought increased political independence from the Danish Crown, Iceland's imperial ruler for five centuries, and the protection of Icelandic culture and language. Icelandic university students who had studied in Copenhagen and were exposed to growing pro-democracy independence and nationalist campaigns in continental Europe fuelled the movement. These campaigns swept the continent in the 1840s and protested the imposition of the governance, culture, and languages of foreign monarchs. The Icelandic independence movement created campaigns to reduce the influence of the Danish language and culture on their island home, while promoting traditions and customs deemed more authentically Icelandic. Some of these traditions included integrating historical Icelandic clothing styles into new, politicized popular fashions that promoted Icelandic autonomy and Icelanders' cultural and historical distinctions from Denmark.

The Icelandic independence movement transformed mid-nineteenth-century Icelandic women's fashion into a political tool using the clothing designs of the artist Sigurður *"Málari"* (the Painter) Guðmundsson. In the 1850s, he criticized the spread of Danish and continental European fashion among Icelandic women and created a campaign to reinstate older, home-grown Icelandic styles. International fashion and materials were already securely embedded in popular Icelandic dress by the 1850s, so Sigurður created new designs from a blend of regional and historical styles, including historical clothing described in ancient Icelandic texts and reflecting elements of Iceland's climate and landscape.[5] He promoted several popular styles for women, including the *peysuföt*, which was used for both ceremonial and everyday dress. This outfit (Figure 1.2) featured a tight, often black, woollen jacket (*peysa*) and a neck scarf; a simple, long, dark, woollen skirt and coloured apron; and a *skotthúfa* (tail cap). This dark, knitted skullcap featured a long, swinging tassel and was incredibly popular with Icelandic women. More elaborate women's costumes designed by Sigurður, like the embroidered *skautbúningur* and flowing *kyrtill*, also based on historical Icelandic fashions, were usually reserved for special occasions like weddings and christenings.

By promoting an alternative to Danish and other continental European styles in Iceland, pro-independence Icelanders hoped that reformed fashion would visually advocate for increased self-governance. Sigurður *Málari* argued that such fashion could engage the growing international attention that Iceland was receiving by the 1860s; the spreading popularity of Viking-era culture in Europe was also fostering a burgeoning tourist industry for curious gentlemen wishing to visit the "land of the sagas." As Sigríður Mattíasdóttir discusses in her research, nationalists used this attention to attract international support for the Icelandic independence movement by casting its people as the descendants of noble and revered rulers who were entitled to self-rule by birth.[6] These leaders sought to address persistent nineteenth-century stereotypes in Europe about Icelanders, which, Kristín Loftsdóttir and Sumarliði Ísleifsson argue, depicted them as superstitious, childlike, and semi-primitive. "Icelanders were generally not represented as complete savages," they caution, but "neither were they seen as fully belonging to civilised peoples."[7]

For Sigurður *Málari* and other members of the independence movement, clothing broadcast a message to international observers about Icelanders' relationship to the "civilized," white European world. By wearing styles influenced by Iceland's medieval golden age, he argued, Icelanders could racially situate themselves as a population deserving

Figure 1.2. Woman wearing *peysuföt* and *skotthúfa*. Undated photograph. EIHC.

of self-governance not afforded to others in the Danish empire, including Inuit Greenlanders and African-descended people in the Danish West Indies. Reformed fashion, he argued, would prove to the outside world that Icelanders "are not slaves' descendants ... but that we bear the signs that we are descendants of the old Norwegian princes, we keep their customs and speak their language, [we] bear their dress."[8]

Dress-reform fashions were generally very popular with Icelandic women and benefited local weavers and wool producers by curbing the country's reliance on imports of cloth and clothing. However, some women resented the movement's attempt to regulate their personal choice of dress. Complaints about reform fashions also circulated, and certain people complained that they were *ljót* (ugly), evident in some women's decisions to continue to "dress Danish" or wear imported styles from Europe.[9] Reformers publicly denounced those stubborn, female fashion devotees, who "wasted" their money on imported cloth and European styles, and they accused them of sabotaging the national cause.[10]

Historians have been critical of this specific focus on women in the independence movement's clothing campaigns and argue that it reflected the questionable effect of the movement on women's status in Icelandic society. Inga Dóra Björnsdóttir argues that dress reform objectified Icelandic women, transforming them into more "territories" that needed to be reclaimed and protected from the corrupting influence of Danish rule.[11] Guðmundur Hálfdánarson writes that campaigns against "fashion-crazed" women who wasted money on imported clothing also helped reinforce a conservative, anti-cosmopolitan agenda and rigid socio-economic hierarchy that benefited the landholding classes.[12] These Icelandic nationalists sought to protect a social order that was, in many respects, strictly divided by property, class, and gender. By restricting the mobility, economic activities, and personal lives of the working poor, the landholding elite could guarantee cheap pools of workers for their labour-intensive livestock and hay farms.[13] This system, along with land shortages and the intervention of church officials, trapped working-class and poor women in cycles of poverty and lifetimes of servitude and hardship. Marginalized women were especially vulnerable in this order, particularly poor or single mothers, who could be denied guardianship of, and separated from, their children.[14] Although independence leaders implied that Danish rule was to blame for the poverty and social problems in Iceland, many future emigrants were pushed to the margins by what was largely, according to Guðmundur Hálfdánarson, a home-grown cycle of inequality that favoured the Icelandic elite.[15]

As plans for Icelandic mass emigration to North America spread in the 1870s, Icelanders from a range of class backgrounds began to seek economic opportunities in areas like Wisconsin, Ontario, and Manitoba, responding to climate conditions and voting with their feet against homeland practices that perpetuated cycles of landlessness and poverty. Early female migrants in these groups regularly boarded ships dressed in independence fashions that were customary in Iceland, particularly the dark *peysuföt* and the tasselled *skotthúfa*. Some migrant women valued these garments as important forms of personal expression and identity, but such items of clothing were also relatively valuable since, as a result of clothing shortages,[16] fewer Icelanders owned more than two sets of clothing, which might consist of a church outfit and an everyday working ensemble. The *peysuföt* could be one of the very few suits of clothing possessed by many Icelandic women in the late nineteenth century, and although they may have been treasured dearly at home, North American photographs reveal that most Icelandic women abruptly discarded these homeland styles after arrival. Why did fashions that were so entrenched in women's daily wear at home disappear from everyday use so quickly in North America?

According to community accounts, Icelandic women's clothing attracted negative attention in North American society; watching immigrants arrive and assessing their character based on appearance was a popular pastime.[17] Icelandic migrants reported that some of these sightseers and other people they encountered openly mocked their clothing, particularly the *skotthúfa* that many Icelandic women wore. Thorstína Walters recalled that when her mother arrived in Glyndon, Minnesota, in 1881, American women tolerated and even appreciated some of her Icelandic clothes, but they openly ridiculed her headwear. "Her Icelander costume of black wool, with its tight fitting skilfully embroidered bodice, full skirt, and multi-coloured silk apron was greatly admired," she wrote. "But the small, tasselled cap under which she turned up her heavy braids of brown hair did not find favour," remembered Walters. "In fact she was advised to keep the costume and send the cap back to Iceland."[18] Other English-language reports of Icelanders' arrival also describe anglophone dislike of, or confusion about, the "peculiar" *skotthúfa*. The *New York Star* described the knitted skullcap as a somewhat bizarre "flat pad about the size of a tea saucer worn directly on the caput" with a long, swinging tassel that "swept the left shoulder at every step the wearer took."[19] These kinds of reactions prompted many Icelandic women to quickly cease wearing their *skotthúfa*. As the immigrant author Einar Hjörleifsson (who later became known as Kvaran) explained: "The clothing had to change.... The women could not go on with the *skotthúfa* if they wanted to avoid becoming a laughing stock."[20]

Fashion encounters with North Americans not only involved pressuring immigrants to abandon the styles of their homeland. As Nelson Gerrard argues in his work on nineteenth-century Icelandic North American costume, educated and curious North Americans were familiar with Nordic literature and history and were very interested in Icelandic clothing. Indeed, Icelandic immigrant leaders continued to use references to their Nordic ancestry and displays of traditional Icelandic dress to bolster their status in North America, just as independence leaders had at home. During his visit to New Iceland in 1877, Canada's governor general, Lord Dufferin, had commented appreciatively on women dressed in Icelandic national costume to celebrate the event. According to the editor-colonist Halldór Briem, Dufferin made special mention of this display and "was especially taken by the festive dress and expressed his hope that the womenfolk would not abandon it."[21] Although immigrant women may have garnered praise for displays of Icelandic clothing in more formal celebrations, it is clear that, in everyday life, any displays of Icelandic difference in public drew unwanted attention. Clothing that highlighted the cultural differences between Icelandic and North American society potentially hindered the acceptance of the immigrant community, particularly since many North Americans already viewed Icelanders as exotic curiosities from the "savage north."

### "A Good Deal Like Eskimos": Clothing, Race, and Perceptions of the North

Pre-existing North American perceptions of the Far North fuelled curiosity about the appearance of Icelanders when they arrived in Canadian and American ports and towns. Aside from well-read and well-travelled government officials, many nineteenth-century Canadians and Americans believed that Icelanders were of "Eskimo" extraction. Dufferin himself observed that "even the most educated people firmly believe the Icelanders to be a 'Squawmuck,' blubber-eating, seal-skin clad race."[22] Reverend Friðrik J. Bergmann recalled encountering these expectations when he arrived in Manitoba. A herd of curious Winnipeggers "rushed aboard the ship and the barges and impatiently asked: 'where are the Icelanders? Show us some Icelanders.'" When the immigrant agent John Taylor pointed to the Icelanders, the crowd did not believe him. Bergmann remembered that the audience protested: "'We know what Icelanders look like ... they are short of stature, about four feet high, rather short and sturdy, long jet-black hair, a good deal like Eskimos! These are not Icelanders, they are white people.'"[23]

After they arrived, Icelanders faced shifting perceptions about their racial identity and prescribed rank within settler society. As scholars such as David Roediger, Thomas Guglielmo, and Noel Ignatiev have well documented, "whiteness" was (and is) not a set category but a shifting designation that could be applied unevenly to nineteenth-century immigrant communities.[24] Immigrants could be considered non-white or ambiguous for a range of reasons in nineteenth-century North America, including their dress, region of origin, general poverty or wealth, and faith. Both Irish Catholics and Italians were famously considered racially inferior due largely to their membership in the Catholic Church. Icelanders' far-northern roots, in addition to their "peculiar" clothing, poverty, lack of English-language skills, and willingness to accept low-paid employment, offered a less certain picture of where these new arrivals might fit into English North America.

Many early Icelanders found employment in industries usually populated by black, Chinese, and South Asian workers, including freighting, construction, and laundry. Icelandic women could also easily find work in local laundries, where they competed with Chinese businesses. As one annoyed Winnipeg observer remembered, laundry customers could expect to be hounded for payment by either "John Chinamen or Iceland Mary."[25] Icelanders' close association with the lowest economic rungs of racialized labour are arguably evident in debates surrounding the roots of the word *goolie* (Manitoba slang for "Icelanders"). Although the origins of this word are contested in the community, some members contend that it came from a variation of *coolie*, slang for the Chinese immigrants who worked in several of the same industries as Icelanders.[26] Magnús Magnússon, a farm labourer, recalled that it was Icelanders' presumed Eskimo roots, in particular, that made them a target for scornful, racist attitudes. "They taunted us and called us 'Greenland Eskimos,'" he remembered of his anglophone co-workers. "They refused to use the same (wash) basin and towels as we used. We bore their contempt with as much dignity as we could summon, but ... the treatment they accorded us was no better than the treatment of convicts at Stony Mountain Prison."[27]

Ólöf Sölvadóttir, an ambitious Icelandic woman born at Ytri-Langamýri in Húnavatnssýslu in 1858, found North American assumptions about race and the north both a curse and a blessing after she immigrated in 1876. Owing to her short stature and a physical condition that inhibited the use of her arms, Ólöf reportedly faced serious health and financial struggles in low-paying positions as a domestic in Winnipeg. After moving south of the border to Dakota Territory in the 1880s, she found work in a hotel. During her frequent encounters with the public, she became "bored, annoyed, and outraged" by enquiries about her national origins and declarations that "we never saw an Eskimo before!"[28] When an American minister offered her five dollars to present a lecture on Eskimo culture to his church group, however, Ólöf decided to embrace this association and created a book-and-lecture performance based on a fictional account of her life in the Far North. She launched a lucrative career as "Olof the Little Esquimaux Lady," announcing to growing audiences that she was a member of a race of Greenland miniature people who lived in snow houses, rode on dogsleds made from giant frozen fish, and drank the blood of polar bears[29] (Figure 1.3).

Ólöf built her performance career on North Americans' hazy vision of the differences between far northern peoples as well as nineteenth-century notions about the relationship between clothing

Figure 1.3. W.E. Bowman, *"The Little Esquimaux Lady," Miss Olof Krarer*, 1889. Collection of author.

and race. Such assumptions took into account dress as well as eating habits, living conditions, and physical characteristics in the classification of populations. In her "autobiography," Ólöf the Esquimaux Lady contended that Greenlanders were originally white Norwegians, but that they had become dark-skinned and black-haired as a result of their constant application of animal grease.[30] Indeed, she convinced many thousand Americans of her so-called Eskimo roots and outlandish claims simply by dressing in a white-fur parka. It is estimated that she delivered as many as 2,500 lectures during her career, including several at American universities. Popular and academic audiences widely accepted her claims and even reproduced them in American school textbooks.[31]

Ólöf's performances offer a relatively dramatic but important example of North American perceptions of northern peoples. North American depictions of Icelanders' purported Eskimo origins endured well into the twentieth century.[32] Icelandic leaders were keenly aware of the potential impact of such perceptions, in part because they were familiar with the racialized systems of power and inequality in the nineteenth-century Danish empire. Indeed, as Kristín Loftsdóttir argues in her analysis of nineteenth-century Icelandic depictions of Africa, before immigration, independence advocates regularly cast Icelanders as superior to other colonized populations in order to respond to accusations that they themselves were a "half-wild" people not suited to self-government.[33]

Eager to achieve better status in Canada and the United States, community leaders replicated independence-movement declarations that emphasized the Norwegian connections of the Icelandic people, attempting to capitalize on the acceptance and relative success of earlier Scandinavian settlements in the United States. As they continually attempted to distance themselves from the "sealskin-wearing" and "blubber-eating" races of the Far North (although nineteenth-century Icelanders did, in fact, occasionally eat seals and use them for their skins), Icelandic leaders issued numerous assurances to Canadian government officials that their community was instead a hardy, white, northern race that was perfectly suited to settler life in the demanding climate of the North American west.[34]

## North American Winters

Assumptions about Icelanders' innate ability to deal with the coldest Canadian and American winter months made them more attractive candidates for the settlement project. But, in spite of their homeland's slightly ominous, wintery name, Icelandic winters were far less severe than those on the Midwestern Prairies thanks to warmer ocean currents, which usually kept average winter temperatures on the island around zero degrees Celsius.[35] Migrants were also upset to find that the preparations made for their arrival, including housing, hay provisions, and bedding, were often inadequate. Simon Simonson (Símonarson) remembered arriving with sick children in total darkness at the Icelandic settlement at Kinmount, Ontario, and being led to unfinished and crowded houses, where they stayed for several nights without blankets. He bitterly recalled losing his infant daughter in this rough shelter.[36] Although many migrants thought that Manitoba would offer an escape from the disastrous conditions at Kinmount, the climate at New Iceland was worse. Temperatures there regularly reached minus-thirty degrees Celsius in the middle of winter and could dip much lower. Immigrants were delayed in arriving at the colony site and were unprepared for the coming winter. Many spent their first winter in tents and often without the clothing and bedding needed to stay warm, work, or venture out in search of food.

In addition to food, bedding, and shelter, adequate clothing was one of the most important factors in surviving winters. Migrants who had brought only their best clothing to start their new lives in rural North America found themselves underdressed for the winter and, by the end of their first year, struggling to save the few pieces they owned. Icelanders brought warmer wool garments with them from home, but working and travelling in the bush could quickly reduce clothing to shreds. In Muskoka, Ontario, Friðríka Baldvinsdóttir reported that "it's good for boys to pack strong clothes which rip in the woods and mittens (because they) don't last long against the cuts."[37] Björn Andrésson wrote, "Anyone planning to join us here should bring all their clothes, both old and new, as they are quickly worn out here.... Constructing houses and working in the bush is hard on the clothes."[38]

Winter clothing shortages were a serious issue, one that also affected food supplies and income. Poorly clad migrants had to simply stay indoors during cold snaps, even when they lacked food. Those who did venture out without sufficient clothing and an understanding of the winter environment around places like Lake Winnipeg risked their extremities and even their lives. In December 1876, Magnús Magnússon and Hjálmur Hjálmarsson got lost in a blinding snowstorm on the frozen lake. When the two men finally made it to Hecla Island, a visiting physician had to amputate one of Magnússon's feet and both of Hjálmarsson's to the instep. Hjálmarsson continued to homestead, but got around by walking on his knees. Anna Sigríður Guðmundsdóttir from Steðji, Þelamörk, was not as lucky: she froze to death that same month.[39]

## *Bóluveturinn*: Clothing and the New Iceland Smallpox Winter

When a second wave of 1,400 Icelanders, many of whom were motivated to leave by the 1876 eruption of the volcano Askja in eastern Iceland, arrived in Quebec City at the end of July, they received medical attention and let their children play with other newcomers in the immigration sheds.[40] According to several community accounts, the Icelanders purchased used clothing and blankets in Quebec City that may have been infected with droplets from one of the city's series of smallpox outbreaks in the 1870s. However it travelled, the smallpox that arrived in New Iceland in 1876 found fertile ground for expansion. The arrival of the 1,200[41] Icelanders in New Iceland that August increased the strain on the colony's precarious housing conditions. The food, clothing, and bedding shortages that resulted from the arrival of such a large group, along with poor housing, contributed to lower body temperatures in the colony and made the migrants more susceptible to illness. The appearance and spread of the dreaded disease sparked a government quarantine on 27 November 1876 as the smallpox assumed a more virulent form.

Cloth and clothing shortages contributed to the spread of the disease in the colony, along with cramped housing. The severe winter temperatures in New Iceland also forced many arrivals to choose between exposing themselves to disease or dying of exposure to the cold. Dr. Augustus Baldwin, who arrived in New Iceland to provide medical service during the epidemic, recalled that body heat and blanket-sharing was one of the only ways to stave off the severe cold, which dropped below minus forty. Baldwin understood the risks of sharing blankets with a smallpox patient but could survive the cold only by sleeping next to his infected guide, the well-known Métis farmer Joseph Monkman, although Monkman had "the eruption out on him."[42] Cloth shortages were so severe that some Icelandic households reportedly even lacked sheets to cover the dead, so they simply left the bodies in their houses or placed them on the roof of their shacks or in nearby snowbanks.[43]

*Bóluveturinn*, or "the smallpox winter," devastated the region, claiming the lives of approximately 10 per cent of the Icelandic population but far more in the neighbouring Indigenous communities on both sides of Lake Winnipeg; this situation will be discussed further in the third chapter. In some instances, Indigenous communities suffered causalities as high as 70 to 100 per cent. Many survivors, including the well-known John Ramsay, one of the Icelanders' main contacts with the Sandy Bar Band, and his daughter Mary, were deeply affected by the epidemic. John lost his wife, Betsey, whom he loved deeply, as well as two sons. In addition to losing her brothers and mother, Mary was forced to carry the physical scars of the disease for the rest of her life. The psychological toll is more difficult to measure, but it is clear that the sight of such devastation left a lasting imprint on survivors and witnesses. One such example was Magnús Stefánsson, from Kelduhverfi in northern Iceland. He reported that when he accompanied Ramsay and Dr. Baldwin to Sandy River, a sizeable village on the east side of Lake Winnipeg, they found not one living person and two hundred dead.[44]

### Indigenous Clothing and Icelandic Settlers

Without detracting from the devastation of the winter of 1876–7, focusing attention on historical clothing in the years surrounding the epidemic complicates and challenges some of the narratives told about John Ramsay and Icelandic-Indigenous relations more broadly. For example, modern public narratives of these relationships often focus on the epidemic and, later, momentarily, the death of John Ramsay as the end point. In so doing, they imagine the disappearance of Indigenous people in the region after 1877, a narrative that erases the continued presence of numerous large communities. It also erases the very real, continued Indigenous legal campaigns for land, treaty rights, and more in the area, such as Elizabeth Fidler's decade-long struggle to secure compensation for the damage that Icelandic settlers caused to her property (a building that had to be burned to prevent contagion) following the epidemic.[45]

From the 1870s onward, some Icelanders had also begun to work near or lived in Indigenous households, and some married into these families. The growth of the commercial fishery on Lake Winnipeg and the sustained contact between Icelandic and Indigenous fishermen fostered many more kinds of relationships, both negative[46] and positive. It is clear, however, that some of these relationships could be profoundly close. When interviewing elderly men and women for an Indigenous history film project with Dave Mulligan in 1965, Margaret Stobie discovered that an eighty-nine-year-old "Indigenous" interviewee was actually born an Icelander. Alfred Thomas was an infant and reportedly the sole survivor in an Icelandic household hit by smallpox during *bóluveturinn*. He was rescued by Reverend Edward Thomas of Peguis First Nation, adopted, and raised as his son.[47]

Focusing attention on clothing practices helps challenge the assumed disappearance of Indigenous communities following the

1876–7 epidemic as well as any tendency to forget other early Icelandic-Indigenous relationships. It is clear that many more Indigenous survivors adapted to the post-epidemic landscape and continued to shape Icelandic community life and economies. Archival evidence reveals that John Ramsay, in spite of his deep personal losses, was still living in the region and conducting a booming trade in whitefish and moose meat for the Icelandic colony in the early 1880s. Icelandic community histories seldom mention Ramsay's life in the area after the smallpox winter, but store accounts reveal that, in the following decade, he forged a friendship and business partnership with Friðjón and Guðný Friðriksson and became a major supplier for the Jónasson and Friðriksson store. Ramsay had remarried and started a new family and placed orders for himself, his wife, and children at Jónasson and Friðriksson. His store accounts in 1881–2 reveal that he ran a thriving business, which helped pay for new clothing and imported commercial goods for his family, including yards of dress fabric and ribbon, new shoes, and a fine woman's shawl, which alone cost $5.50, or the equivalent of ninety pounds of moose meat.[48]

Beyond his role in colony business and food supplies, Ramsay was also a fashionable agent of style, considered by some New Icelanders as one of the best-dressed men in the area. Guttormur Guttormsson, the famed Icelandic Canadian poet born in 1878 at Víðivellir in New Iceland, recalled Ramsay's distinctive and expensive "going-to-town outfits," including his "star white trousers of expensive and thick material," a sash, and a red-chequered shirt. "I must say how fond I was of [his] wonderful costumes which were so different from the way Icelanders dressed," he remembered.[49]

While John Ramsay's wardrobe reflected the influence of a man of status in the area, it is clear that much larger networks of exchange existed between Icelanders and many other regional Cree, Ojibwe, and Métis seamstresses, brokers, friends, and family. Letters, memoirs, and store accounts from New Iceland suggest that Icelanders' adopted Cree, Ojibwe, and Métis moccasins and garments not just because they were better suited to the local climate but also because some appreciated their style. Many early Icelandic immigrants wore moccasins. Account books, immigrant memoirs, and letters reveal that this style of footwear was essential for those working in land-clearing and the growing fishing and transportation economies around Lake Winnipeg. Some Icelanders continued to wear and use more affordable homemade *skinnskór*, traditional Icelandic slipper-style shoes made from cowhide or sheep hide, for decades after arrival, but many seemingly preferred Indigenous footwear. Guttormsson recalled that moccasins were far more comfortable and better suited to the geography and climate of the Prairies than *skinnskór*. Icelandic shoes, he reported, could be slippery on the ice, hard, uncomfortable, and prone to shrinking. Many Icelanders also valued the beauty of beaded and embroidered moccasins, he wrote, including those "made from light-brown cured hide and embroidered with silk roses all around." There was no comparison to "our rock-hard, Icelandic leather shoes! What a difference! ... I can't describe how great my joy was when I received my first pair of moccasins."[50]

The appearance of clothing produced by skilled Cree, Ojibwe, and Métis seamstresses in the community reveals some of the numerous networks that Icelanders could use to access Indigenous clothing. Many early New Icelanders often lacked anything of value to trade for moccasins and other garments from local First Nations producers except Icelandic knitwear, which quickly became a trade item. John Ramsay himself reportedly appreciated the warmth of Icelandic socks.[51] For decades afterwards, Icelandic families continued to produce knitwear, just as they had for generations in Iceland, and it was common to find Lake Winnipeg fishermen wearing a blend of Icelandic and Indigenous clothing, including moccasins with tightly knit, knee-high woollen socks and parkas with felted or distinctive *sjómannavettlingar*, double-thumbed fishermen's mittens, a style imported by Icelanders.

Expensive but beautifully decorated moosehide jackets were also particularly popular with turn-of-the-century Icelandic fishermen around Lake Winnipeg. New Icelanders called these special coats and jackets *moccasintreyjur* (moccasin jackets)[52] and wore them for special occasions, including dances and semi-formal portraits (Figure 1.4). Beyond ornamental clothing, however, Icelanders often relied on Indigenous seamstresses and brokers for working clothing, including parkas, gauntlets, and winter moccasins, which were better suited to the local climate than mass-produced North American clothing and fabrics. The expert seamstresses who produced these garments could find an eager market among Icelandic fishermen journeying north as the Lake Winnipeg commercial ice fishery expanded since wearing those garments was essential to survival and working in the severe winter weather on the lake could easily claim the lives of workers and travellers (Figure 1.5). Responding to a friend's concern about the severe climate in Manitoba, Jón Jónsson explained that migrants owed their winter survival to local Indigenous clothing producers, who were "geniuses" when it came to garment production and, in fact, "knew how to clothe themselves better than those in the homeland."[53]

Figure 1.4. L.B. Foote, *Thordur G. Thordarson in Winter Clothing*, ca. 1915. Provincial Archives of Manitoba (PAM), Winnipeg.

Figure 1.5. L.B. Foote, *Fishermen Posing with Catch Taken through the Ice of Lake Winnipeg near Riverton, Manitoba*. Undated photograph. *Winnipeg Free Press* Archives.

### Fashion and Life beyond the Colony

Good-quality, homemade Icelandic and Indigenous clothing in the Icelandic colony was essential to everyday working-class life and adaptation in New Iceland. However, the general poverty of the colonists and their sometimes very visible difference in Anglo–North American society intensified class tensions in the immigrant community and debates about progress, assimilation, and the direction of Icelandic culture on the continent. Upwardly mobile Icelanders were a profoundly image-conscious population and often Anglophiles, ardent devotees of anglophone style, literature, and culture. These business owners, religious officials, agents, and their families often embraced the status and upward mobility associated with "dressing English" and the styles of the anglophone middle class. For these Icelanders and anglophone observers, the distinctive, unusual dress and poverty of New Iceland represented potential problems with immigrants' "backwardness" and their resistance to assimilating English styles, work habits, and language.

In the 1870s and 1880s, Icelandic migrant leaders began to promote the idea of young people working on farms and in homes outside New Iceland. Employment beyond the colony could help supplement its struggling households and reform what the leaders saw as the undesirable habits of poor migrants. Such positions, they argued, would encourage industry, address public concerns about Icelanders' isolationism and rejection of English influence, and help "reinvigorate" the Icelandic people in North America. Halldór Briem wrote in 1878, "By paying careful attention we can learn so infinitely much from [anglophones], especially where working methods and public service are concerned."[54] Mired in disease, poverty, floods, and internal strife in the colony, many Icelanders energetically sought out such positions and left. The booming construction industry in Winnipeg and the high demand for domestic servants there encouraged many to leave for the city and send wages home. The immigrant agent, John Taylor, reported that the Icelandic youth who worked outside the colony spoke English, dressed in English-style clothes and were generally almost indistinguishable from anglophone Canadians. "I am often misled by their appearance, their dress, and their speech, so much and so closely resembling our own," he attested. "A perfect identification in all respects with our people will eventually take place."[55]

Changes in immigrant style reflected both the internal and the external pressures that Icelanders experienced in the tense years following the epidemic. Einar Hjörleifsson reported in his lecture on the community in 1895 that anti-immigrant sentiment and anglophone popular opinion against immigrants had taken their toll in these early years. Some Icelanders even "began to hate themselves for being Icelanders," he recalled, and strove to change their external appearance as much as possible.[56] Icelandic immigrant leaders also energetically responded to criticisms and doubts raised by the colony's disastrous early years, which undermined notions about Icelanders' hardiness and adaptability as well as the status and future of the community in Canada. Icelandic organizations and newspapers eagerly promoted an image of the community as able and willing to assimilate in the decade following the founding of New Iceland.

The colony's founder, Sigtryggur Jónasson, and a local merchant, Friðjón Friðriksson, were already sympathetic to and public admirers of Anglo-Victorian society, which they saw as a democratic political and cultural alternative to Danish influence.[57] For these leaders, establishing business deals, land opportunities, and social networks with North American state officials and society meant that Icelanders needed to speak English flawlessly, understand anglophone North American culture, and dress according to its notions of taste, modernity, and respectability.

Immigrant photography as well as the account book of the Jónasson and Fredrickson Sawmill and Store reveal much about early clothing practices at Icelandic River in northern New Iceland, where fashionable North American style was a marker of affluence and success in the colony in the late 1870s and early 1880s. Möðruvellir, the home of immigrant leader and business owner Sigtryggur Jónasson and his wife, Rannveig Briem, as well as their social circle (Figure 1.6) was a showcase of North American goods and styles. The house was carpeted at a cost of $31.50, and Sigtryggur's purchases of imported Trinidadian cigars and a $14 smoking jacket reveal a love of luxury that stood in stark contrast to the local immigrant shanties.[58]

To replicate North American styles at Möðruvellir, elite women, including Rannveig, Guðný Friðriksson, Lára Bjarnason, author Torfhildur Holm (Rannveig's companion), and the widow Sigríður Jónsdóttir (mother of the renowned Icelandic children's author, Nonni), could place orders in Winnipeg, establish their own sewing circles, and buy imported clothing at New Iceland stores. Having spent time in urban centres,[59] the Icelandic middle class and elite acted as agents of both social reform and style in isolated Icelandic communities. In addition to their devotion to North American fashion, Möðruvellir's inhabitants opened an English-language school in the house in 1878–9. The school was relatively popular, but class tensions arose over attempts at the store to profit from the poor colonists and the elite's conspicuous displays of wealth in the struggling colony. Poorer Icelanders criticized members of this circle, reportedly referring to women like Sigríður Jónsdóttir sarcastically as *meirihéttar Sigga* ("*fabulous* Sigga") because of her love of elaborate fashions and "air of superiority she had acquired during her years of association with the upper class in her homeland"[60] (Figure 1.7).

Working-class women and girls from New Iceland also engaged with North American clothing markets when they went south to find work in Winnipeg. Urban wages kept a number of the earliest New Iceland farms afloat. Even mothers with young children travelled south to take up positions in urban laundries and households to supplement their families' efforts at farming or fishing in the struggling colony in the late 1870s. As Simon Simonson explained in his 1904 memoirs, "The wages were not high, and nowhere else were they high but generally they were better for women in domestic service than elsewhere – for at that time there was little prosperity in the land."[61] A construction boom

Dressing Up

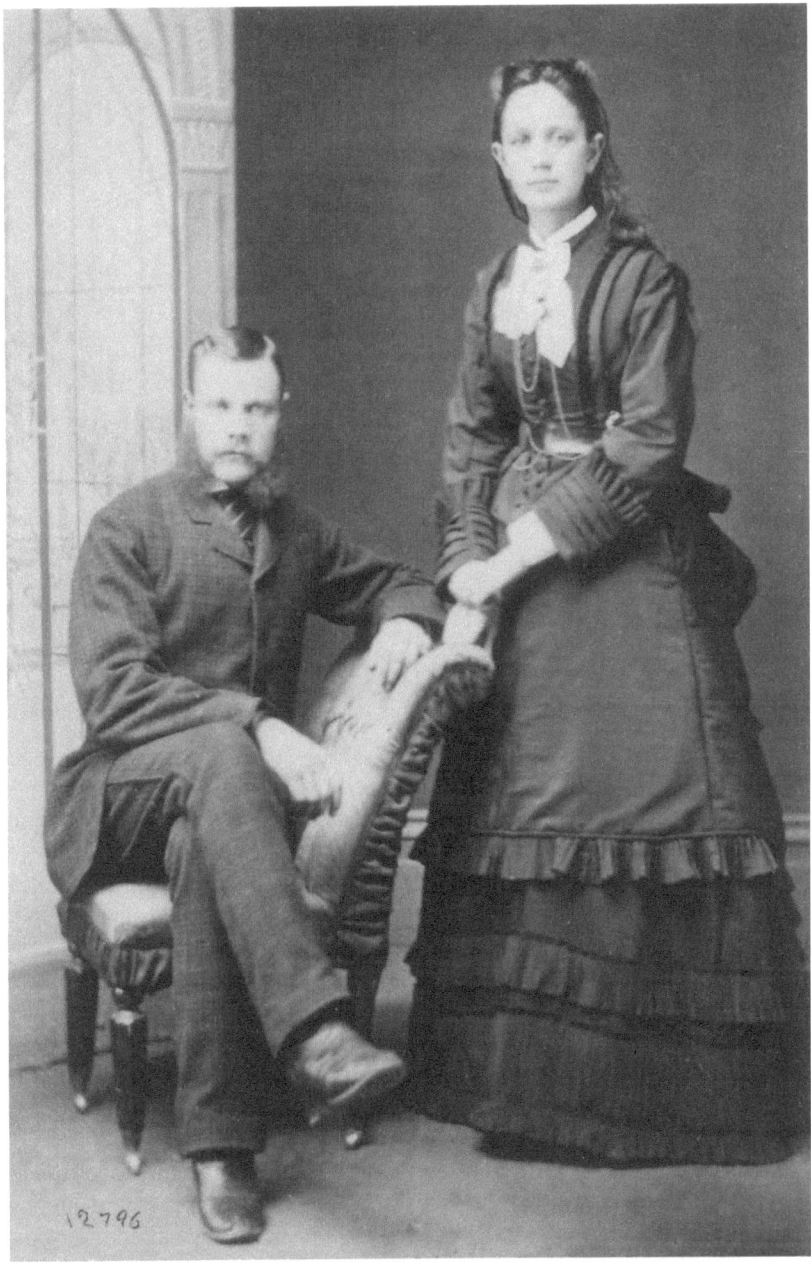

Figure 1.6. Sigtryggur Jónasson and Rannveig Briem.
Undated photograph. EIHC.

Figure 1.7. G.W. Searle, portrait of Sigríður Jónsdóttir, Winnipeg, ca. 1885. EIHC.

in Winnipeg in the early 1880s improved conditions and wages. Since most Icelandic women could easily find work in the city, many began to bypass New Iceland after arriving in Canada and went straight into more established, urban centres to work. As the urban immigrant community grew, so too did the agricultural resettlement of Icelanders beyond the bounds of New Iceland. New money earned to save up for or support immigrant homesteads enabled Icelanders to establish more prosperous farms in new territories like Argyle and Baldur in Manitoba and Dakota Territory and the regions that eventually became Saskatchewan and Alberta. Although often under-acknowledged in the community, the wages of many young, unmarried, urban female relatives played a critical role in the establishment of those farms.

Merchant Friðjón Friðriksson responded to the demand for good positions for Icelandic working women by establishing an employment agency specializing in Icelandic domestics, while other women swelled the ranks of the city laundries. Positions were relatively well paid, compared to women's indentured positions at home in Iceland, where working-class women often remained trapped in servitude and where single women on the margins, including widows and unmarried mothers, faced restrictive laws that stripped them of their property and children. In contrast, single working women in North America enjoyed far better economic opportunity and wages. Pro-immigration publications like *Landneminn* advertised and at times glamorized the economic opportunities for working-class women. It published accounts from women like Rósamunda Guðmundsdóttir from Eyjafjörður, who reported in 1893 that although she had previously worked in the best household in Iceland, better conditions and pay in North America were incomparable. At home she had worked from 7:00 a.m. to 11:00 p.m. cutting hay and tending animals, sometimes in the pouring rain, for thirty-five kronur per year. But in North America, she wrote, "no one would ever dream of asking maids to work such hours, and least of all for such an insulting wage. Since I've arrived, I've never earned less than $10 a month and for the last year have had $20."[62]

Access to capital through domestic work, even when limited, could transform the lives of immigrant women. In one lucky episode, Guðrún Jónsdóttir, a young, unmarried domestic from Máná in Þingeyarsýsla, had saved $20 of her own money by 1881 during Winnipeg's construction boom. She used her savings to put a down payment on a city lot and built a small house there, which she sold two months later for $1,000.[63] Other Icelandic domestics in the city played the marriage market. A large population of single, male workers had been made rich by the Winnipeg construction boom in the early 1880s, as a result of which "the demand for marriageable females was perfectly wild." As Charles Napier Bell recalled, young domestic workers in the city could invest their saved wages or meet eligible and wealthy potential suitors – or do both. Female domestics in the city in the early 1880s, he reported, could "choose from among a host of admirers, the best of them obtained good husbands and well-furnished homes of their own."[64]

### Fashion, Morality, and Working Urban Women

Clothing was integral to both the fantasy and the lived reality of Icelandic immigrant women in Winnipeg, and early immigrant fashion reflected the dramatic fluctuation of class in the Icelandic community. After leaving Iceland, members of some of the poorest, lowest economic and social ranks could be transformed into the wealthiest, most fashionably dressed Icelanders on both sides of the ocean – in some cases, in the span of a few years. Women like Aðalbjörg and Sigríður Jóakimsdóttir, sisters from Árbót in Aðaldalur, sent home portraits of themselves dressed in the latest North American fashions, along with letters attesting to their new-found successes or struggles (Figure 1.8). The independence and wages available to women

Figure 1.8. Portrait of Aðalbjörg and Sigríður Jóakimsdóttir from Árbót in Aðaldalur, Þingeyjarsýsla, Iceland, after their arrival in Milwaukee, ca. 1874. EIHC.

in the city stood in stark contrast to the menial status of working women at home in Iceland. In 1877, just after the quarantine had lifted on a struggling New Iceland, Björn Andrésson described the stunning, fashionable clothing of the Icelandic working women in Winnipeg, noting that "I have seen several here with whom the finest in Reykjavík could not compare."[65]

Accounts and photographs of fashionably dressed Icelandic North American women, particularly those who had come from the lowest rungs of Icelandic society only a few years before, fuelled women's dreams of escape, wealth, and independence beyond nineteenth-century Iceland's rigid society. In an article promoting migration, Rósamunda Guðmundsdóttir compared the wardrobes of Icelandic and Canadian working women to describe the freedom the new land offered. "Hired girls here have more control in financial matters," she reported in 1893. This kind of financial power meant better financial independence – and wardrobes, she continued. "In Iceland I never had more than three outfits at any one time, while here I have 10–14."[66]

The fine dress of some working women, however, concealed some of the enduring inequalities they faced in North America. Immigrant letters and newspaper reports document the dangers and pitfalls of domestic work for young women and the ultimately insufficient wages they earned. Ingveldur Jónsdóttir of Ytri-Hraundalur in Hraunhreppur warned family members in 1892 that "there is by all means never a shortage of work for women ... but few women get rich."[67] Migrant letters and accounts also describe the isolation, homesickness, and physical exhaustion of domestic work, while scholars like Constance Backhouse and Karen Dubinsky have documented female workers' vulnerability to unwanted pregnancies and sexual assault.[68] Working-class immigrant women faced language barriers and new sets of sometimes unfamiliar and restrictive Anglo–North American gender roles, which may have made them more vulnerable to economic and sexual exploitation. Although seldom discussed in Icelandic community historiography, police reports from Winnipeg during this period reveal several documented cases of sexual assault against Icelandic female domestic workers in their employers' homes and suggest many more undocumented cases.[69]

In the Icelandic immigrant community and in North American society more broadly, women's dress also fuelled anxieties about working women's sexuality and sexual availability. As Mariana Valverde argues in her analysis of nineteenth-century discourse of fashion and sexuality, a woman's "love of finery," particularly working-class women's wearing of "showy" clothing or dress associated with upper-class women, could also act as a potential sign of moral and sexual corruption.[70] Indeed, the morally compromised daughter with a taste for finery is a reoccurring theme in Icelandic immigrant literature,[71] and signs of Icelandic unmarried women's wealth in Winnipeg, like expensive fashions, were part of the code through which the community discussed their potential engagement in *other* economies. From the 1870s to 1914, there were numerous informally tolerated brothels in the city's red-light districts,[72] and locals might easily mistake independently wealthy, single domestics wearing expensive clothing for being morally suspect. The booming sex-trade economy in late nineteenth-century Winnipeg made local madams and sex-trade workers well-known consumers of fashionable dress. Their clothing reflected, in part, their greater access to capital outside marriage, but brothels also commonly relied upon well-dressed women to attract better-paying male clientele (and charged sex workers for their wardrobes at inflated prices).

Young Icelanders in suspiciously fancy dress represented the moral dangers of the city and the other "most prosperous economy" open to immigrant women. Winnipeg arrest records suggest that some

Icelandic immigrant women could find employment in local brothels as sex workers, but also as laundresses and domestics. Occasionally, madams hired local young women as domestics and then withheld wages to pressure them into taking on additional duties in the brothel. In 1878, an Icelandic woman going by the name Elizabeth Goodman found herself in such a position after her employer, a local madam named Alice Hamilton with links to local police, refused to pay her wages for domestic work, possibly as an attempt to pressure her into sex work.[73] While many desperate working-class women may have been too embarrassed to pursue the matter in court, Elizabeth Goodman grabbed the madam and "beat her soundly with her broom." She then marched down to the local police station to file a complaint.[74] While Goodman resolved her own situation in police court, the Icelandic Women's Society took action to divert future recruits from morally precarious and dangerous workplaces. The society, popular with the wives of the Icelandic elite, hoped to protect new arrivals from exploitation by offering "guidance to young girls in selecting suitable places of employment"[75] (Figure 1.9).

Many single, working Icelandic women saw up-to-date, anglophone-style clothing as being beyond a sign of moral ambiguity; it was essential to securing better jobs. Appearing English was essential to securing better-paying work, and image-conscious North American employers often expected their immigrant employees, particularly domestic staff who worked in the home, to dress in a way that complemented their own sense of respectability, hygiene, and style. For some employers, the worn-out shoes and strange, threadbare, or awkward clothing of poor immigrant women were unwelcome. Author Laura Goodman Salverson recalled how the fashion expectations of her employer, "Mrs. H.," thwarted her attempts to save money to help her parents while she was working as a domestic, dressed in her mother's hand-me-down clothes.

> Out of my first week's salary (bless the word!) I had to pay the employment bureau and buy blue percale for two dresses. I would look so nice in blue, Mrs. H. thought.... A pair of shoes ate up the next week's earnings, then I paid my debt, and now I had only to wait six weeks to get a spring coat.[76]

Beyond their external appearance, workers strove to sound and seem English. Wages for Icelandic immigrant women depended on supply and their ability to fit into English-speaking homes and establishments, and the financial compensation for these adjustments was considerable. Icelandic women who could speak English received almost double the wages of those who could not. Working men and women often took on English names more familiar to anglophone employers and

Figure 1.9. The Icelandic Women's Society, Winnipeg, mid-1880s. EIHC.

neighbours. Icelandic women often removed the customary female demarcation in their last names and anglicized both their first and last names, turning names like "Ólöf Sveinsdóttir" and "Ragnheiður Jónsdóttir" into "Olive Swanson" and "Ruby Johnson." Other migrants opted for total reinvention, choosing and changing names as circumstances demanded. Migrants' sometimes wild, new English names could be the source of confusion and humour.[77] As the Icelandic newspaper *Lögberg* noted in 1888, someone named Sveinn Grímsson might be known by two or three other names, including "George Byron" and "Thomas Edison." One Icelander in Winnipeg, it reported, had even recently registered to vote under the name "Mr. Christ."[78]

The urbanization of Icelandic migrants and the continuing stream of arrivals from the home country resulted in the rise of Icelandic-language clothing markets to meet the dress needs of the community. Icelanders were known as a significant consumer force in Winnipeg, with an interest in fashionable clothing. In 1883, there were at least twelve Icelandic tailors operating in the city,[79] including Erlendur Gíslason, who ran a small shop on Ross Avenue.[80] English-speaking Winnipeg merchants also recognized the purchasing power of the rapidly urbanizing Icelandic community and used Icelandic-language advertisements and the promise of respectful treatment and respectability to attract its business. "Many businessmen and others would willingly take Icelanders into their employ, if for no other reason than the hope of obtaining as many Icelandic customers as possible,"[81] reported the Icelandic newspaper *Framfari*. Such stores capitalized on the relationship among fashion, respect, and belonging desired by many migrants, and they used Icelandic staff and advertisements claiming Icelandic-language services to create an image of special treatment and dignity for Icelandic patrons. In their storeroom filled with *fínum tízkufötum* (fashionable clothing), Icelandic women could also peruse the largest selection of women's hats in the city at Carley Brothers' Clothing Company. The store had even hired a team of Icelandic clerks to assist, announcing, "We have Icelanders in the store especially for Icelanders."[82]

## Conclusion

Twenty years after the establishment of New Iceland, Einar Hjörleifsson was on a lecture tour in Iceland, and he told a story about an immigrant woman in a silk dress. The immigrant author, also known as Kvaran, was describing some of his experiences after spending a decade in Icelandic North American settlements and the profound differences between the treatment of working women in Iceland and *Ameríka*. He recalled visiting a well-established Icelandic-immigrant farm on a Sunday. Although she was clad in a beautiful silk dress for church, the lady of the house stopped to haul water on her way to the service. In Iceland, such a scene might be considered bizarre since the well-dressed wives of the elite seldom performed lowly tasks usually assigned to domestic servants. Yet, he announced, Icelandic immigrants valued and respected women's waged and manual labour, which had financially, mentally, and aesthetically transformed the community. Fashionably clad immigrant women workers enjoyed better money and better respect in North America, he informed his compatriots, while the "disdainful" treatment of female domestic workers in Iceland "would be considered a disgrace."[83] "Manual labour in the New World is an honourable occupation," he reported, "and to honour work is the same as honouring the person doing it."[84]

Kvaran's speech eloquently captured the close relationship among immigrant fashion, the making of a new social order in the immigrant community, and the many larger shifts that immigrants' new suits of clothing represented. While scholars have previously understood the decline of Icelandic "traditional" dress as a sign of cultural deterioration, changes to immigrant clothing, including the embrace of new North American styles, reveal much about migrant experiences and identities. Indeed, the popular decline of Icelandic nationalist fashions in North America represented more than their assimilation – it also signalled their disruption of rigid homeland hierarchies based on gender and class. At home, Icelandic costume embodied nationalist leaders' notions of natural and national order, ideas that justified the privileging of independent male landowners over working-class, poor, and marginalized Icelandic men and women. Although many migrant women had eagerly embraced these fashions at home in Iceland, it became clear when they arrived in North America that this clothing, including the "peculiar" *skotthúfa*, could represent something different, a marker of excessive ethnic and racial difference in the eyes of white, anglophone North Americans.

The history of clothing in the Icelandic community also offers a road map to the rapidly changing circumstances of migrants' lives. Icelanders initially felt the xenophobic scorn and biting cold of North America through fabric and fabric shortages, and cloth was the medium through which they fractured Old World hierarchies, built wardrobes suited to a new landscape, and pursued upward mobility. In addition to being their link to new work, wages, and survival in a radically different environment, immigrant clothing practices were part of the larger fashioning of new lives, values, and identities.

*Chapter Two*

# The Coffee Pot and King Bacchus: Icelandic Immigrant Drinking Cultures

In every Icelandic home the coffee pot sits on the stove and is never cold. It is their household god.[1]

While early migrants may have eagerly embraced anglophone fashions upon arrival, as discussed in the previous chapter, that embrace often stopped short of the beloved English teapot. Icelanders came from a coffee-centred culture, and jokes abounded about their desperate attempts to find good, strong coffee in a new land devoted to tea. Caffeine addiction even fuelled migration, according to a popular joke in Eyjafjörður in Northern Iceland. According to the story, when news spread about the possibility of emigrating to Brazil in the 1860s, two *kerlingar* (old biddies) "thought it would be paradise to be there, where there was more than enough [coffee] for them." The two women decided to emigrate, packed up their possessions, and left their homes. Their coffee plot came to an end when they came to the nearby, relatively small river, Fnjóská. This little river was only their first barrier to reaching a country ten thousand kilometres away, but the two women stopped on the bank and said to one another, "No, this is too difficult," and thus ended their journey to Brazil.[2]

This chapter explores the cultural and political history of drink in Icelandic North American society, with a focus on two of the most popular and contentious kinds of beverage: coffee and alcohol. Icelandic coffee culture was integral to the nineteenth-century society from which Icelanders emerged. In spite of the expense and poor quality of coffee beans on the Prairies in the 1870s and 1880s, and pressure from English suppliers to consume tea instead, early migrants devoted scarce money and considerable time and effort to re-establishing Icelandic coffee culture. Indeed, many immigrants viewed this coffee culture as essential to everyday life, labour, and the social fabric of the community. Conversely, alcohol was a powerfully divisive force, one that fuelled gender- and class-based rifts as many respectable Icelanders waged war against *Bakkús* (Bacchus), the god of wine. While Icelanders may have eagerly imported coffee practices to North America, many hoped that this other form of thirst – for alcohol – could be purged from their new society.

This chapter begins by exploring the roots of Icelandic coffee culture and tracing its controversial relationship to social life, hunger, and survival in nineteenth-century Iceland. Criticized by reformers as a tool of Danish colonial control, luxury items like coffee were nonetheless central to gendered identity and working and social life, even in instances of near-starvation. Coffee was also a surprisingly integral part of immigration and settlement. It reflected Icelanders' engagement with international flows of people and goods, and migrants' devotion to re-establishing Icelandic coffee culture in the new land transformed local coffee markets.

Alcohol was also a traditional part of Icelandic social life, particularly among men, but one that generated heated debate. Anxieties about male alcohol consumption reflected older antagonism towards Danish monopolies and their perceived connection to Icelandic social ills. The temperance movement was popular in the immigrant community, particularly among women, and it grew as part of a campaign to create a new, better Icelandic society devoid of homeland evils, inequalities, and abuses. It was also fuelled by fears that Anglo–North Americans might detect what many Icelanders believed was an inherited "Viking" weakness for drink. Fears that they might earn the label of rough, rowdy, intemperate foreigners, Icelandic reformers energetically targeted working-class Icelandic men for carousing in public as opposed to more affluent community members who drank, usually in private. Although they never eradicated drinking in the community, Icelandic chapters of organizations like the Good Templars did succeed in creating a public image of the community as sober, serious, and devoted to temperance. Still, alcohol consumption endured as an integral part of social life for many, revealing the considerable divide between the public face and private reality of Icelandic-migrant popular culture.

## Transnational Food and Drink Voices

Since the 1990s, scholarship on gender, migration, and North American ethnic communities has benefited from investigations into food and beverage consumption.[3] This chapter proceeds both from the growing scholarship on ethnic food history and from histories of the debates and divides over alcohol to describe a much broader range of conflicts and relationships.[4] Although historians have provided good coverage of the temperance movement since the 1970s,[5] scholarly research on the history of alcohol beyond prohibition campaigns has gained traction more slowly.[6] In addition to the scholarship of Hildigunnur Ólafsdóttir on changes to alcohol culture in Iceland, the work of scholars such as Craig Heron and Julia Roberts has moved away from the anti-alcohol discourse of the temperance movement to refocus on a much broader range of relationships and experiences surrounding drinking, including the pursuit of pleasure, male sociability, and the effects of alcohol cultures and economies on the construction of class, cultural identity, and space.[7] By studying coffee and alcohol together, this chapter seeks to understand both sides of the debate, from the reformers who struggled to purge Icelandic culture of "bad desire" to the dedicated patrons of coffee and alcohol who sometimes stood in their way.

### *Kaffi* and *Brennivín*: Drink in Nineteenth-Century Icelandic Society

Coffee was a fundamental part of nineteenth-century Icelandic social life. Although it was fashionable in England and continental Europe by the late seventeenth century, this exotic import did not take hold in Iceland for at least another century. During the eighteenth century, Icelandic accounts suggest that it was religious officials who first acquired a taste for it during their education in Denmark.[8] However, other Icelanders, including fishermen, students, and travellers, also likely encountered and tasted coffee on their voyages. Because it was expensive, *kaffi* began as a drink of the elite, but by the 1840s, coffee beans could be found in many Icelandic households due to a general period of economic improvement and the island's growing engagement with non-Danish foreign markets and traders. When the Danish crown relinquished control of trade for the island in 1854, new economic possibilities, trading partnerships, and opportunities for engaging with global export markets emerged.

While this change ushered in a new period of economic opportunity in Iceland, the newspaper *Íslendingur* reported that too much of this new-found money and purchasing power was going straight into Iceland's coffee pots. Reports indicate that the import of beans nearly quadrupled in the mid-nineteenth century, rising from 87,808 pounds in 1849 to 327,272 pounds in 1859, or roughly five pounds of coffee per person per year.[9] The large quantities of coffee that Icelanders consumed reflected its central place in mid-nineteenth-century Icelandic life, where drinking good-quality coffee was integral to the rhythm of most Icelandic households. As one priest reportedly declared in 1860, "Anyone who can't brew up coffee, among our people, can hardly be called a Christian."[10]

Unless household members were part of the minority who abstained from the beverage, coffee breaks punctuated Icelanders' working day. The first cup of coffee was often served in bed. A servant or the lady of the house often rose before the rest of the household to prepare the first pot. "After drinking this cup of coffee, everyone dressed and quickly went to work."[11] Coffee breaks throughout the day also helped labourers stay warm and energized when working outside in Iceland's often cold, damp weather (Figure 2.1). As a stimulant, coffee helped workers cope with strenuous labouring and travelling conditions, as did alcohol, which was an important part of both working and social life for many Icelandic men. The coffee-pot habit, however, was an expensive one. Beyond immediate family, established Icelandic households often consisted of numerous members who needed to be included in the household coffee budget, such as hired labourers, servants, extended family, and visiting travellers.

Although Icelandic men made coffee as needed and tea could be found in Icelandic homes, it was generally considered the responsibility of the female head of the household to regularly provide good-quality coffee for her guests. A woman's ability to provide good-quality coffee contributed to her status in the household and the larger community. Guests' assessment of coffee quality in a household, even during periods of shortage and crisis, could positively or negatively affect a hostess's reputation. As Icelandic cookbook author Þóra Andrea Jónsdóttir contended in 1858, Icelandic women should strive to brew up the best possible cup using pure, freshly roasted coffee beans.[12] Whether they sacrificed sometimes scarce funds to purchase beans, sugar, and coffee cups and saucers and other accessories or blended and roasted their own beans, by the 1870s, middle- and working-class women alike regularly devoted significant portions of their personal or household incomes to the production of good-quality coffee.

Both women and men enjoyed coffee as a social beverage, but Icelanders' consumption of alcohol was more rigidly policed according to gender and varied according to other factors, including preference and class. Taboos against alcohol consumption by women meant that "it was uncommon to see a drunken woman," although some were known to consume alcohol.[13] Some older children tried alcohol, particularly male children, who might have associated alcohol consumption with manliness and male sociability.[14] *Brennivín*, the 37.5-per-cent-proof, anise-flavoured liqueur, dominated commercial alcohol sales in nineteenth-century Iceland, although some Icelanders, especially those

Figure 2.1. "Kaffi fært rakstrakonum um 1910" [Coffee being served to women raking hay around 1910]. PMS.

of means, also imported wine and spirits such as rum. While Icelandic immigrant reformers in North America would come to focus on the drinking habits of working-class Icelanders, Hildigunnur Ólafsdóttir reports that, for much of the eighteenth and nineteenth centuries, discussions about problem drinking usually focused on heavier consumption by wealthier farmers, civil servants, and church officials. The Icelandic labouring class and subsistence farmers, she argues, simply could not afford such a habit until the middle of the nineteenth century.[15]

After the demise of Denmark's trading monopoly in 1854, larger quantities of imported alcohol, including brandy and cognac, flooded into the country, ushering in a period of heightened alcohol consumption in mid-nineteenth-century Iceland.[16] Heavy alcohol use among Icelanders was a common feature in travelogues from this period[17] and resulted in public reports of intemperance among Icelanders from all walks of life, including the clergy.[18] Frederick Metcalfe asserted that while Iceland had bred fine literary minds, the island's isolation had also fostered visible alcohol-related ills. Visiting the home of a brilliant but inebriated priest in 1860, he remarked, "On the book-shelves I saw a Virgil, Ciceronis de Officiis, a Handbook of Mythology, a Greek Lexicon, and several volumes of sermons; while under the table, upon the table, and in various parts of the room, were bottles, mostly empty."[19] Metcalfe reported to English readers his guide's explanation that alcohol use among the clergy was common and reflected the larger acceptance of heavy drinking in Icelandic society since "if the old fox swallows the poison, is it any wonder if the cubs do the same?"[20]

People consumed store-bought alcohol in a variety of places: at home, on the road, and in local merchants' establishments, which substituted as pubs, where men could purchase fractions of a bottle and drink and visit with friends. The increased availability of cheaper alcohol, coupled with a period of economic improvement for a larger segment of the population, caused both a spike in drinking and more concentrated discussions about the problems that it caused. The early immigrant generation in North America grew up in this particular moment of both alcoholic excess and campaigns for reform in the 1860s and 1870s. Moreover, reformers saw alcohol and coffee, as imports usually funnelled through Danish merchant networks, as somewhat morally ambiguous luxury goods. By the 1880s, temperance societies were flourishing in Iceland, and alcohol imports had dropped by almost half.[21]

Critics attributed countrywide poverty to working-class Icelanders' appetite for imports like alcohol and coffee, in much the same way that fashion reformers criticized their consumption of imported fabrics like silk. Alcohol was doubly cursed as both an intoxicant and a lucrative import that mainly benefited foreign producers and the merchant elite. Ann Pinson argues that Icelandic views on drinking reflected the close relationship between the country's temperance and independence movements, noting that, in the mid-1870s, "the prohibition movement was an important symbol of Icelandic independence from Denmark."[22] Indeed, *brennivín* was one of the main commodities in the Danish-dominated import economy of nineteenth-century Iceland. Although Denmark's trade monopoly on the island had been lifted in 1854, the Danish merchant class and Danish-owned stores and businesses remained powerful throughout the century.

Mid-century reformers noted with distain that the lower classes were far too accustomed to a steady supply of coffee, alcohol, and other "luxury items" from these merchants, even when it meant forfeiting farm supplies and food.[23] Indeed, archival evidence suggests that these stimulants and sources of comfort were still desired and occasionally located during times of crisis. In 1869, Sveinn Þórarinsson, a sheriff's clerk in Eyjafjörður in northern Iceland, included coffee news in his detailed diary of daily life during one of the region's cold summers, which thwarted fishing, prevented haymaking, and blocked the arrival of supplies. Shortages caused by the weather were killing his cattle, he reported. "Everywhere news of people near death ... no fish to be caught, the nets drag nothing. Hunger closes in on us, rich and poor alike."[24]

Two pounds of coffee and two pints of *brennivín* were among the last of Sveinn's family's food stocks in June 1869, and both remained a source of fixation for him and other members of his social circle. "We walked over to Siglunes to get some coffee; but what we got was thin and poor,"[25] he wrote with disappointment that month, but reported with satisfaction on 18 June that "Friðbjörn Steinsson [had] sent his wife a pound of coffee, and I got a taste of it."[26] His family tried to replace coffee with wild thyme water, but his desperation for coffee motivated him to create an experimental coffee replacement "made of beans and grain." Alcohol, he noted, was also a source of desire and badly needed relief. Just one month before his death, Sveinn "stayed overnight in town with Ólafur and several others" when a cargo ship and several shark-fishing boats docked in the harbour. The men socialized and "did some drinking," which offered them a familiar reprieve from a dire summer.[27]

## Immigration and Drink

Coffee, alcohol, and the debates they inspired were woven into the fabric of the Icelandic society that produced the emigrant/immigrant generation. As coffee and alcohol were commonly accepted symbols of pleasure and good living, potential immigrants also often imagined their lives in North America in terms of the potential availability and expense of their favourite commodities, and enquiries about the expense of these items can often be found in their letters. Frequent questions and articles about the cost of "essential" household goods like coffee were one of the ways in which Icelanders attempted to imagine and plan life across the Atlantic.[28] Imported goods were also one of the ways in which isolated Icelanders could experience contact with global networks and the outside world before departure. The coffee plantations of Brazil, for example, rendered the country at least slightly more familiar to the Icelanders who considered moving there in the late 1850s and early 1860s. In 1859, circulating reports of mass European emigration included word of opportunities in Brazil and prompted pledges from 150 Icelanders to join this move if conditions were good. Brazil emerged in the Icelandic popular imagination as a dream-like land of sun and plenty. As Einar Ásmundsson wrote in a circular on the plan, "Winter never comes there, and many kinds of fruits and vegetables grow excellently ... on cultivated land one can grow an abundance of coffee, sugar cane, cotton, tobacco, rice, maize and so on."[29]

While images of plentiful *kaffi*, alongside sugar, tobacco, and fruit, may have seduced some Icelanders into considering a new life in Brazil, most new arrivals to North America were unhappy with the lack of access to good coffee there. Some Icelandic migrants to the United States found commercial markets more accustomed to providing coffee for the large Norwegian, Swedish, and other coffee-drinking immigrant groups, but its quality and availability could still vary considerably. Migrants to Canada, where the British teapot reigned supreme, were even less fortunate. Early aid sent to the struggling New Iceland colony by the Canadian government in the 1870s reflected Anglo-Canadian tastes, including a preference for economical tea. As Jón Jónsson of Mæri recalled with disappointment, "I could get tea from the government, but little coffee."[30] Guðbrandur Erlendsson also recalled with a slight hint of bitterness that he had been "restricted to drinking tea" while working in a predominantly anglophone Nova Scotia because there "was no coffee available in the stores."[31]

Some Icelanders would go to great lengths to rectify coffee shortages. After she ran out of coffee beans in the winter of 1886, Helga Johnson was too nervous to travel by herself to the nearest neighbouring Icelandic farm in the Lögberg area (Saskatchewan). She waited for three days until she could stand the craving for coffee no longer. That Sunday, she grabbed a pair of her husband's overalls and disguised herself as a man. When she finally arrived at the house in search of beans, it was filled with Sunday company, who were horrified at the sight of the housewife in men's clothing.[32]

Indeed, limited access to good coffee was a significant source of displeasure, and some went to great lengths to brew a pot. Augustus Baldwin, a medical official who was working in the New Iceland colony during the height of the smallpox epidemic, recalled that although many lacked food, one Icelandic woman offered to pour him a cup of coffee. Shocked to find such a luxury amid the squalor of the early settlement during the winter quarantine, Baldwin eagerly accepted, but was horrified to see his host clean the cup by licking it out with her tongue first.[33] Even after the smallpox quarantine was lifted in the summer of 1877, poverty continued to restrict regular access to coffee for years. "Fabulous Sigga" Jónsdóttir, marooned without coffee on Hecla Island in 1879, described her inability to satisfy her deep-seated cravings for *kaffi*. "Much did I long for coffee in the fall when I got better – and I would get weak in the middle of the day for it, but we never had the remedy," she reported.[34]

Even for those who could afford coffee, numerous early reports attest to its poor quality in Winnipeg and Dakota Territory. Icelandic immigrants often encountered coffee of a "very inferior quality"[35] and considered much of the pre-ground, pre-roasted coffee they encountered "unbearable for the Icelandic palate."[36] Thorstína Walters recalled that the poor-quality coffee available in Dakota Territory stores was very unpopular with women, who "preferred to buy the green coffee and roast it at home."[37] Such demands for better coffee led to greater availability and an improvement in the quality of beans in Icelandic districts. In Winnipeg, Icelandic grocers provided shoppers with unroasted coffee beans, but non-Icelandic stores quickly caught on to the demand. In the 1890s, Moses Finkelstein, an immigrant from the Ukraine and Winnipeg's future first Jewish councillor, took out Icelandic-language advertisements boasting that his store had the *bezta grænt kaffi*, or the "best green coffee," in Winnipeg.[38]

Green beans, rather than pre-roasted and pre-ground, North American–style coffee, were the norm in rural Icelandic homes at the turn of the century. "The smell of roasting coffee and the purring sound of the coffee grinder," wrote Magnús Guðlaugson, were familiar smells and sounds in migrants' homes.[39] "No sooner had a visitor arrived at a farm home," he reported, and "the coffee-rites were in full swing!"[40] (Figure 2.2). In addition to having their own coffee-roasting practices, Icelanders rejected the methods of brewing coffee found in Manitoba and Dakota Territory and preferred their own method of preparing it using a handmade cloth filter, also called a *kaffi poki* (coffee bag, or coffee sock). Coffee bags, made from dense flannel or cotton, were first

Figure 2.2. Coffee in a turn-of-the-twentieth-century Icelandic farmhouse in Brownbyggð, MB. Undated photograph. EIHC.

stitched to a thick, metal-wire circle about four inches across, outfitted with a handle. Next, the fabric was seasoned with coffee grounds. Freshly roasted, freshly ground coffee was then placed in the bag and boiling water poured over top. The semi-watertight bag would hold the hot water and grounds as they steeped and slowly allow the coffee to drip into the pot.[41] At the time of writing, this method of making coffee could still be found in the households of some migrants' descendants.

Once early financial and geographical obstacles to its acquisition had been overcome, *kaffi* resumed its mandatory place in social and economic interactions in the late nineteenth and early twentieth centuries. Although they were initially offered more economical tea by their employers, Icelandic labourers began to demand coffee from other Icelanders as a condition of their employment.[42] Oral accounts frequently reference the central place of coffee in immigrant social life as well as the multiple coffee breaks that punctuated the working day on Icelandic farms.[43] This passion for coffee led to several eccentric customs, which became widespread in the community, including drinking coffee from saucers instead of cups and the Scandinavian custom of drinking coffee through sugar cubes held in the mouth, also known as *molakaffi*.[44] The Icelandic quest for good coffee was also the source of numerous Icelandic-language jokes and stories. Albert Kristjanson recalled one about a man named Sigurður who arrived to work on the farm of a wealthy Icelandic immigrant. To his surprise, the employer failed to provide him with coffee. Shortly afterwards, the employer found Sigurður kneeling next to a hay bale in prayer and approached him once he got up. "I see, dear Sigurður, that you are at prayer," said the employer. "Yes," replied Sigurður, "I was asking the Holy Spirit how it was that He sent me to the only Icelandic home that doesn't offer people coffee in the afternoon."[45]

Icelandic coffee culture also permeated immigrant space in urban centres such as Winnipeg, where patrons could get a good, strong cup at one of several Icelandic *kaffihús* (coffeehouses). These early coffeehouses provided Icelandic migrants with more than strong coffee; they offered a welcoming Icelandic-language space where patrons could meet, visit, and debate. In 1888, migrants could congregate at an Icelandic coffeehouse at 17 Market Street that offered chessboards and cards for patrons to use, along with Icelandic-language service and newspapers.[46] Later incarnations, such as the Wevel Café, were widely recognized sites of cultural production and political debate. This café opened in 1915 at 692 Sargent Avenue, in the heart of the Icelandic neighbourhood in the city's West End. Its proximity to local Icelandic businesses meant that the editors and staff of the local Icelandic newspapers and publishing houses frequently met there. Famed artist Charlie Thorson was also a regular, due in part to his personal interest in a beautiful, dark-haired waitress named Kristín Sölvadóttir. The Walt Disney Company later hired Thorson, and he contributed to the development of cartoon characters such as Bugs Bunny. He also reportedly used sketches of Sölvadóttir while being involved in the creation of Snow White in 1937. This led to claims in the community that Snow White was not only Icelandic – she had also served coffee at the Wevel Café.[47]

### Drowning the "Old Icelandic Adam": The Icelandic Temperance Movement

While the re-establishment of coffee culture was a priority in Icelandic immigrant society, many hoped that another appetite – for stronger drink – would disappear in the new land. Icelanders may have been relatively united in their pursuit of good-quality coffee, but no force divided the nineteenth-century immigrant community like alcohol. In response to the reign of *Bakkús Konungur* (King Bacchus) in Iceland, the Good Templar movement emerged and began to flourish in the immigrant community in the 1880s. Reformers at home in Iceland blamed the sales of spirits like *brennivín* for weakening the Icelandic nation, destroying the health and welfare of Icelanders, and undermining the independence movement. Across the Atlantic, Icelandic immigrant leaders also feared that alcohol would sabotage the future of the Icelandic North American community.

Temperance became central to the way that many Icelandic immigrants imagined the future of their community in North America. Icelandic chapters of the Good Templar movement and temperance supporters used protests against alcohol as a catch-all for critiquing the perpetuation of poverty, corruption, and abuse on both sides of the Atlantic. Many migrants involved in or sympathetic to the temperance movement saw alcohol as representing the poverty, underdevelopment, and inequalities of life in nineteenth-century Iceland and used temperance to discuss the social progress that was possible for the Icelandic people in North America. Frances Swyripa writes that many late nineteenth-century migrant communities saw the west as "virgin land capable of regenerating a tired and corrupt civilization."[48] Yet, as Friðjón Friðriksson wrote to the Reverend Jón Bjarnason, the establishment of a new Icelandic society liberated from Danish control also meant purging the old "sins" and negative desires embedded within Icelanders themselves – particularly men. "First the old Icelandic Adam – along with all his sins and bad desires – must be drowned," wrote Friðrikson in 1881. "Then the new American can emerge."[49]

**Sons of Egill: Drinking and "Viking" Masculinity**

Ideas about gender helped fuel some of the fiercest debates over temperance in the Icelandic immigrant community. Like their Anglo–North American counterparts, Icelandic women became involved in the temperance movement as a response to male violence and sexist economic disparity. Alcohol was part of the coded language through which nineteenth-century North Americans discussed gender inequality and domestic violence, as Katherine Harvey and other temperance historians have written.[50] Women with alcoholic husbands faced drains on family budgets, potential violence, and strains on family relations. Heavy drinking also threatened the lives and health of male breadwinners, upon whom women depended.[51] The growing popularity of feminist and temperance sentiment in Iceland in the 1870s led to a lively Icelandic-language exchange about temperance and women's rights across the Atlantic around the turn of the century. During a tour of Icelandic settlements in Manitoba and North Dakota in 1897–8, prominent Icelandic activist Ólafía Jóhannsdóttir reported that she was energetically welcomed by the thriving temperance and suffrage movement while addressing what she saw as the intertwined issues of alcohol abuse and gender inequality. Through the temperance movement, many Icelandic women could also rise to positions of leadership otherwise reserved for men. Housewife Guðrún Búason of Winnipeg, for example, was a prominent leader in the Hekla Lodge. Her duties took her to international conventions in Washington, DC; Antwerp; and Hamburg between 1893 and 1911, and she was celebrated as a shining example of Icelandic honour[52] (Figure 2.3).

For many Icelandic temperance advocates, alcohol also represented what they thought was a hidden secret in their community: that some Icelandic men had inherited a violent "Viking" gene, which could bring out their uncivilized side. Temperance was a prerequisite for self-governance and progress, they believed. As one Icelandic MP declared in 1934, during the country's ongoing debates about alcohol laws, "Icelanders are not able to use alcohol as civilized persons, their nature is still too much of the Viking kind, they get too excited and brutal with alcohol usage."[53] Although nineteenth-century Icelandic immigrants associated alcohol with the unruly Viking potential of Icelandic men, some did so proudly. For example, when Halldór Þórgilsson from Hundadalur got into an argument with a Quebec City bartender in 1876, he proudly announced that he was a "descendant of Egill" – Egill Skallagrímsson, a tenth-century Viking settler from the sagas and arguably Iceland's unofficial patron saint of altered states. After spending three weeks at sea, Halldór had decided to slip away and celebrate his arrival in Canada with a drink at a local pub. His travel companions reportedly later found him on the street in a confrontation with a local bartender. The bartender accused him of walking out on a fifty-cent whisky bill and demanded payment, but Halldór refused to back down. Accompanied by a few of his countrymen, he defiantly told the bartender "that we were Vikings" – and left.[54]

If thirsty and rough, working-class immigrant Vikings in Winnipeg had a main representative, it was probably Gísli Jónsson from Saurar, also known as "Dirty Gísli." Born in West Iceland in 1820, Gísli became a symbol of the dangers that alcohol consumption by individuals posed to the reputation of their community. Dirty Gísli ran a Winnipeg

Figure 2.3. Guðrún Búason, 1913. Reprinted from Guðmundur Árnason et al., *Minningarrit Stúkunnar Heklu Nr. 33 af Alþjóðareglu Good Templara [Memories of the Hekla Lodge of the International Order of the Good Templars]* (Winnipeg: Prentsmiðja Ólafs S. Thorgeirssonar, 1913), 51.

boarding house that was popular with many in the working-class Icelandic community, but condemned by the local Icelandic-language newspaper *Framfari* as a centre of drinking and disreputable conduct. "There is a considerable amount of irregularity going on among the Icelanders here," a letter to the newspaper reported in 1879, "especially in that building known as 'The Icelandic House,' which Saura-Gísli is now renting. There are dancing and drinking parties, often every evening, and the police have begun to keep their eyes on it," reported *Framfari*. Dirty Gísli himself, they claimed, had even been arrested "when he lay in the street drunk."[55]

Although some Icelanders from all class backgrounds drank alcohol, it was the more public drinking habits of working-class, city Icelanders like Dirty Gísli and patrons of the Icelandic House who provoked the most concern among respectable Icelanders in the 1870s and 1880s. The Icelandic community in Winnipeg had been founded in the same autumn as New Iceland, in 1875, and image-conscious Icelandic immigrant leaders had long expressed concern that the more publicly visible conduct of Icelandic labourers in the city, particularly drinking, might tarnish the reputation of the community in the eyes of anglophone society. "Such behaviour brings down upon the Icelanders in the eyes of other people," asserted an 1879 editorial in *Framfari*, "for many people are inclined to judge foreigners on the basis of only a few examples, and so blame a whole people for the faults of only a few individuals."[56] Much to the horror of ambitious and image-conscious Icelanders, news of arrests and public disruptions appeared on the front page of the *Manitoba Free Press* for the reading pleasure of English audiences around this time. Such reports included the 1879 arrest of an "Icelander with an unpronounceable name," who was found drunk on the street and arrested after "giving his tuneful voice too full scope in an Icelandic version of 'Pinafore' yesterday."[57]

Despite the editorials in *Framfari*, there were some Icelanders who respected Dirty Gísli, who also had a reputation as a poet and champion of the impoverished and marginalized.[58] His clashes with the immigrant elite also reflected his reputation as a well-known "thorn in the side of his superiors" on both sides of the Atlantic.[59] In rumours that circulated about his character, including stories that he had run a poly-amorous household in Iceland and had once struck a priest for criticizing him, Gísli emerged as a general opponent of those who sought to impose Christian, middle-class order on others.[60] *Framfari* recommended that temperate and respectable Icelanders stay at Jón Thordarson's boarding house in Winnipeg, away from Dirty Gísli's and those who squandered "their money and time in saloons."[61] They also publicly requested that intemperate Icelanders "raise themselves above such conditions and engage in some finer and better activity" to become "men among men."[62] Urban labourers resented the accusations and interference coming from New Iceland's elite. The "Shanty Town Dwellers," as they were known, fired back an angry letter to the editor of *Framfari*, protesting the "false propaganda" about their character and habits.[63]

An analysis of early arrest records and conflicts in Icelandic Winnipeg reveals the historical conditions in the city that made alcohol so central to discussions of the future of the Icelandic people in North America. Many Icelandic men were drawn to Winnipeg because of the availability of construction and other labouring jobs in the 1870s and 1880s. This period also saw an explosion in the number of saloons and breweries in the city to serve the influx of labourers and businesspeople flooding into the city from across the continent. By 1882, Winnipeg boasted five breweries, eighty-six hotels (many with saloons), and sixty-four grocers who sold whisky, the drink of choice for many working-class men during this period.[64]

For many Icelandic migrant men, even those from temperate backgrounds, life in North America often meant immersion in a working-class social life in which alcohol was often essential to both Icelandic and North American notions of masculinity. Such attitudes are perhaps best summarized in a posed, cowboy-style photograph of Jóhannes "Long-haired Jo" Stefánsson, the wild brother of the explorer Vilhjálmur Stefánsson, enjoying a drink with a friend in Dakota Territory around the end of the nineteenth century (Figure 2.4). Individual Icelandic workers might have their own opinions about drink, but they had to reconcile them with the central place of alcohol in working-class, male-leisure, and male-identity culture, especially if they hoped to be accepted by new co-workers. Boarding a crowded train of men bound for lumber camps in Ontario, Magnús Árnason recalled that most of his Swedish, African American, French, Norwegian, and Slavic co-workers were already drunk.[65] Drinking fostered a sense of belonging, which meant that temperate men risked isolation and alienation in remote work camps. Even devout temperance men like Thorvaldur Thórarinsson accepted a drink at the urging of his co-workers on a construction job on the Canadian Pacific Railway in 1876–7. It was his first and last. He disliked the feeling of dizziness and lack of control and snuck away by himself to sleep it off under a tree.[66]

Anxieties about working-class drinking in the urban community intensified after the Winnipeg construction boom collapsed in 1883. As unemployment and urban poverty in the Icelandic community grew, a large group of 900 new Icelandic immigrants arrived in the city. Most of them had relied on older news of the fortunes being made in the province, but arrived instead in the midst of a financial crisis and labour glut. This influx of impoverished new arrivals placed a strain on many established community members, who themselves were also suddenly in need of work and affordable housing. These stressful conditions, immigrant poverty, and a plentiful supply of alcohol fuelled a steep rise in the number of arrests of Icelandic immigrants in Winnipeg. In 1883, twenty-four Icelanders were charged with public drunkenness and related charges amid a larger spike in alcohol-related charges in the city.[67]

Figure 2.4. Long-haired Jóhannes ("long-haired Joe") Stefánsson and unknown companion. Undated photograph. EIHC.

Concerns about public drunkenness, as well as the growth of moral reform campaigns, helped inspire the formation of the first Icelandic chapters of the Independent Order of Good Templars (IOGT) in Winnipeg. The creation of multiple IOGT lodges in rural Icelandic centres followed, including two named at Icelandic River and Gimli.[68] By the mid-1880s, numerous religious and political divides had already emerged within the Icelandic community, and separate temperance lodges were established along these various lines. The Hekla IOGT lodge served readers of the conservative newspaper *Heimskringla* and opposed membership in the Lutheran Synod, while membership in Skuld consisted mainly of *Lögberg* readers and supporters of the Lutheran Synod.[69] Most major Icelandic associations, including Framfarafélagið (the Progressive Society), the Icelandic Student Society, women's church guilds, and later the Jón Sigurdsson Chapter of the Imperial Order Daughters of the Empire (IODE), established in 1916, were affiliated or ideologically aligned with the temperance movement, but engaged with it in their own particular ways. Still, temperance emerged as an unusually unifying force within such a politically and spiritually divided community. It was a requisite for accessing resources and public space in the community, especially for those who wished to use the large, well-equipped Icelandic Good Templars Hall, built in Winnipeg's West End in 1906. The "Goolie Hall," as it was also known, was the site of many types of events, including plays, dances, lectures, and sales, and was a focal point of social activity for the city's Icelanders. It was restricted, however, to dry gatherings that respected temperance principles.

### Temperance and the Homebrew Line: Drinking in New Iceland

Just as divisions between the wet and dry communities shaped space and social life in Icelandic Winnipeg, so clashes over drinking and temperance occurred throughout rural Icelandic settlements. Heated discussions emerged in New Iceland over the availability of alcohol in the area as community members clashed over the place that alcohol could occupy in the area. New Iceland was subject to the ban on liquor in Rupert's Land until 1881,[70] but in the last decades of the nineteenth century, access to alcohol shifted according to the development of transport and mail infrastructure and the growing availability of local goods and services. From the 1880s onward, for example, New Icelanders could order patent medicines being advertised in Icelandic newspapers to "correct nervousness" and other disorders. Some of these, like the Burdock Blood Bitters advertised in *Heimskringla* in 1889, were 19 per cent alcohol, while others, such as Hoffman's Drops and colic remedies, could contain ether, morphine, or cocaine.[71]

More than simply trying to close down taverns or restrict access to commercially produced alcohol, however, rural temperance advocates faced a more diffuse, private culture of alcohol consumption and home-brew production. New Iceland and other rural Icelandic settlements may have appeared temperate by outward appearances, but it is clear that here too alcohol had resumed its place as an important part of Icelandic male social life in the 1880s and 1890s. "It is considered little better than a profanity to state that liquor is sold here in New Iceland, but it is easy to prove," an anonymous commentator noted of the numerous tipsy attendees at an 1891 election debate at Icelandic River. "Things are just as they were back in Iceland," they reported.[72]

It is difficult to trace the extent of the undocumented production of home brew by Icelanders in the earliest decades of settlement. However, it is clear that some immigrants were familiar with homemade alcohol production; at least a few Icelanders produced home brew in small batches in their own homes, often just "enough to get a few guys drunk."[73] Community lore associates the larger-scale, cottage-industry production of alcohol in Icelandic settlements with the opening of New Iceland to non-Icelandic immigrants in 1897. Ukrainian immigrants began arriving in the area around this period, and some enjoyed a reputation for skilled production of powerful home brew. Ukrainian-produced alcohol gained an infamous reputation among Icelanders, who also called it *Gallahland* (Galician swill).[74]

By the beginning of the twentieth century, the popularity of home brew in the area surrounding Riverton (Icelandic River) had left an imprint on the local landscape. In keeping with the Icelandic tradition of naming places, a survey line between Riverton and Víðir was known as *Brugglínan* (the Homebrew Line) because of its association with the local economy.[75] During Prohibition, residents of Riverton could reportedly "go in any direction, and you'd find somebody bootlegging."[76] To avoid detection by local officials, bootleggers legally distanced themselves from direct transactions by accepting, as payment, information about the locations where bottles were hidden.

Home-brew production and consumption could also be found in and around fishing camps around the northern basin of Lake Winnipeg, where people could escape the legal regulation of alcohol production during times of prohibition. "It was against the law to make it, so some guys would build a still out in the bush," remembered Joe Johnson, a veteran fisherman whose parents had emigrated from Iceland at the turn of the twentieth century. "Some of it was good, some of it was not ... but it packed a punch." Even in the isolation of the Manitoba bush, however, the conflict over alcohol continued, much to the chagrin of men who operated stills. As Johnson recalled, some temperance activists could be proactive and aggressive, and "If they dared, they'd go and break your still ... oh, they were just wicked."[77]

While some Icelanders and their descendants maintained a pro-temperance stance for decades afterwards, membership in Icelandic temperance organizations fluctuated dramatically in the former colony. Advocates also lost a crucial battle in 1905 when the first liquor licence was granted to a hotel owner in Gimli. Still, alcohol consumption remained a tense subject in the region well into the twentieth century, and oral history interviews and memoirs quickly reveal the continued power of temperance convictions in many Icelandic North American homes. Many women and temperance supporters continued to impose strict personal and household rules that restricted the spaces where alcohol consumption was permitted. Some women established total bans on alcohol in their homes and sometimes in their marriages. George Asgeirson remembered, for example, that before his parents emigrated to Canada in 1913, his mother had set a precondition for marriage, making his father swear that he would never touch a drop of alcohol.[78]

Men who wanted to drink might also find themselves ostracized by women and temperate male friends and relatives. Metta Johnson recalled that her parents' strict views on alcohol forced those who wished to have a beer or a whisky into the family's icehouse.[79] In a humorous *drykkjuvísa* (drinking poem) from south of the border, Pembina County poet Kristján Niels Júlíus (also known as Káinn) echoed this description of the less glamorous spaces where he and his drinking buddies were forced to spend their nights when they *"lentu á túr,"* or "went on a drunk."

> Our countrymen were mighty then,
> Mightier than giants in cliffs.
> Many got a blow to the chops, I remember still,
> When we drank in outhouses.[80]

## Conclusion

Icelandic immigrant drinking practices and divisions provide us with a unique window through which to view some of the rich subtleties of the early community's heated debates about the shape of the immigrant future in North America. Unlike the dramatic transformations in fashion described in the previous chapter, coffee and alcohol consumption and production endured in the migrant community, although the transition to Anglo–North American society shaped the way that migrants accessed these mainstays. In Iceland, despite criticisms that the working poor forfeited farm supplies and food for such addictive luxury items, coffee and alcohol were integral to working and social life, even during periods of deprivation. Good, strong cups of coffee and nips of *brennivín* were woven into the nineteenth-century Icelandic gender norms, notions of hospitality, and daily life. The disruption of coffee and alcohol supplies during immigration was a clear source of displeasure among the migrants, who invested considerable time, energy, and money in re-acquiring good-quality supplies in their new homes.

The immigrant generation's passionate pursuit of good coffee also illuminates the boundaries of migrant acculturation, including Icelanders' resistance to tea-centric markets in Anglo–North America. Icelanders may have altered other parts of their public appearance to fit into mainstream society, including clothing, but they rejected more personal and immediate changes in their beverages of choice. The endurance of traditional coffee practices reflected not only migrants' refusal to change but also their ability to transform local markets and public spaces, evident in the rise of Icelandic coffeehouses and the commercial availability of better-quality coffee beans, particularly green beans, in response to their demands.

While Icelanders may have been relatively unified in their quest to re-establish their own coffee culture in North America, no issue divided the community like alcohol. Patterns of private consumption of alcohol reflected the ways in which drink was part of larger internal debates about Icelandic masculinity, social reform, and the community's relations with Anglo–North American society. Rooted in migrant critiques of Danish rule, socio-economic stagnation, and gender inequality at home, anxieties about alcoholism resulted in the community creating a public facade that emphasized temperance. As Icelandic-language forums and oral accounts reveal, however, this public image reflects a larger division within the community itself, one that relegated drinking and drinkers to the margins of Icelandic migrant society and space. According to many sources, drinking was commonplace and a source of contention in multiple communities, including Winnipeg in the 1880s and New Iceland after 1897. Moreover, it was an integral part of male culture and relationships, including those with men outside the community. The popularity of the temperance movement with Icelandic women, however, revealed that alcohol consumption was also part of a larger, gender-based contest over power and definitions of appropriate masculinity in the immigrant community.

In nineteenth-century Iceland and North America, coffee and alcohol acted as both cohesive and divisive forces that illuminated debates over character and conduct in Icelandic society. Reflecting older reform movements at home, the desire of Icelandic community leaders in North America to "drown the old Icelandic Adam" and rejuvenate Icelandic culture and people on North American soil required purging select, undesirable aspects of Icelandic society. This resulted in the establishment of early divisions between those who observed temperate, hospitable, and "good" Icelandic practices and those who did not. The reappearance of old drinking patterns not only endangered the dream of a reformed and rejuvenated migrant society, it also threatened the social and economic status of the community in Anglo–North American society. Respectable middle-class and temperate Icelanders feared that the more visible drinking habits of working-class Icelanders in Winnipeg might damage the collective reputation of the community, while many working-class Icelanders found themselves in work camps and neighbourhoods where alcohol consumption was integral to male sociability and belonging. Yet, whether it was *kaffi* or booze, Icelandic drinking traditions endured as much desired sources of pleasure and comfort in a new land.

*Chapter Three*

# Unsettling Apparitions: Power, Ghost Stories, and Superstitious Belief

According to one of many Icelandic ghost stories from Riverton, Manitoba, a boy called Skrámur almost died after attempting to impersonate the supernatural. The local youth decided to frighten two girls who lived next to the community's notoriously haunted smallpox cemetery at Nes (Graftarnes, or Burial Point). In local lore, the cemetery was a terrifying site, one where memories of the smallpox epidemic lingered. The riverside site was nicknamed Náströnd (Corpse Beach),[1] a corpse-filled underworld in Viking Age mythology, because of the bones of epidemic victims that regularly eroded out of the riverbank.[2] Skrámur delighted in scaring the girls by telling them some of the many ghost stories he had heard about Nes. These included descriptions of apparitions of First Nations children, undead men that emerged from the ground, and wild, black horses that appeared there, but belonged to no local farm.

As the story goes, Skrámur decided to stage a ghost sighting at Nes to frighten the girls while their father was away working on a threshing gang. He hid in the long grass with a white sheet, waiting for them to make their evening trek near the haunted cemetery to get the cows for milking. When they approached, he draped himself in the sheet and swayed back and forth in the long grass, terrifying the pair, who ran back to their house, crying. Meanwhile, their father, Björn of Víðimýri, had just returned from his harvest tour. He quickly grabbed his shotgun and went in search of the "ghost." This time, when Skrámur stood up in his sheet, he received a round of buckshot in his backside. Skrámur survived, but spent several weeks convalescing in hospital in an embarrassing position.[3]

The story of Skrámur's trip to the hospital is a more obvious illustration of the real power of the ghost story in Icelandic immigrant culture and what Icelanders believed were the deserved results of tampering with, or making light of, the supernatural. Actual belief in these kinds of stories varied; however, it is clear that distinctive Icelandic ideas about the supernatural, some of which were rooted in medieval traditions, continued to shape community life, outlooks, and even uses of space for generations in the new land.

While the previous two chapters have focused on Icelanders' engagement with and adjustment to anglophone North American culture, this chapter turns inward to examine supernatural belief as a form of popular community expression that was largely hidden from outside observers. It begins with a discussion of the historical significance of the ghost story as a resource for understanding ways of speaking about trauma and power in an immigrant community. A discussion of some of the distinctive properties of Icelandic ghost stories and superstitious traditions in the nineteenth century makes clear that these narrative traditions arrived in North America with Icelandic immigrants and were altered and adjusted to help community members understand and make sense of difficult experiences in a new context.

As an oral tradition, early Icelandic immigrant ghost stories usually relied upon Icelandic language forums and were translated into and shared in English only very selectively. This special relationship to the Icelandic language meant that, for decades, many Icelandic ghost stories circulated behind the veil of language, in spite of taboos against ethnic and non-Christian forms of superstitious beliefs in Anglo–North America. Interestingly, some of the compelling and distinctive ghost stories that emerged in nineteenth- and early twentieth-century Icelandic immigrant communities preserved sometimes centuries-old narrative structures and beliefs, blended with North American content and conditions. They also offer important windows into understanding more complex power relations within the community, including spiritual beliefs about the exploitation of children and young labourers and spaces of colonial displacement and trauma that surrounded New Iceland. By exploring stories about revenge ghosts and followers (*fylgjur*) as well as powerful First Nations ghosts, whom Icelanders believed could bar them from certain spaces, this chapter argues that supernatural stories helped establish alternative hierarchies of power and spatial boundaries, which sometimes stood in stark contrast to official patriarchal and colonial order on the Prairies.

## *Hjátrú* and Hauntology

*Hjátrú*, the Icelandic word for "superstition," translates roughly as something that is "beside" – or an addition to orthodox faith or religion. "Folk belief" is perhaps the closest English-language translation, although the term *superstition* is also widely used. These terms carry their own connotations in English, including an association with ignorance or backwardness. Moreover, they do not fully capture the nuances of the Icelandic term, which suggests that such beliefs and narratives do not compete with Christian authority and faith, but exist alongside and outside them. Indeed, numerous Icelandic tales of the supernatural reference Christian religious figures involved in *hjátrú*, including dream interpretation, ghostly sightings, and even sorcery.[4] This outlook reflects the larger history of traditional belief in Iceland. *Hjátrú* persisted among many nineteenth- and twentieth-century Icelanders on both sides of the ocean, often without the same negative stigma that often characterizes discussions of the "occult" in English-language North American culture. It also offers a rich area of study that has long attracted interdisciplinary attention. Iceland's centuries of relative isolation, late industrialization, and sparse, predominantly rural population provided conditions favourable for the preservation of older narrative structures about superstition, some of which are rooted in the country's pre-Christian past.

G. Turville-Petre and other mid-century scholars frequently commented that some of the large body of supernatural narratives show "little discontinuity between Norse pagan times and the twentieth century."[5] Although Icelanders officially accepted Christianity in 1000 CE, the terms of the conversion permitted practitioners of the old pre-Christian faith to continue to worship in private. Scholars, therefore, generally caution against a rigid separation of pre-Christian and Christian belief in Iceland, arguing that elements of the two belief systems could, instead, co-exist. "Because of the nature of the Conversion of Iceland to Christianity," argues Loftur Reimar Gissurarson and William H. Swatos, Jr., "it cannot be assumed that ancient beliefs and superstitions were ever entirely repudiated."[6] The enduring, powerful influence of the sagas in Icelandic culture and their frequent references to Norse mythology over the centuries further fostered continued attachment to older ways of thinking about the world.

Many immigration historians tend to dismiss ghost stories in community studies, often viewing them as unreliable and even backward by-products of immigrant cultures. Unfortunately, as Peter Buse and Andrew Stott contend, other scholars often approach ghost stories with the intent of identifying "fact or fiction, real or not-real ... either a positive or negative facticity that the notion of ghostliness continually eludes."[7] However, a renewed scholarly appreciation for supernatural narratives, figures, and landscapes reveals how ghost stories can also offer important insight into histories of trauma and the formation of historical consciousness, hierarchies, and dialogues. As scholars influenced

Jacques Derrida's work on hauntology argue, the study of haunting is not about proving or disproving the existence of ghosts. Instead, it offers a compelling way for understanding and thinking through the spectre of belief.[8] More recent works on the cultural implications of ghosts and hauntology have become an increasingly popular subject in cultural and literary studies since Derrida's 1994 publication of *The Spectres of Marx*, which uses the term *hauntology* to play with and challenge established notions of ontology (the study of the nature of existence). For Derrida, the in-between state of the ghost – as something that exists between life and death, real and unreal, past and present – offers a critical space for challenging notions of order and historical reality.[9]

Ghost stories also offer a compelling framework for thinking about alternative cultural conceptions of time. The idea of the ghost disrupts notions of linear time and the separation between the past and present, suggesting that – at times – they may become entangled and coexist. The ghost suggests that the present never exists separately from the past, thereby defying established chronologies and systems of logic. Such an approach is particularly useful for thinking about the relationship between historical colonial trauma and the present. Fredric Jameson argues, in his review of Derrida's work, that the ghost reveals that "the living present is scarcely as self-sufficient as it claims to be [and] that we would do well not to count on its density and solidity, which might under exceptional circumstances betray us."[10] Elizabeth Stern asserts that such stories also offer valuable resources for understanding social change and crisis in the lives of the tellers. "Ghostly activity presented physical danger," she writes, "but also manifested spiritual and social dislocation in the community of the living."[11]

Proceeding from Stern's assertion that ghost stories link the traditions of the past with the concerns and dislocations of the present, this chapter focuses on the ways in which Icelandic immigrants used stories about the supernatural to make sense of parts of life in the new land. Such stories are a particularly rich resource for understanding how immigrants discussed their own relationship to past and present and, particularly, how they made sense of traumatic episodes. Beyond the repressed desires of individuals, traumatic episodes are central to popular ghost stories, and such narratives should be understood in conjunction with the growing scholarship on memory and trauma. Indeed, ghosts often behave in ways that signal their connection to the unique ways that the brain records and processes traumatic data. Just as ghosts, trapped in certain points in time, return to haunt the living, individual traumatic memory appears "fixed or frozen in time, refuses to be represented as past, but is perpetually re-experienced in a painful disassociated, traumatic present."[12] The intergenerational transmission of these stories within the Icelandic community, as discussed below, illustrate that the ghost also acts as a stand-in for traumatic incidents and a vehicle for telling stories that evoke community memory, values, history, and even critiques of power, which can last for several generations.

## "A Greater Than Average Preoccupation": Icelandic Superstitious Beliefs

In the nineteenth-century Icelandic culture from which migrants emerged, there were no fewer than eighteen terms describing ghostly apparitions or incidents.[13] While many Icelandic immigrants might have declined to discuss such stories in English and in mixed company, the supernatural remained a vibrant part of immigrant culture. Substantial collections of community lore reveal that many Icelandic settlers and their descendants maintained and adapted relationships to spiritual beliefs, practices, and narratives that fell outside Christian doctrine and were arguably particular to Icelandic language forums. Indeed, *hjátrú* refers to a large number of practices and beliefs, including prophetic dreaming (*berdreymi*) and the belief in a range of non-Christian spiritual phenomena, such as human and animal fetches, or spirit followers (*fylgjur*), ghosts (*draugar*), land spirits (*huldufólk*), and psychic ability (*skyggni*).

The Icelandic North American *hjátrú* tradition reflects a unique blend of older Icelandic narrative structures and North American and regional-specific components, including Canadian and American landscapes, technological developments (for example, ghosts who rode in cars), and non-Icelandic populations.[14] Immigrants transported these systems of belief to their new lands according to customary beliefs about the characteristics of certain kinds of ghostly figures. For example, different kinds of ghosts could behave in radically different ways since, according to Icelandic belief, their character was often defined by their origins. There are, for example, separate beliefs and names for the ghosts of drowned men, exposed children, and improperly buried corpses – even the greedy *fépúki*, the ghost of someone who cannot bear to leave worldly wealth behind. Many possessed names that reflected the locations that they haunted, while others could be recognized for their attachment to certain people and families. Some ghosts might also retain a few of the characteristics they possessed when they were alive and could inspire in the living feelings of fear and terror as well as pity, attachment, and affection.

In nineteenth-century Iceland, different kinds of ghosts were assigned distinct characters and behaviours, and Icelandic believers considered that while some spirits remained at home in Iceland, some were able to emigrate.[15] For example, various immigrants reported that some *ættarfylgjur* (family followers) followed North American Icelandic families as they moved, usually as the result of a curse. Often these *fylgjur* appeared as human children who could age into short adults, known as *skotta* (female) or *móri* (male), and a few re-established themselves in North America. Kristín M. Jóhannsdóttir, a linguist specializing in North American Icelandic, reports that early narratives generally located Riverton, Geysir, and Víðir (Vidir), Manitoba, as centres of the Icelandic "ghost settlement."[16] Community stories from these areas indicate a relatively widespread belief in *fylgjur* within the community and in renewed sightings of figures like *skotta*, *móri*, and *Þorgeirsboli* (Thorgeir's bull), a half-flayed bull whose appearance signalled disease and disaster. These narratives report that such figures continued to wreak havoc in New Iceland, where some allegedly terrorized livestock and caused accidents.

Hrund Skulason reminds us, however, that some of these figures could also have a sense of humour and were capable of playing funny tricks on people – for instance, causing women to spill chamber pots on themselves.[17] *Skottur*, or little follower girls, were particularly well known in New Iceland. One, *Leirár-skotta*, was a powerful and violent girl said to have left Borgarfjörður with her family in 1889. Another *skotta* was less malevolent but had caused mischief in the Skagafjörður district of northern Iceland, where she followed a woman named Þóra Eiríksdóttir. When Þóra's descendants emigrated to Canada and settled in Riverton, she was said to have followed all of them and begun appearing in the settlement.[18] More than spooky apparitions, figures like *Leirár-skotta* could strike fear into local community members, who blamed her for terrifying livestock and even killing cattle.[19] Immigrants believed that some of these followers continued their work in North America, but they thought that others, including *staðardraugar* (place ghosts), remained behind because they were stationary spectres that could haunt only specific places. Although many ghosts lived on in stories about home, most immigrants believed that many older, active spirits necessarily remained in Iceland.

Ghost stories dating from turn-of-the-century New Iceland also clearly reflect the influence of North American spiritualism and popular Anglo-Victorian superstitious narratives. Spiritualism, a popular religious movement that spread throughout the United States and Canada in the late nineteenth century, was intensely popular with some members of the Unitarian faction of the Icelandic North American community.[20] Spiritualist leaders promised their followers contact with deceased relatives, friends, and even figures from the sagas through seances, mediums, and other forms of communication.[21] One devotee, editor and author Einar Hjörleifson (later Kvaran), helped spread interest and information about spiritualism following his return to Iceland, where, around 1900, this movement found a receptive audience.[22] Although the spiritualist movement helped to enrich and popularize older "preoccupations with the supernatural" in the Icelandic community, this development must be viewed as a twentieth-century phenomenon and one that was remarkably different from older Icelandic superstitious narratives and beliefs.

*Hjátrú* narratives from the Icelandic migrant community attracted significant attention from folklorists in the 1960s and 1970s. This attention resulted in the creation of two large oral collections: a translated folklore collection assembled by Magnús Einarsson of the Canadian Museum of Civilization and the extensive collection of stories gathered by Hallfreður Örn Eiríksson and Olga María Franzdóttir at the Árni Magnússon Institute in Reykjavík, published in Iceland in 2012 as *Sögur úr vesturheimi* (Stories from the New World). Although the interviews in both collections were conducted almost a century after the founding of New Iceland, psychic experience, dreams, ghosts, and non-Christian spiritual figures remained one of the most popular forms of oral tradition in the Icelandic immigrant community. Einarsson recalled the surprise he felt when he began a mission "to collect Icelandic and Icelandic-Canadian folklore ... anything they cared to tell me that was humorous, strange, or somehow out of the ordinary." Inundated with *hjátrú* narratives, Einarsson remembered that he "didn't expect to find alive such a keen and pervasive interest in dreams and ghostly visions."[23] Other Icelandic anthropologists working in the 1970s, such as Eiríksson and Franzdóttir, experienced little trouble in amassing extensive collections of mostly Icelandic-language *hjátrú* narratives from oral history interviewees. They collected over 120 separate narratives during their research in 1972, while Einarsson notes that most of his 462 narratives express some degree of belief in the supernatural.[24] Although fragmentary, evidence points to the subsequent continuation of certain elements of these belief systems in the community, particularly in Manitoba.[25]

Although *hjátrú* stories are one of the most popular forms of Icelandic migrant oral narrative, they have been both protected by language barriers and publicly suppressed, in part due to concerns about the stigma surrounding the occult in anglophone North American culture. A reluctance in the community to speak openly about superstition might reflect the decline of certain forms of belief, but it was also clearly linked to the storytellers' fears of being labelled backwards or ignorant.[26] Nineteenth-century migrant leaders such as Friðjón Friðriksson and Rev. Jón Bjarnason also considered superstitious belief as one of a series of ills associated with cultural stagnation and ignorance that needed to be purged from the community.[27] Even *hjátrú* narratives collected by Icelandic scholars frequently begin with a negation of belief in the supernatural. When Magnús Einarsson asked Margrét Arngrímsson to tell him a ghost story, she replied, "I – I have nothing to say. Well, I could tell you one thing that happened to my uncle." She then told the story of a family in Iceland that had been haunted by the ghost of a Norwegian man who had drowned in the area and had banged loudly on the walls of their house until his body was found and buried. Arngrímsson concluded the story by stating, "I am certain of that – that my kinsmen didn't make this up."[28] Similarly, Bergljot Sigurdsson provided Eiríksson with an extensive list of narratives associated with Nes, but concluded her stories by stating, "But I, I don't really believe in ghosts."[29]

Regardless of the stance they might take in public, Icelanders commonly held superstitious beliefs. Even sceptics who denied belief in the supernatural clearly valued the ability of these stories to move and frighten their audiences. Icelandic clergy members too might still identify themselves as superstitious in private. Rev. Albert Kristjanson, when interviewed in the 1970s,[30] confessed to avoiding certain spaces and being concerned about premonitions. Icelandic "non-believers" could also be reluctant to wholly refute such narratives, and such beliefs were simply accepted as part of the everyday mental landscape of Icelandic communities.[31] As Jón Árnason explained, "Sure I was superstitious, just like any other Icelander."[32]

## *Huldufólk*

The persistence of superstition in modern Icelandic popular culture is a contentious topic on both sides of the ocean. Icelanders at home in twentieth- and twenty-first-century Iceland have wrestled with the implications of the country's reputation for folk belief, which has attracted the interest of tourists and anthropologists for decades. The most notable and problematic of these superstitions is a reported belief in *huldufólk*, or "hidden people," also popularly referred to in English as "elves." *Huldufólk* are better understood as land spirits of normal human stature, who occupy a parallel landscape and are visible only to certain people. Varying degrees of belief in *huldufólk* persist in Iceland, particularly in rural areas. Tourist brochures and anthropological surveys of the country frequently cite the decisions of developers and construction workers not to disturb certain hills or stones, including the rerouting of a main road in Kópavogur, now a large suburb of Reykjavík, because of concerns about *huldufólk* habitation.[33]

While stories about *huldufólk* accompanied nineteenth-century Icelandic immigrants to North America,[34] Nelson Gerrard and Magnús Einarsson contend that, according to traditional beliefs, *huldufólk* were land-based spirits, who were therefore unable to leave Iceland.[35] Some scholars have argued that the relative absence of *huldufólk* narratives in migrant communities reflects the impact of immigration on popular spiritual belief. In spite of nineteenth-century beliefs about the inability of *huldufólk* to migrate, it is clear that some new *huldufólk* stories were produced in the immigrant community, although they were less common than other *hjátrú* narratives.

Well into the twentieth century, a few Icelandic North Americans still admitted to avoiding certain spaces or suspecting *huldufólk* when searching for missing objects.[36] For example, in 1967, in Arborg, Manitoba, Margrét Bjarnason recalled searching everywhere in her home to find her gloves before heading out to hang laundry on the line. "I discovered that my gloves had disappeared ... that I often used when I was spreading out laundry in the wintertime." A year passed with no sign of the gloves – until Margrét found "them lying in the clothespin box where I had always kept them.... Naturally [I] had often opened this little box. The hidden people had returned them."[37] In another narrative from the early 1900s, Rósa Oddsdóttir Vigfússon of the Geysir district found herself at a mysterious house, which she believed to be that of a hidden person. In keeping with an association of *huldufólk* with wealth and finery, local lore describes how Rósa was "walking back and she saw this house – a black, black house – and she noticed that the windows were all decorated and the doors had silver filigree around the door knobs – a really strange house." Other women in the community also reported seeing children who fit the description of hidden people.[38]

While these narratives suggest that some of the *huldufólk* tradition endured in the North American community, migration signalled a rupture in certain forms of popular spiritual belief and an alteration or adaptation of others. These alterations reflected changing conditions in North America and cultural change within the community itself. Thorstína Walters writes that some migrants told stories about why certain ghosts did not come to North America, including one that was too afraid of being enclosed in migrant ships. Walters wrote that her own parents were plagued by a *skotta* known as *Kelduskóga-skotta*. She recalled her grandfather telling stories about the "shadowy little girl" who had followed the family as the result of a curse as well as his explanation of why she had not emigrated with the family. According to this story, "*Kelduskóga-skotta* took one look at the outward bound vessel on which the family left for America and decided to remain in Iceland.... For when it came to putting up with the immigrant quarters in the steerage and becoming used to the new land, [she] just 'could not take it.'"[39]

Ghost stories in immigrant districts in North America often described and explained the actions of figures like *skotta* and other ghosts in accordance with the Icelandic belief in their reality and physicality. While many popular English ghost stories describe ghosts as physically benign, wispy, and translucent figures that hover and elicit chills, Icelandic ghost narratives often emphasize their physical reality as well as their potentially violent nature. Icelandic ghosts not only terrified people but could also bite, beat, scratch, and even kill their victims. For example, Björn Bjarnason of Arborg, Manitoba, claimed that the ghost of a "feeble old woman" who had lived with them in life had, as a ghost, killed a girl in their household at home in Iceland. The girl "had been rather a tease and made it her habit to provoke the old woman until she had become so difficult of temperament that she swore a curse on her and said that ... since she could not repay her while still alive, she would do it when she was dead."[40] The old woman committed suicide, and "the same evening this young girl was so violently attacked [while she was sleeping] that people rushed to her, and were only just able to get to her and awaken her, and she woke up alive." The girl left the farm for the sake of her safety, but later returned after the house had been thoroughly swept out with juniper, which Bjarnason explained "was an antidote, [since] ghosts were, supposedly, more reluctant to seek out a well swept place." She went up to bed, "but after a short while a terrible racket is heard from the bed where the girl lay," and when the household rushed to her, they found her dead. He argued that when they "started investigating whether everything had been carefully swept [they realised that] they had forgot to sweep the loom and the ghost had been able to stay there."[41]

As the Bjarnason narrative illustrates, Icelandic believers who emigrated to North America brought with them a belief in both the seriousness and the power of ghosts and their potential effects on the health and well-being of the living. *Hjátrú* acted as an unpleasant and sometimes dramatic index of the spiritual, mental, and physical future health and well-being of community members. Stories about premonitions of *feigð* (pending death) and accidents were particularly common. As a young girl, Lára Gudmundsson saw an apparition of a woman "dressed like she had just gotten off a ship" while she lay in bed with her sleeping grandmother in Riverton, Manitoba. Gudmundsson asserted that this was a premonition of the death of a girl whom her grandmother was sponsoring to come to Canada. When she woke her grandmother to tell her, however, the grandmother blamed the apparition on Lára not saying her prayers and added, "Don't tell anyone you saw that."[42]

North American–born descendants of the Icelandic community clearly felt uncomfortable with the fatalism embedded in Icelandic *hjátrú*, including its association with predetermined death and the ability of some to foresee the future – or "too much" knowledge. This discomfort contributed to the decline of certain narratives and practices. For example, Icelandic-speaking descendants frequently enjoyed fortune telling through coffee-cup readings, but the practice's affiliation with "bad news" may have contributed to its decline in popularity. Both Cliff and Lilja Holm of Geysir, Manitoba, remember their *ammas* (grandmothers) reading coffee cups for local people. Lilja's *amma*, Stefanía Friðrika Stefansdóttir, was a particularly reputable cup reader. In one family story that Lilja recalls, a man at a wedding approached her *amma* for a reading. "She just went white, and she wouldn't say what she saw," she remembered. "And then she said, 'He'll never make it home.' And he drowned that night." As her husband, Cliff, then remarked, "There's nothing but bad news in those cups; [people should] just leave them alone."[43]

The persistence of *hjátrú* narratives in the immigrant community reveals that even when they conveyed unsettling messages or upset members, such stories still fulfilled certain functions that were considered valuable. The large body of narratives dedicated to apparitions of fishermen or labourers reflects how community members attempted to foresee and make sense of the dangers, tragedies, and isolation entailed in working on Lake Winnipeg. *Hjátrú* beliefs could help people build a sense of understanding or knowledge of sudden and unnerving traumatic incidents, including drownings and disappearances, and potentially provide a sense of comfort by creating the possibility of communication after death. Magnús Elíasson (perhaps best known as a founding member of the Canadian Commonwealth Federation) confirmed to Hallfreður Örn Eiríksson and Olga María Franzdóttir that the belief that dreams could carry messages from the living or dead was common in northern fishing camps on Lake Winnipeg.[44] Numerous fishermen, himself included, apparently, believed that *nákvæmur draumur* (a precise dream) could accurately predict accidents or death. In a narrative that resembles Margrét Arngrímsson's family story about a drowned Norwegian making his demise known to her family in Iceland, Elíasson asserted that Canadian-made spirits could make themselves known through dreams under similar circumstances. He recalled how his cabin mate, Jón Melsteð, had told him that "he was afraid something had happened" after having a dream in which he saw "men come into his cabin and they were wet ... and they had ice frozen into their clothing."[45] He went on to say that a party of men, an Icelander named Magnússon and two unnamed Ukrainians, were discovered dead from exposure on the frozen lake several days later.

This story about the enduring but evolving *hjátrú* tradition is one example of the flexibility and vitality of such beliefs in some communities and families in which migrants and their descendants adapted Icelandic narratives and beliefs to North American conditions. Migrant narratives of superstitious belief also offer a critical window for understanding power dynamics within the community, particularly since ghosts in many (if not most) Icelandic narratives are marginalized figures – including women, children, elderly people, and even abused animals.[46] In one story from around Arborg, Manitoba, a two-and-a-half-year-old boy spooked local farmers when he reported seeing a dog following a local man. The farmer was visiting his neighbours when the couple's little boy asked who had "cut" the dog that accompanied him. According to the story, the farmer had come to the farm alone, but had recently killed his dog by cutting its throat.[47] This inversion of power in ghost stories, in which the abused and marginalized assume positions of spiritual authority over adults in positions of relative authority, criticized the actions of the most powerful members of the community and exposed their wrongdoings.

Stories involving children and animals are clear examples of how ghost stories acted as a form of critique and defiance in the Icelandic community. The frequent appearance of ghosts in the form of abused foster children and young labourers reflected community concerns about poor working conditions, employer negligence, and the precarious well-being of workers on the lowest rung of the economic ladder. Tímoteus Böðvarsson reported that one man who ran a fishing outfit on Lake Winnipeg was "followed" by a *fylgja* in the form of a young man who had died while working for him.[48] The employer, whom Einarsson refers to only as "Axxx," and his two young employees had run into "an earth-tossing storm" on the lake with their dog team. The sled dogs instinctively began to head for shore, "but the foreman, he didn't trust the dogs ... took the lead away from them and took a wrong turn ... before they got to shore one of the boys had died of exposure. They tried to keep him warm on the sled, bundle him up, but he was both exhausted and cold through and through." The surviving employee froze his feet, which had to be amputated at the instep. Böðvarsson explained that the appearance of the *fylgja* around the boss was proof of his responsibility for the young man's death. Böðvarsson reported that his wife, who had known the dead employee quite well, saw him long afterwards outside her window, and "a man who was there said 'then Axxx will probably be coming today.' That was the foreman on this – the cause of this man's death. He died because of him. Oh yes, yes, after about an hour, Axxx has arrived."[49]

In such oral narratives, people who lacked physical power in life could often, in death, possess a tremendous physical and spiritual power that surpassed that of the strongest community members. Such stories helped enforce social taboos against the abuse of vulnerable community members by threatening abusers with supernatural retribution, as in the case of several stories about the ghosts of abused foster children. Fostering was a relatively common custom in Icelandic migrant families and part of long-standing practice at home. According to Gísli Ágúst Gunnlaugsson, fostering was particularly common at the start of the mass migration period in Iceland as it helped people adapt to housing shortages, poverty, and the social pressures that accompanied having children out of wedlock in the late nineteenth century.[50] Some childless couples and kind families eagerly welcomed and loved foster children, while others found themselves in placements filled with hard manual labour, abuse, and neglect.

The appearance of the ghosts of children who had died while working for or being fostered by other families reflected larger anxieties in the nineteenth-century immigrant community about these stories of exploitation and abuse. For example, Lárus Nordal's narrative about the noisy and unsettling *fylgja* of a girl shot and killed by her employer served as a disturbing warning about the spiritual consequences of neglecting or harming child labourers, even by accident.[51] Nordal and his wife reported hearing the loud wailing of a girl in the poplar woods surrounding their new house outside Leslie, Saskatchewan, one night. The cries were so loud that Nordal's concerned wife sent her husband and neighbours out as a search party, but with no result. That evening, an Icelandic man arrived. He had accidentally shot and killed his young female employee several years before. Nordal argued that the man was haunted because the girl's mother, a spiritually powerful woman who had refused to accept her daughter's death, had sent her daughter's noisy spirit after him in revenge as a follower. Nordal recalled the effects of the haunting on the afflicted man. He was "always singing, as if he was trying to silence something else."[52]

## Unsettling Apparitions: First Nations Ghosts and Space

Just as ghost stories reflected the anxieties and beliefs of Icelanders regarding abuse, power, and dangerous working and living conditions in the community, so they acted as forums for discussing the community's relationship to trauma and tragedy involving nearby communities, including First Nations. In some instances, Icelandic ghost stories suggest that many immigrant believers acknowledged that they had entered a territory that was already populated by both First Nations people as well as their territorial spirits, although they interpreted that presence through an Icelandic lens. Often detached from First Nations people's own spiritual beliefs,[53] the Cree, Ojibwe, and Métis ghosts that appear in *hjátrú* narratives reflected the world views of Icelanders. For example, Ingólfur Bjarnason, a fisherman working in a station on Lake Winnipeg, reported to his colleagues one morning that he had dreamed a strange dream the night before. In the dream, he passed his Métis co-worker's bed and saw "lying there in his bed a totally naked Indian."[54] As in the Melsteð narrative described earlier, Bjarnason responded to the Icelandic belief in the importance of dreams by informing the bed's owner when he arrived at the camp the next day. Upon hearing the account, the young man "blanched" and reported that his grandfather had robbed and murdered a man of the same description many years before. Bjarnason explained this apparition as part of the Icelandic belief in intergenerational ghosts, which reminded descendants of their ancestors' transgressions. The naked man, he argued, *"hafði verið fylgja drengsins,"* or "was the lad's follower."[55]

In the psychological landscape of Lake Winnipeg, First Nations spirits could loom large in the minds of fishermen, farmers, and townsfolk alike, although they were arguably more popular with those who inhabited the northern edges of the old Icelandic reserve and more northerly communities surrounding Lake Winnipeg. Many stories emanated from the Icelandic and Indigenous smallpox cemetery, Nes, where graves peppered a field just north of Icelandic River (Riverton). Such stories were also arguably more common in the landscapes north of the Icelandic reserve itself, particularly in predominantly Indigenous northern communities and along routes where turn-of-the-century Icelandic labourers increasingly worked in the commercial fishery and other resource-based industries.

Superstitious stories offered Icelanders a forum for more critical analyses of power and space in relation to their Indigenous neighbours and debates about notions of right and wrong. As a result, the numerous immigrant stories about Indigenous ghosts provide scholars with important insights into popular Icelandic attitudes towards aggression and displacement involving Cree, Ojibwe, and Métis individuals and communities. Icelandic-language ghost stories featuring Indigenous figures were relatively common in the late nineteenth- and early twentieth-century community, but such accounts stand in stark contrast to the published, translated narratives of settler-Indigenous relations that came to dominate community memory in the era after the Second World War. One is an often-referenced story about John Ramsay of Sandy Bar. Tales about John Ramsay are still told and observed in the twenty-first-century Icelandic community. Still, Anne Brydon and others have been critical of the ways in which these now anglicized stories, including the story of the dream of John Ramsay, tend to sanitize Icelanders' role in the colonial project. This particular narrative describes how a poor Icelandic farmer named Trausti Vigfússon dreamed that John Ramsay appeared and asked the carpenter to fix the picket fence that surrounded the grave of his wife, Betsey, who had died in the 1876–7 smallpox epidemic at Sandy Bar, near Riverton (Figure 3.1). Ramsay himself had recently been buried beside her. After consulting with his family and possibly a lapse of some time, Trausti collected enough sawn boards to construct the fence and made the long trip to the grave.[56]

In some variations of the John Ramsay dream story, Trausti delayed his task, and Ramsay had to remind him in another dream.[57] The delay was also accompanied by incidents of bad luck, and when Trausti told his wife of both the second request and his own delay, she reportedly scolded him for failing to fulfil his promise to Ramsay and pressured him to complete the task as soon as possible. In keeping with beliefs about the relationship between spirits and the well-being of the living, some versions of the story report that fishing in the area, which had been poor that season, improved dramatically as soon as Trausti had completed the task. After Trausti died, other community members occasionally took on the responsibilities associated with his dream and continued to maintain the fence and site of John and Betsey Ramsay's graves. Although it is located in the middle of a farm field and is inaccessible for much of the year, the white wooden fence surrounding the two graves is still maintained by local farmers.

Brydon argues that the enduring popularity of the John Ramsay dream story has helped create a myth of "good relations" between First Nations and Icelanders, "purified" of the Icelandic community's larger role in Indigenous displacement.[58] Indeed, using the story of John Ramsay and Trausti Vigfússon to characterize Icelandic-Indigenous relations in Manitoba frames and suppresses a much larger and far more complex and problematic history. Excluding the work of Brydon, Eyford, and

Figure 3.1. Guttormur Guttormsson visiting Betsey and John Ramsay's graves near Riverton, MB. Undated photograph. PAM.

Ögmundardóttir, both popular and scholarly histories of the Icelandic community have often treated Icelandic settlement and First Nations displacement as separate, detached events.[59] This is typical of popular Canadian and American visions of migration to the west, which often imagine a wider separation between First Nations dispossession and European arrival and ignore the important role of immigrants, especially ethnic immigrants, in colonizing North America.[60] Interestingly, the extensive archive of Icelandic *hjátrú* narratives from the Icelandic community reveals that while certain narratives about Ramsay were translated into English and reused, more disturbing or ambiguous narratives about other spiritual Indigenous figures were not.

Although anglicized narratives of Ramsay's ghost may reveal much about how ethnic communities collectively try to replace difficult histories of colonial violence with stories of friendship, this story must also be understood as an Icelandic *hjátrú* story, related to a larger body of untranslated stories in the community that dealt with similar subjects. There are two reasons for thinking critically about the Icelandic *hjátrú* components of the Ramsay story. First and foremost, the Ramsay dream story reflects the serious obligations that many Icelanders felt they should observe when it came to the spiritual or supernatural world. In Iceland and, to some extent, in North American communities, this sense of obligation had no expiration date and could last for generations. Such narratives suggest that, like the *huldufólk* tradition, many Icelanders saw the well-being and health of the living community as related to the respect for the unseen, including fulfilling requests or demands made by singular figures. This explains why so many Icelanders understood and arguably continue to understand the "gravity" of Ramsay's request in the dream.

Second, the John Ramsay dream story was only one of many stories that earlier generations of Icelanders had told about a range of First Nations figures, trauma, and the smallpox epidemic. Many of these other, often untranslated *hjátrú* narratives highlight Icelanders' understanding of the direct, very uncomfortable relationship between immigration and colonialism. They also reveal that Icelanders believed that North American land was already occupied by a much broader cast of First Nations spiritual figures whose title to the land could not be taken lightly. Icelandic ghost stories involving Indigenous figures reveal powerful community beliefs about observing territorial boundaries established by the supernatural populations – even when that spiritual occupation contradicted colonial claims to land. Although the Canadian or American state may have legally claimed land and encouraged Icelanders to farm or fish in certain areas, community members might strictly avoid them because they believed they were already occupied and subject to a different set of rules.

In keeping with the belief in the physicality of ghosts in Icelandic *hjátrú*, stories about First Nations ghosts often describe the dangers of trespassing on territories inhabited by these powerful figures. In one narrative from Lake Winnipeg, Björn Bjarnason described how a party of Icelandic fishermen was caught in a storm and was forced to take shelter in an abandoned house. According to local stories, the spirit of an Indigenous man haunted the house. "Few wanted to stay there," he reported, "because it was said that – or to have a reputation for being haunted."[61] Bjarnason related that the men were worried about the stories they had heard about the shack, but one said "he wasn't afraid of things like that" and went in, prompting the others to join him. The man fell asleep. Shortly afterward, however, he "start[ed] moaning so loudly that the others called out to him and it didn't seem to do any good, until [another man]) grabbed him and shook him." The man finally came to and "said that it had seemed to him as if someone had lain on top of him, as if he were being strangled." He called it "one of the greatest trials he had ever endured." Afterwards, all the men in the group "put on their clothes and stayed up for what was left of the night."[62]

Other narratives involving Indigenous spirits include encounters with ghosts appearing on "old Indian trails" used by freighters[63] and areas considered off limits to camping and settlement because of their affiliation. Hallgrímur Stadfeldt reported that a strange visitor terrorized the dogsled team of an Icelandic man while he stayed on Devil's Island on Lake Winnipeg. The island was haunted, he explained, because it was the site of a terrible accident at a lumber mill that had claimed the lives of several men and a large number of "abandoned Indian shacks."[64]

## "A Well-Known Ghost Den": Náströnd / Graftarnes

The prolific appearance of First Nations ghosts in *hjátrú* narratives testifies to the concern that a significant number of Icelanders felt about their historical proximity to the deaths and displacement of local First Nations people. While Icelanders may not have formally voiced these concerns about episodes like the 1876–7 smallpox epidemic in public, it is clear that, in private, many believed they had inherited an obligation to some of its victims. Home to both Icelandic and First Nations victims of the epidemic, Nes was described by locals as so haunted that it became virtually uninhabitable (Figure 3.2). The site became the source of numerous tales that described both the hauntings as well as the gravity of ignoring the claims of spirits to the site.

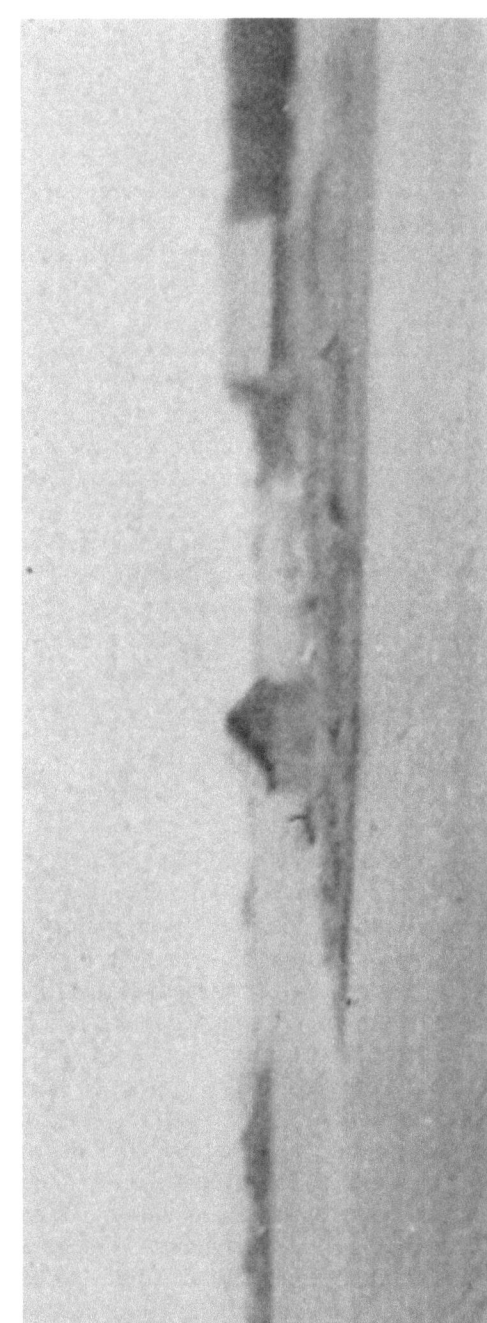

Figure 3.2. Top: Graftarnes, MB, and surrounding farms. Undated photograph. EIHC. Bottom: To the left is the only known image of what was likely the infamous house of Magnús Hallgrímsson.

Some of these stories, such as the one about Skrámur that opens this chapter, were told for entertainment and shock value, but it is clear that they also helped instil a healthy fear of the site. Poet-farmer Guttormur J. Guttormsson, who was born and raised at Víðivellir, next to Nes, remembered, "I never saw anything unusual there, but that might have been because I never dared go near the place once evening approached."[65] He relayed several stories about the site and recalled that an elderly couple who lived across the river from Nes "were eyewitnesses to the fact that all was not peace and serenity at the Ness when darkness fell." The old woman, in particular, "thought she saw too much and seized the opportunity, whenever a child was christened in the church, to wash her eyes with christening water at the end of the ceremony."[66]

In local narratives, the reason for the intense hauntings at Nes stemmed from both its traumatic association with the epidemic and its disturbance by a local Icelandic settler. Less than ten years after the epidemic, Magnús Hallgrímsson, a settler from Hecla Island, inexplicably decided to occupy the site and build his new house on top of the smallpox cemetery. His house dominates ghost stories about the cemetery, and although an explanation of his actions is strangely absent, after he died in the house a few years later, reports of haunting spread. The farmer had succumbed to a ruptured abscess on his neck[67] and, according to local accounts, was discovered dead in his bed, drenched in his own blood.

Most of the Nes-related stories recorded in 1972–3, almost a century after the cemetery was created, deal with the house that Hallgrímsson had built on the site because it was plagued by aggressive and disturbing ghosts. At various times, travellers and haymakers attempted to take shelter inside, but accounts report that they invariably came banging on the doors of neighbouring homes, "snow white," looking for shelter, and unwilling to speak about their experiences in the middle of the night.[68] Other stories describe the appearance of unearthly spirits in the shape of strange animals. In one, Tómas Jónasson, a stalwart sceptic who lived at Engimýri, one farm upriver from Nes, chose to ignore local warnings and walked past the house at night on his way home. When he looked over at the house, he saw "six black horses coming out from around the house," although none of the neighbours owned black horses.[69] Around 1910, he and his family were once again unnerved when two male boarders asked why there were so many red and brown sheep at Nes. The two travellers, who had stopped at Engimýri for dinner, said that they had seen a herd of about fourteen distinctively coloured sheep coming out of the abandoned house and running around in the snow outside. The men thought that a sheep farmer must have lived there, but were informed that the house was abandoned and no one in the area owned such a flock. When community members went to check on the house, they found it empty, with no prints in the snow around it.[70] According to the story, the men who reported seeing the sheep were non-Icelanders from outside the community who were unfamiliar both with the history of the house and with the site.

Ghosts at Nes, locals reported, could also assume the form of human Icelandic and Indigenous figures. Bergljót Sigurdsson grew up next to the infamous stretch of land and had heard numerous stores about the site (Figure 3.3). She recalled hearing stories about men who had tried to stay in Magnús Hallgrímsson's house and reported seeing "gruesome" things there. When the saddle maker Hallgrímur Stadfeldt tried to stay in the house, he asserted that six undead Icelandic men began crawling out of the cellar part-way through his stay.[71] In spite of these appearances, some local Icelanders viewed Nes as a primarily First Nations cemetery, an idea that was reinforced by memories of local Indigenous peoples coming to the site to leave tobacco.[72] Anne Brydon and other postcolonial scholars have challenged the archetype of the Indigenous ghost in popular North American lore as part of a larger fossilization of the colonial past. The appearance of First Nations spirits in Icelandic *hjátrú* narratives, however, must be understood as part of a distinct oral tradition and set of beliefs that reflect how Icelanders experienced trauma, difficult histories, and their relationship to them.

A closer examination of these stories reveals, significantly, that several accounts of First Nations ghosts at Nes involve children who had died in the smallpox epidemic. These reflect lingering local memories about the unspeakable and unsettling toll of the epidemic. Rather than fossilizing the colonial past, these powerful little ghosts reveal that Icelanders not only were highly cognizant of this unsettling history but also saw that history as a kind of autonomous actor that continued to inhabit the area. Rather than fossilizing or erasing First Nations populations and histories, the *hjátrú* tradition created for Icelanders an enduring, powerful, and active Indigenous presence in the community, which remained for generations after settlement. Growing up next door to the infamous cemetery, Guttormur Guttormson reported that, as a child, he had encountered the ghost of a First Nations boy of his own age. The boy appeared inside Guttormson's family home. When Guttormur spoke to the boy, "He didn't say anything or look ... just looked out the window."[73]

Several other Icelanders reported seeing the ghost of a young First Nations girl, who sat on three graves at Nes, presumably those of family members, and refused to vacate the site. The little ghost appeared so

Figure 3.3. Bergljót Sigurdsson. Undated photograph. Courtesy of Heather Ireland.

frequently that women in the community even expressed concern for her well-being, reminiscent of the affection that community members developed for certain well-established versions of *skotta* and *móri* back in Iceland. One woman who was not afraid of the ghost "always put flowers on these graves, but the ghost of the little Indian girl still sat on them."[74] In keeping with *hjátrú* tradition, this narrative reflects belief that sympathy for the ghost – as well as for victims of the epidemic and colonial displacement – did not absolve the people to whom she appeared or end the hauntings. Instead, such narratives suggest that the epidemic and the cemetery *haunted* community members. In other words, it maintained a painful, continued presence in the community's collective imagination, one that stood in stark contrast to the erasure of First Nations claims and celebration of settler progress that characterized public narratives.

## Conclusion

The landscape at Nes, as well as the larger adaptation of the *hjátrú* tradition in Icelandic settlements, reveals the complex and unique roots and implications of immigrant ghost stories. Immigration signalled a compelling transformation of Icelanders' belief in the supernatural, including both the virtual disappearance of old ghosts and spirits who decided to stay at home and the birth of new figures that reflected changing conditions, lives, and relations in North America. Such stories manifested community beliefs and memory that blurred the lines between physical and psychological landscapes, the living and the dead, the past and the present.

In keeping with theoretical work on both trauma and hauntology, ghosts and *hjátrú* narratives existed between, and could potentially unsettle, established hierarchies of power and authority. Although clearly valued for their ability to entertain and terrorize, Icelandic ghost stories are compelling for their frequent critiques of regimes of power based on gender, age, class, and race. In these Icelandic *hjátrú* narratives, a range of figures who might wield only marginal power in life, from children to animals and the elderly, could return to plague white, adult, male employers and landowners in some of the most powerful ways possible. This reoccurring dynamic makes such stories important resources for understanding popular community discussions of justice and authority.

Reflecting the etymology of *hjátrú* as a system of beliefs alongside formal Christian faith, these often Icelandic-language narratives offered a third space for expressing alternative voices and notions of justice. As Elizabeth Stern asserts, the appearance of ghosts in Icelandic narratives "manifested spiritual and social dislocation in the community of the living,"[75] offering us an important window into how Icelanders understood rupture, trauma, and power. Indeed, the ghost's powerful ability to remind community members of their connection to others, while undermining settler claims to space and authority in the present, imbue these narratives with a subversive quality. Rather than reinforcing white colonial claims and boundaries by relegating First Nations people to a shadowy, unreal presence, the appearance of First Nations ghosts in the lore of the Icelandic community had real-life connotations. Indeed, the substantial body of *hjátrú* narratives in the Icelandic community shows that different generations and members of different ethnic groups could view their relationship to the colonial past in culturally specific ways. Rather than attempting to suppress or downplay migrants' relationship to the displacement and deaths of Indigenous people, *hjátrú* narratives reflect the fact that they also felt haunted or perhaps even cursed, to some extent, by their role in colonial displacement. In the larger context of Icelandic superstitious belief, the appearance of First Nations ghosts signalled not the separation of a fossilized Indigenous past from a progressive settler present, but a living inheritance – and obligation – for migrants and their descendants.

*Chapter Four*

# Main Street Vikings: Anglicization, Spectacle, and the Two World Wars

At her August wedding in 1933, Signy Stephenson walked down the aisle with her father, Friðrik (Stefánsson) Stephenson, a Winnipeg publisher from Skagafjörður, Iceland (Figure 4.1). The immigrant publisher's daughter was marrying John David Eaton, heir apparent to the T. Eaton Company, at that time Canada's largest retail corporation. The wedding was one of the most celebrated public events in North America's Icelandic community in the years between the First and Second World Wars. Reporters, who regarded the Eatons as Canadian royalty, eagerly provided extensive media coverage of the ceremony, hosted by Lady Eaton at her summer home – and of her somewhat unusual new daughter-in-law. Signy Stephenson was not an affluent Anglo-Ontarian society girl, they reported, but a "blonde Nordic beauty," a former shop girl from Winnipeg and the child of immigrants.[1] Her acceptance into the Anglo-Canadian elite represented a larger symbolic acceptance for many Icelanders, particularly since she chose to highlight her background in the wedding ceremony with Icelandic songs, the Icelandic flag, and a silver "Viking headdress."[2]

In addition, the glamorous summer home of the Eaton family at Rosseau, Ontario, stood in stark contrast to the early childhood home of Signy's father, who had survived the cold, cramped shacks of New Iceland's 1876–7 smallpox winter. Although Signy and her children enjoyed a privilege and mobility in English society that was unimaginable for early New Icelanders, some authorities had once counted the father of the bride among the most undesirable classes of immigrants. This chapter uses the "Viking" socialite's walk down the aisle with her father, survivor of the earliest, most tumultuous days of New Iceland, as a symbolic moment in a larger era of intergenerational change in the first half of the twentieth century. It links the decline of the Icelandic language of the immigrant generation and the growing popularity of Viking imagery with their descendants, arguing that many Icelanders ultimately saw both

Figure 4.1. John David Eaton and Signy Stephenson on their wedding day, Winnipeg, 1933. Reprinted from *Lögberg*, 17 August 1933, 5.

as a way to deflect anti-immigrant sentiment and achieve acceptance in Anglo–North American society during periods of intense pressure.

This chapter begins with a discussion of the political and cultural roots of the Viking imagery that came to dominate public festivals in the twentieth-century Icelandic community. It argues that because the Viking image was admired and accepted by anglophone North American society as a symbol of Protestant whiteness, it offered Icelanders a convenient avenue for both acknowledging and neutralizing immigrant difference during wartime and other periods of potentially volatile anti-immigrant sentiment. While many Anglo–North Americans might have accepted and approved of the Viking events staged by Icelandic and Scandinavian communities, the languages of these immigrant groups suffered a different fate. Icelandic-language use and the Icelandic publishing industry declined during the first half of the twentieth century due, in part, to changing identities and internal pressures, including the linguistic standards that North American descendants found difficult to maintain. It is clear, however, that anglicization was also partially a defensive move for many against the anti-immigrant sentiment that surrounded the world wars, the Winnipeg General Strike, and the Great Depression.

This chapter then proceeds to a discussion of some of the effects of anglicization and the growth of Viking-style festivals in the community, particularly as they pertained to women's and radical expression. While the Icelandic-language press had previously sheltered radical and feminist sentiment from some of the pressures of the wider North American society, the anglicized festivals of the 1920s, 1930s, and 1940s offered far more limited public roles for women and much more conservative messages to the Icelandic North American public and anglophone onlookers. While women could and did exercise some control over these events, as a discussion of the bald *Fjallkona* scandal of 1924 will indicate, they were often relegated to silent and symbolic roles behind the public facade of the Icelandic immigrant community, with its declarations of national loyalty to Canada and the United States.

Finally, this chapter closes with an analysis of the shift away from Viking imagery during the Second World War. Hitler's appropriation of the Viking past in Nazi propaganda, and tensions surrounding the Allied occupation of Iceland in 1940, led to a temporary decline in the popularity of such imagery during the war. Instead, Icelandic wartime events and campaigns strove to promote an image of Icelanders as friendly, hospitable hosts to their armed "guests" during the later Allied occupation. Just as images of the Viking-age past had been played out on women's bodies in earlier immigrant events, so too did debates about Icelandic hospitality for Allied personnel. While struggling to control reports of widespread protest against the unwelcome foreign military presence in Iceland, including those of the country's "icy" women who rejected the advances of Allied soldiers, Icelandic immigrant leaders also balked at sensational reports and fictionalized American depictions of "Eskimo love rituals" between American GIs and Icelandic women that were far too "friendly."

### The Icelandic Community and the World Wars

Twentieth-century conflicts and pressures on both sides of the Atlantic defined Icelandic North American identity as much as the nineteenth-century experiences and culture of the Icelandic immigrant generation. However, the intergenerational changes that transformed immigrant culture and identity in the first decades of the twentieth century are often overlooked in community historiography, which too often concludes its coverage with the end of Icelandic mass immigration after 1914. With a few exceptions, works that do examine the community in and around the time of the First and Second World Wars usually restrict themselves to discussions of individual and organizational sacrifice or accomplishments.[3] Missing here is an understanding of how Icelandic immigrant culture was affected by a major generational shift – namely, the aging and death of the older, Icelandic-born population and the intense social, cultural, and political pressures that their children and grandchildren were forced to navigate during the two world wars.

### Race and the Viking Immigrant: The Politics of Heritage

Viking imagery in the form of statues, names of sports teams, and commercial logos that adorn grocery stores, street murals, gas stations, and bars are still easily found in twenty-first-century Icelandic and Scandinavian immigrant centres in North America. The phenomenon has roots in the nineteenth century. Icelanders frequently invoked their connections to the Viking Age in nineteenth-century writing and continued to do so as the popularity of ethnic spectacles, including parades and pageants, grew in the early twentieth century. For example, on 18 June 1924, an Icelandic Viking ship float won $200 in Winnipeg's Diamond Jubilee parade (Figure 4.2). An English-language banner at the helm of the ship reminded the throngs of Winnipeggers who packed the parade route, "Leifur Eiríksson, an Icelandic man, discovered North America in the year 1000."[4] Another float, launched in Winnipeg in 1930, depicted the meeting of the first "Viking" parliament in Iceland at Þingvellir in 930, filled with modern-day chieftains wearing Viking-era dress and long, fake beards. Since the early twentieth century, innumerable Viking-ship-style floats have similarly sailed down small-town main streets in

Figure 4.2. Viking ship float featuring costumed Icelanders during Winnipeg's Diamond Jubilee celebrations, 18 June 1924. EIHC.

Icelandic centres like Mountain, North Dakota, and Gimli in jubilees, annual festivals like The Deuce of August and *Íslendingadagurinn*, or the Icelandic Festival, as well as centennial parades to visibly acknowledge and celebrate the heritage of the local population.

In common use, the term *heritage* usually refers to the inheritance of traditions, possessions, and practices from previous generations. However, as historians of memory and heritage have documented, commemorative cultural displays are not simple re-enactments of the past, but strategically chosen performances of certain histories, selected to meet the needs and ambitions of present generations.[5] While the Viking Age is an important part of contemporary culture in Iceland, Icelandic immigrant Viking spectacles emerged in distinct ways from a blend of immigrant culture, twentieth-century North American pageantry, and public debates about "desirable" and "undesirable" immigrant communities in anglophone North America. In her critical analysis of myth making within the Icelandic community, Kirsten Wolf argues that references to the Viking past from 1,000 years earlier provided immigrants with "a moral continuity from a historic past," which helped them respond to anti-migrant sentiment in both Iceland and North America. At home in turn-of-the-century Iceland, nationalists increasingly accused emigrants of being "disloyal to their home country," while British North Americans similarly viewed non-anglophone migrants who maintained their native language and culture as dangerous or disloyal foreigners.[6] Icelandic immigrants could respond to critics by simply replying that they were the descendants of "Leif the Lucky" (or Leifur Eiríksson) and other beloved saga-era heroes. This sense of historical continuity not only helped Icelandic immigrants justify their departure from their homeland, it also became an important tool for promoting improved status, prestige, and acceptance for the community in anglophone North American society. As loaded symbols of power for the Anglo-Protestant majority, nineteenth- and twentieth-century Viking symbolism and festivals also acted as shorthand for *white* and *Protestant*. Immigration critics and xenophobes approved of this Viking branding, which counteracted rumours of Icelanders' "Eskimo" roots and contributed to their special status among mass migrants. As A.R. Ford explained in 1909, Icelanders were the "sober, industrious and thrifty" descendants of "Viking sea-rovers"[7] and, like the Swedes, a "clean-blooded" and "serious-minded" people that "easily assimilate with the Anglo-Saxon people and readily intermarry."[8]

Viking symbolism was firmly entrenched in North American discourse around whiteness, Protestantism, and immigrant desirability. Although they may not have appreciated other aspects of Icelandic culture, or the Icelandic language, Anglo-Europeans and North Americans accepted Icelandic and Scandinavian immigrants, in part, because of a growing fascination with Viking culture in the nineteenth and twentieth centuries. As in Europe, North American audiences eagerly consumed scores of romantic, Viking-themed, English-language novels, texts, and eventually movies in the late nineteenth and early twentieth centuries.[9] References to Viking history were popular with Anglo-Canadians and Anglo-Americans from all walks of life, and resurrected, retooled, and romanticized images of the heroic Norse and Icelandic past reflected larger pressures and movements in North American society. Although Leifur Eiríksson predated the Protestant Reformation by five centuries, he became a powerful figure in the religious and political dimensions of Anglo-Protestant North American mythology since he could supplant Christopher Columbus, a beloved symbol of the growing population of Catholic Italians in late nineteenth-century America.

Geraldine Barnes writes that interest in the Vinland voyages expanded following the 1837 translation and publication of the Icelandic sagas, which contained accounts of these voyages. Anglo–North Americans eagerly embraced these accounts as a challenge to the Catholic figure of Christopher Columbus as the 400th anniversary of his voyage approached. The Vinland voyages, writes Barnes, created a new founding narrative more compatible with American democratic nationalism and Protestant, white, Anglo-American culture by placing "a Northern hero from an Atlantic 'republic' at its helm."[10] Conversely, Anglo-Protestant Americans such as author Marie A. Brown argued in 1887 that by spreading the story of "the false claims of Columbus," the Roman Catholic Church, the "foulest tyrant the world has ever had," was trying to expand its influence in American society.[11] Frequent references to the perceived "blondness" of the Vikings also informed larger notions of preferred populations and belonging in white, anglophone North America. The Ku Klux Klan even had a "Leif Ericson" chapter in Dexter, Maine, where local Anglo-Protestants launched campaigns of violence and intimidation against local minorities, particularly Catholics.[12] As Elisabeth Ward explains, Anglo-Protestants appropriated Viking symbolism, in part, to highlight and solidify the cultural differences between Protestant, northern Europeans and those from the Catholic south.[13] In a move that reflected the intensifying anti-Columbian sentiment in the United States, a large Viking ship, having just sailed from Norway, figured prominently at the World's Columbian Exposition, held in honour of Columbus in Chicago in 1893.[14]

The anglophone fascination with "Viking explorers," coupled with late nineteenth- and early twentieth-century racial and religious tensions, offered Icelanders a strategic foothold in North American social hierarchies as a determined, desirable, white, and self-governing class of migrants. As Salome Halldorson, an Icelandic schoolteacher and member of the Legislative Assembly (MLA) from Lundar, Manitoba, explained, the Viking heritage of Icelanders made them perfect Canadians. "My parents came to this country as pioneer settlers from Iceland, the land of the Vikings, so I come of a strong and sturdy race, who had an instinctive love of freedom and were the first to establish a representative parliament," she announced in the Manitoba Legislative Assembly in 1937. "I identify with the history and ideals of my race. I too am a freedom-loving pioneer with a strong will to set out in search of a new and better world."[15]

Viking festivals and references to the Viking roots of Icelanders might be understood as strategic responses to racial tension and anti-immigrant sentiment in both the late nineteenth century and the first few decades of the twentieth. The declaration of war in 1914 sparked an intensification of those attitudes. During the First World War, higher-than-expected levels of recruits who had been rejected for medical reasons fuelled anxieties about the general fitness of North American populations. These anxieties intensified racism and anti-immigrant sentiment, and they fuelled the rise of the eugenics movement in Canada and the United States in the 1920s. Although the war ended in 1918, Icelanders and many other immigrant groups faced new government policies that barred immigration from other countries, thus effectively curbing future arrivals to North America.

## Anglicization and Language Decline

Despite the general public acceptance and popularity of Viking imagery that helped foster the growth of Viking-style events and displays in the Icelandic community, other noticeable cultural markers, particularly the use of the Icelandic language (like most other languages other than English), were not welcome in everyday interactions with most Anglo–North Americans during the First World War. Many reformers and critics welcomed the arrival of different immigrant communities to Canada and even tolerated cultural and religious differences to varying degrees, but any perceived refusal to assimilate linguistically often created tensions. Commentators in the *Manitoba Free Press* railed against immigrant-language education in the province, arguing that it eroded Canada's fundamentally British character. "Different cultures and qualities can only be blended by a common language," argued one editorial, "and it [is] for that specific purpose that a common language (English) is insisted upon."[16]

Within the Icelandic community, anglicization intensified as many young immigrants, such as Signy Stephenson, married into non-Icelandic families during the first decades of the twentieth century. Although intermarriage dated back to the earliest years of settlement in North America, it accelerated in the decades surrounding the two world wars. By 1914, approximately 20 per cent of recorded marriages in the community involved a non-Icelandic bride or groom, and by the end of the Second World War, the rate had increased to approximately 50 per cent.[17]

Oral history interviews suggest that intermarriage directly affected the transmission of the Icelandic language. Some Icelanders considered it rude to speak it in front of non-speakers, including non-Icelandic spouses, in-laws, and guests. Such forms of linguistic politeness also limited the amount of Icelandic spoken in the home.[18] In "Lost Tracks," a short story about an Icelandic woman who marries into an affluent anglophone family, Guðrún H. Finnsdóttir discusses the role that class and intolerant in-laws could play in language transmission. Guðrún's protagonist, Ragnhildur, changes her name to Ruby at the request of her wealthy English mother-in-law because she wants to avoid an association with several local Icelandic washerwomen with the same name. Her father-in-law also forbids "Ruby" from teaching her own daughter Icelandic after he hears his granddaughter singing an Icelandic song. "I won't allow you to teach this child any of this foreign nonsense," commanded her father-in-law. "English is sufficient."[19]

Census data suggest that Icelanders had largely succeeded in retaining their language in the six decades following arrival. In 1931, 82 per cent of Icelandic Canadians identified Icelandic as their native tongue, but in 1941, this figure dropped to 72 per cent.[20] Between 1913 and 1940, the Jón Bjarnason Academy offered Icelandic-language education to students in Winnipeg's West End, and, in 1951, the University of Manitoba created a Chair in Icelandic Language and Literature to promote the study of the language. In spite of these programs and statistics that show that most Icelanders may have been able to speak Icelandic early in the twentieth century, actual opportunities to speak and learn the language were restricted by conditions during the First and Second World Wars, internal linguistic pressures, intermarriage, and xenophobia. Birna Arnbjörnsdóttir writes that the North American–born children of Icelandic-born parents became "English-dominant bilinguals" – that is, they understood Icelandic, but more commonly used English outside the home.[21] A range of personal and social forces steadily eroded opportunities for later generations to hear and learn Icelandic, including, as Arnbjörnsdóttir contends, internal community demands for perfection in the Icelandic language, which discouraged North American–born generations from speaking it.[22] Older generations of Icelandic immigrants could be staunch linguistic purists who considered it their "sacred duty ... neither to forget their own language nor to mix it into some kind of slang."[23] Speakers of what poet Guttormur Guttormsson called "Winnipeg Icelandic," Icelandic immigrant slang mixed with words borrowed from English, could expect teasing and ridicule from older, fluent Icelandic speakers.

For the children of Icelandic immigrants, however, perfect English-language skills had long since taken precedence over Icelandic because English was often so crucial to work, upward mobility, and acceptance in North America. Albert Kristjánsson moved to Canada around the age of ten in 1887 and remembered how using flawless English was incredibly symbolic because it rebuffed English assumptions about the inferiority of "foreigners."[24] He reported that much of this same sentiment was still common among his anglophone colleagues when he served as an MLA in the early 1920s. In spite of his remarkable and lengthy career, Kristjánsson said that "the greatest victory" he ever won was beating his anglophone classmates at an English spelling bee as an immigrant schoolboy. Anglicization and integration did not contradict their identity as Icelanders in the minds of early twentieth-century migrants and their descendants. Instead, they were necessary for survival, success, and self-respect in societies that could impose xenophobic limits on upward mobility. "The Anglo-Saxons, who are the lords of laws and promises, [looked down] on the Icelanders and all foreigners," remembered Kristjánsson. "They were called foreigners, *foreigners*.... We had to fight for recognition as men among men."[25]

Indeed, as Kristjánsson's quote suggests, by the turn of the century, Icelanders often experienced negative treatment in everyday situations because of negative attitudes towards foreigners in general rather than specific assumptions about Icelanders in particular. This encouraged many Icelanders to simply build up thoroughly anglicized public personas, which would encourage acceptance in Anglo–North American society. Ryan Eyford reminds us that, by the 1920s, members of the Icelandic community had attained positions of relative prominence in Canada.[26] Indeed, numerous individual Icelanders had risen to impressive stations of professional, political, and military leadership by the time of the celebrated Stephenson-Eaton wedding in 1933. Among these were Thomas H. Johnson (Tómas Hermann Jónsson), who became attorney general of Manitoba in 1917; Vilhjálmur Stephansson, the Arctic scholar born at Árnes, Manitoba, who by 1915 had become one of the most famous Icelanders in North America, gracing the front page of publications like the *New York Times*;[27] and the Winnipeg Falcons, the predominantly Icelandic Olympic-champion hockey team, which won gold at Antwerp in 1920.

While official English-language discourse celebrated the promise of the Icelandic immigrant community, everyday interactions in the wider society could still be problematic. The use of the term *goolie*, for example, was widespread in Winnipeg throughout the inter-war period, although its role as an ethnic slur is unclear. Eyford points out that, by 1920, many Icelanders affectionately embraced the name and considered it "a humorous expression of familiarity."[28] Some interviewees for this project shared this view of the term; however, some older community members still disliked it and considered it offensive.[29] Helga (Olafson) Gerrard remembered that she landed a good job in Winnipeg in the 1940s, but that she and the other Icelandic women in the office were excluded from their English colleagues' women's softball league "because they were goolies."[30] Many of her Icelandic work friends anglicized their names to blend in, alongside their Ukrainian co-workers, but Gerrard resisted the recommendation that she change her name from Helga to Helen because it was an old family name. She remembered that although Icelanders were generally considered acceptable because they were related to Scandinavians, markers of difference, like Icelandic names, could spark tensions in everyday interactions with English co-workers. These tensions did not necessarily keep young Icelanders down, remembered Gerrard. As in Albert Kristjánsson's testimony, she worked hard to achieve and earned a promotion above those who looked down on ethnic workers.

> I finally got a job. I was 21. On the first day of work it was mostly Scotch and English workers (and) I was being introduced to one woman as "Helga

Olafson." She said to me: "what kind of a name is that?" and I said, "it's a Scandinavian name." She said, (with a sour tone) "well, we'll let you stay." I looked at her and I thought to myself, "I'm going to beat you."[31]

For many Icelandic immigrants and their descendants, accomplishment, acculturation, and especially service in North American society were integral to identity and upward mobility. During the First and Second World Wars, Icelandic organizations also launched pro-war campaigns and celebrated rates of enlistment and wartime service. Although Icelandic attitudes towards the First World War were mixed, a vocal group of pro-war Icelanders strove to create an image of their community as unified in its support for North American forces and the British Empire. Newspaper board members and influential public figures and organizations supported the war, including women's organizations like the Jón Sigurðsson Chapter IODE. Named for the Icelandic independence leader, but devoted to service to king and country, this Icelandic chapter of the IODE helped organize major initiatives during both world wars. It was founded in 1916 under the leadership of Jóhanna Guðrún Skaptason, a woman whose husband was serving overseas.[32] The chapter offered Icelandic women who supported the war effort a significant outlet for organizing large knitting drives, fundraising campaigns, and plans for a memorial for Icelandic war casualties and returned soldiers. It also helped create and publish a special Icelandic-language, commemorative volume to honour the known Icelandic veterans of the First World War, and it later published an English-language version dedicated to veterans of the Second World War.[33]

In addition to the charitable works of Icelandic organizations supporting the war effort, the image of the Viking immigrant soldier emerged as a powerful wartime figure representing Icelanders' loyalty to, as well as their rightful belonging in, North American society during a period of xenophobic pressure. An estimated 1,245[34] identified Icelandic Canadians and Americans enlisted for service, forming battalions with heavy Icelandic representations, such as the 223rd Battalion (Canadian Scandinavians) and the 197th (Vikings of Canada) Battalion, which recruited Icelandic and Scandinavian Canadians for service during the First World War[35] (Figure 4.3). In addition to their regulation uniforms, each of the burly soldiers of the 197th wore a Viking-ship crest emblazoned with the number 197. Members of the 223rd bore an image of a Viking with a massive moustache and battleaxe standing in front of a maple leaf (Figure 4.4). In a special tribute to the 197th, the *Winnipeg Tribune* reported, "The best-known and highly honoured names of the Scandinavian countries" were sending

Figure 4.3. Enlistment advertisement for the 223rd Canadian Scandinavians. Reprinted from *Lögberg*, 16 March 1916, 8.

Figure 4.4. Badge from the 223rd Canadian Scandinavians. Collection of Joe Martin. Image courtesy of the Manitoba Museum, Winnipeg.

their sons, "blonde-haired Vikings, few of whom stand less than six feet tall" to fight for Canada.[36] Such demonstrations of the loyal "Viking spirit" in war and civic life, agreed Laura Goodman Salverson in her award-winning novel, *The Viking Heart*, was the best way to "prove to Canada the worth of her Icelandic subjects."[37]

### Language, War, and Radicalism

While the English media celebrated the Viking immigrants who enlisted for service, the everyday actions of immigrant Icelanders at home in wartime North America could still raise suspicions about community and individual loyalty. During both world wars, intolerance towards the use of the Icelandic language and linguistic markers of Icelandic difference – including names and accents – intensified. In wartime, undiscerning English-language speakers easily mistook a range of foreign languages and names for German or those belonging to other enemy alien groups. Although Icelanders were not considered enemy aliens, English officials viewed Icelandic-language publications as potentially dangerous sources of radicalism and anti-war sentiment. During the First World War and the Winnipeg General Strike, newspapers such as *Lögberg* and *Voröld* were monitored and subjected to translation and review.[38]

Fears of enemy spies, traitors, and radicals, as well as a general distrust of non-English languages, strongly discouraged a range of North American immigrant groups from using their own languages in public during the war. In the United States, aggressive campaigns against the German language could make speaking many other "foreign" languages in public a risky activity. Anti-bilingual sentiment in Canada, aimed at both French Canadians and immigrant communities that sought to preserve their home languages, was also intense, but had been so in the years leading up to the war. As Royden Loewen and Gerald Friesen argue in their analysis of the debates over French and immigrant bilingualism, the *Manitoba Free Press* published at least sixty-four anti-bilingual articles and editorials "advocating English as the sole language of instruction."[39]

In 1916, the Manitoba government bowed to these pressures, officially revoking bilingual-language education rights and mandating school attendance as well as the sole use of English in publicly funded schools. Although anglophone intolerance towards preserving immigrant languages had long targeted French-Catholic education in the province, the laws mandating English-only education sought to quash any resistance, real or perceived, to the anglicization and assimilation of immigrant children. Moreover, the law passed just two years into the First World War. As Loewen and Friesen contend, the timing of the legislation meant that any non-English speakers who opposed such measures could find themselves to be targets of pro-British fervour and wartime English-Canadian nationalism and hysteria.[40] As Frances Swyripa discusses in her work on the Ukrainian-Canadian community, English commentators saw immigrant-language education and preservation campaigns as an expression of ethnic "disloyalty."[41] English critics might respond sharply to the very act of speaking another language during the war since, as Howard Palmer asserts, ideas about "loyalty and cultural and linguistic uniformity were synonymous" during this period.[42]

The decision of Icelandic immigrants and their offspring to use the English language in public during wartime reflected not only legislative changes but also larger, often undocumented pressures that non-English speakers faced in everyday life during a period of increased scrutiny and suspicion. Several Icelandic leaders, including MLA and future Manitoba attorney general Thomas H. Johnson, openly supported the new English-language schools policy; this attitude reflected intensifying Canadian nationalism and older (sometimes Anglophilic) devotion to English ways of life that dated back to the Icelandic community's earliest years, when English society and culture were cast as a preferable alternative to Danish.

Still, the nationalist sentiment of such leaders represented only one side of the debate in the Icelandic community. In the years leading up to the First World War, Icelandic-language forums and publications sheltered and fostered politically diverse and dissenting voices, despite external pressures in Canada and the United States. The prolific Icelandic-language press provided a forum in which immigrants from a range of political perspectives and backgrounds could critique inequality, discrimination, war, and each other. English critics who worried that the Icelandic-language press might be sheltering radical and subversive sentiments during the war and the Winnipeg General Strike were, to some extent, correct. Although they might have expected arguments from conservative Icelanders, they were not aware that radical immigrant writers and editors like Margrét Benedictsson and Dr. Sigurður Júlíus Jóhannesson – or "Siggi Júl," as he was known – were expressing themselves in Icelandic with relative freedom and much less fear of reprisals from mainstream North American society.

**Political Diversity, Radicalism, and the Icelandic-Language Press**

In the years leading up to the First World War, a booming Icelandic immigrant press had offered Icelanders from a range of political and religious backgrounds – including Unitarians, socialists, and feminists – an outlet for expression and critique. In addition to innumerable books, the prolific immigrant press produced more than thirty-five Icelandic-language newspapers and periodicals in Canada during this period. Before the amalgamation of the two largest newspapers in 1959, Conservative Icelanders often subscribed to the paper *Heimskringla*, while Liberal community members supported its rival, *Lögberg*.[43] Socialist-leaning Icelanders read and published in more radical papers such as *Voröld*, and Icelandic women could read about feminist, temperance, and suffrage issues in Benedictsson's monthly *Freyja* (1898–1910). Beyond newspapers and periodicals, immigrant Icelandic publishing houses in Winnipeg, such as Friðrik Stephenson's Columbia Press, Hecla Press, and the Viking Press, produced many Icelandic-language books of poetry, fiction, biographies, and autobiographies, which often discussed life, culture, politics, and faith in North America. Some of the most revered of these works were those by esteemed *skáld* (poet) and pacifist Stephan G. Stephansson of Dakota Territory and later Markerville, Alberta, who clashed with conservative and nationalist supporters of the war.

Stephansson, alongside socialist editor Dr. Siggi Júl of *Voröld*, wrote and spoke about their doubts and criticisms when Canada entered the war in 1914. In spite of events supporting enlistment and service in the Icelandic community, oral testimonies suggest that anti-war sentiment and political analysis found receptive audiences in Winnipeg's West End Icelandic neighbourhood. Einar Arnason, who grew up there, recalled that there was less than overwhelming support for the war in this urban community. "Most of the people were pacifists," he asserted. "The war in Europe was very remote."[44] In print and at community gatherings, pacifist Icelanders used Icelandic-language forums as alternatives to the propaganda and misinformation that filled the mainstream, English-language papers.[45] During his time as editor of *Lögberg*, Siggi Júl refused to reprint translated English reports of the war, instead replacing them with anti-war articles and editorials. According to oral histories and newspaper reports, intense political divides occasionally led to threats and vandalism in the Icelandic community, particularly during the Winnipeg General Strike.

Icelanders were similarly divided by the strike, which erupted in response to the dismal economic and labour conditions that arose after the war ended. Hrund Skúlason remembered that when editor and Icelandic National League vice-president Jón Bildfell tried to drive some Icelanders from the train station during the transit strike, he had his windshield smashed.[46] Many Icelanders in Winnipeg's West End feared that Siggi Júl would be shot for his public pro-strike stance, and, eventually, the elderly doctor was arrested for seditious speech after translations of speeches he had given at the Good Templars Hall were submitted to the Winnipeg Police in 1919. In the wake of the strike, the well-known doctor entered into a public legal battle with conservative Icelanders whom he identified as police informants.[47] The trial, which was covered in the English-language media, offered non-Icelandic readers a relatively rare glimpse into the political tensions that had engulfed the immigrant community.

As Siggi Júl's arrest suggests, Icelandic-language forums shielded, but did not offer total protection from, restrictions on freedom of speech in the early twentieth century. State surveillance of immigrant newspapers intensified during the First World War, and conservative Icelanders who had opposed Siggi Júl successfully lobbied for his removal as editor of *Lögberg*.[48] Icelanders who ardently opposed critics like him also provided information to law-enforcement officials about community activities hidden behind the veil of the Icelandic language. Viðar Hreinsson reveals that the first Icelandic Canadian MLA and attorney general, Thomas H. Johnson, even tried to silence the pacifist work of respected *skáld* Stephan G. Stephansson.[49] He offered the Royal North-West Mounted Police (RNWMP) English-language translations of *Vígslóði*, Stephansson's anti-war book of poetry, for their register of subversive publications. The RNWMP, unsure of what to do with a book of poems written by an elderly farmer in Alberta, decided not to take action against Stephansson.[50]

### Gender and the Decline of the Immigrant Press

As the children and grandchildren of Icelandic immigrants anglicized, they grew more detached from the Icelandic-language press that had been central to community expression in their parents' and grandparents' generations. This growing separation between older Icelandic-language media and younger Icelandic audiences had political implications for community expression. The anglicized ethnic festivals that increasingly replaced the immigrant press were largely stripped of the diversity and nuance of immigrant voices that had thrived in Icelandic-language newspapers and books.[51] This had a range of implications, including a shift in opportunities for women's expression in the community. Although male editors and commentators occasionally ridiculed them, the Icelandic-language press offered women like Margrét Benedictsson and contributors to *Freyja* a forum for a political, cultural, and spiritual expression that challenged the bounds of both traditional Icelandic and North American femininity. For example, Icelandic women could use the immigrant press and ideas about the community's Viking Age past to create a far more diverse range of political debates. Indeed, the Viking Age was not anchored to any particular political side in the immigrant community and could offer fertile ground for nineteenth- and twentieth-century women's political expression. As Annette Kolodny writes, medieval Scandinavian and Icelandic laws governing women's political and economic rights also fascinated and energized some Anglo-American feminists. Activists referenced these laws to describe a European tradition of "enlightened policies" for women that might naturalize and lend external legitimacy to the modern feminist movement.[52]

Conversely, Viking-themed public heritage displays in the Icelandic community often consigned women to more passive and largely silent models of Icelandic femininity. Removed from such events were more complex and unsettling narratives from the Icelandic sagas, including stories about Leifur Eiríksson's gender-bending, warrior-like sister, Freydís Eiríksdóttir, who also reportedly made the trip to Vinland and incited several murders – and even took up the sword while heavily pregnant.[53] Instead, when immigrant women boarded the Viking ship floats that sailed down various North American parade routes, they often appeared as passive and nameless "carriers of culture" dressed in nineteenth-century national costume.[54]

## The *Fjallkona*

After the First World War ended, a new public female figure who evoked the Viking past – the *Fjallkona* – emerged in the Icelandic immigrant community. The *Fjallkona* (Mountain Woman) was a female embodiment of the Icelandic nation crafted in the nineteenth century but created using a number of references to its Viking Age past. This female figure, first evoked in literary form, became intensely popular after Eiríkur Magnússon commissioned a German artist, J.B. Zwecker, to create a much-reproduced etching of a beautiful, long-haired woman for a nineteenth-century book of folk tales (Figure 4.5).[55] Icelandic immigrant organizers further popularized the *Fjallkona* by bringing her to life through North American–style pageantry in 1924. That year, organizers in Winnipeg and Icelandic communities such as Winnipegosis (Manitoba) and Blaine (Washington) decided to expand their Icelandic Day celebrations by having an Icelandic woman dress up as the *Fjallkona*, based on the Zwecker etching, in an attempt to draw in larger, younger audiences. The Winnipeg *Fjallkona* pageant, however, received the widest coverage in the Icelandic press, due in part to a scandal that erupted around the election of its *Fjallkona*, Sigrún Lindal. Lindal, complained older Icelanders, could never be the *Fjallkona* because she was a *skollótt kona* (bald woman) – a reference to the fact that she, like many fashion-conscious daughters of immigrants, had cut her hair into a 1920s bob (Figure 4.6).[56]

In 1924, Sigrún Lindal and her haircut became the centre of a symbolic conflict between new, North American–born generations of Icelandic women, who defied Old World gender rules – and socially conservative male community leaders, who clung to nineteenth-century Icelandic values. A chorus of these conservative male leaders protested the

Main Street Vikings 119

Figure 4.5. J.B. Zwecker, *The Fjallkona*. Drawing based on J.B. Zwecker illustration reprinted from the cover of *Almanak Ólafs S. Thorgeirssonar*, 1909. EIHC.

prospect of having a *Fjallkona* with "castrated" hair – who violated the more traditional, long-haired, nineteenth-century image of the figure. Organizers in rural Hnausa, Manitoba, issued a formal statement against Sigrún Lindal's hair, arguing that the *Fjallkona*'s "beauty and nobility will be reduced if [her hair] does not get to her waistline."[57] Jón Bildfell, editor of *Lögberg*, launched an editorial attack on the larger "bald women epidemic" afflicting the Icelandic community and its daughters who wanted to look, and work outside the home, like men. The gender equity pursued by these unrecognizable Icelandic women, lamented Bildfell, would destroy the ancient cultural values (and traditional gendered order) embodied by the *Fjallkona*.[58] *Heimskringla* also published a "scientific" warning that women who cut their hair "like

Figure 4.6. The "bald" *Fjallkona*, Sigrún Lindal, 1924. Reprinted from Elva Simundsson, *Fjallkonas of Íslendingadagurinn 1924–1989* [Fjallkonas of the Icelandic Festival 1924–1989] (Gimli, MB: s.n., 1990).

men" killed the blood cells under the scalp and would also eventually grow beards like men. The report contended that such women would even pass on beardedness to their female offspring.[59]

On the day of the *Fjallkona* pageant, short-haired Sigrún Lindal bowed to pressure and wore a long wig. However, this attempt by male leaders to control the personal style of the *Fjallkona* candidates was short-lived. When Stefanía Magnússon acted as the *Fjallkona* in 1925, she appeared as a modern incarnation – with her own fashionably cropped short hair. The campaign against the so-called bald women epidemic was over, and the requirement for long hair was dropped from the pageant. Although the *Fjallkona* scandal reveals the limits of male leaders' control over women's personal style at public festivals, women's otherwise silent role stood in contrast to the much richer and more diverse opportunities for expression in the Icelandic-language press.

### Immigrant Politics, the Second World War, and the Occupation of Iceland

Anglicization, however, did not deprive Icelandic North American women of political voices and opinions. Aside from the *Fjallkona* pageant and other public events, Icelandic women enjoyed a growing number of English-language opportunities for political participation by the start of the Second World War in 1939, although in a far different political context. Influenced in part by the community's strong suffrage and temperance movements, some Icelandic women pursued positions of leadership in English society in the 1930s and 1940s. In 1937, as war in Europe loomed, Icelandic Canadian author Laura Goodman Salverson won the Governor General's Award for her pacifist-themed novel, *The Dark Weaver*. Nevertheless, by the time she assumed editorship of the newly formed, English-language magazine the *Icelandic Canadian*, which sought to connect with English-speaking people of Icelandic descent, she had become a tireless supporter of the war effort, and the periodical published features on, and odes to, Icelandic servicemen and servicewomen as well as news of the war.

Salverson's support of the Second World War reflected the distinct ways in which the community responded to this conflict. Whereas the responses of Icelanders to the First World War had been very mixed, few spoke publicly against the Second. This was to some extent due to the death of older radicals, such as Stephan G. Stephansson, but even surviving older radicals curtailed their critiques. Siggi Júl, for example, was an ardent anti-fascist, and the Icelandic community was relatively unified in its opposition to Hitler. A few radical Icelanders continued to issue criticisms behind the veil of the Icelandic language, including MLA Salome

Halldorson. The former schoolteacher, whose brother had died from the effects of poison gas during the First World War, remained a steadfast pacifist and delivered anti-war speeches in Icelandic to local communities in the early years of the war. She even organized a vote of no confidence in the wartime administration and launched fiery attacks against Icelandic women involved in the war effort.[60] However, Halldorson increasingly operated on the fringes of the community after 1940 and lost her seat in the 1941 election. In addition to less political opposition, events displaying immigrant support for North American forces in the Second World War were also remarkably different from their campaigns in the First. Viking imagery declined sharply as it became linked to Nazism.[61] As Julia Zernack explains, Nazis appropriated romanticized, nineteenth-century depictions of Viking Age Iceland, which they argued represented the "epitome" of Germanic society.[62] Images of Viking warriors and ships appeared in Nazi propaganda in Germany,[63] and the Nazis even reprinted special German translations of the medieval Icelandic text, the Prose Edda, for distribution to the Hitler Youth.[64] Nazi ideas about the Viking past also shaped campaigns in occupied Denmark and Norway, where German troops depicted themselves as modern-day Vikings engaged in a war against Bolshevism (Figure 4.7).

Icelandic-press editorials wrestled with the Nazi uses and abuses of the Norse past. Salverson contended that the community was composed of a more anti-fascist brand of the Viking spirit, which, she argued, fundamentally battled "racial hatreds, racial pride and ignorance."[65] References to the Viking spirit and especially "Viking blood," which had been popular during the First World War, assumed far more ambivalent and potentially damaging associations.[66] This new spirit clearly contributed to a temporary decline in the use of Viking themes in the Icelandic media,[67] which, instead, frequently focused on the themes of friendliness and hospitality, particularly once their cousins back home became the "hosts" of a controversial Allied occupation of their country on 10 May 1940.[68]

Although Iceland remained neutral during the First World War, it became strategically essential during the Second World War due to developments in aviation technology and the country's proximity to North America. Advancements in flight fuelled fears that a Nazi occupation of Iceland could put enemy bombers "within striking distance of such vulnerable points as New York, Chicago, Pittsburgh and Detroit."[69] Intelligence reports of suspicious German activity in Iceland in the months and years leading up to the outbreak of war strongly suggested Hitler's interest in the island,[70] and fears of a Nazi occupation of Iceland increased following the German invasion of Denmark,

Figure 4.7. Norwegian SS poster, 1943. Collection of Stanford University, Stanford, CA.

Iceland's colonial ruler, on 9 April 1940. Allied nations saw the invasion as a display of seemingly unstoppable Nazi military expansion, but Icelandic nationalists regarded it as a critical opportunity to effectively extinguish the last vestiges of Danish rule, and they pursued an independent position of neutrality.[71] Following the severance of communication with Denmark, the Alþingi, Iceland's Parliament, abruptly freed itself from the authority of the Danish king on 10 April 1940 and assumed control of its own foreign relations.

Iceland's lack of a powerful ally and its own standing military fuelled fears that it would either partner with Axis forces, which promised funding and support for sovereignty, or quickly succumb to German invasion. Despite Iceland's assertions of neutrality and sovereignty, a unit of 746 British marines landed in Reykjavík harbour one month after the Nazi invasion of Denmark. Responsibility for the occupation briefly changed hands between Britain and Canada before the United States assumed control in 1941. The occupation was intensely unpopular with many local people, Daisy Neijmann notes, and symbolized "a shameful repeat of Iceland's colonial history."[72] Allied soldiers seldom met with organized resistance, but some Icelanders responded to the occupation when they met servicemen in public by heckling, spitting at them, and even starting barroom brawls.[73] *Þjóðviljinn*, the Icelandic Communist Party newspaper, became a very active opponent of Allied operations in Iceland and issued condemnations of the occupation and frank discussions about its potential permanency.[74] In the summer of 1940, Canada's high commissioner to Great Britain sent a telegraph to the secretary of state for external affairs in London, warning that the "local and political situation is a delicate one ... you should do your utmost, in collaboration with His Majesty's Minister, to cultivate friendly relations with local authorities ... and community at large."[75]

### Cold Women: Gender, Hospitality, and the Allied Occupation

Facing organized resistance was one thing. But Allied military leaders were particularly concerned about everyday forms of resistance, which affected the strength of the forces stationed in a sometimes harsh and unfamiliar landscape and damaged the international image of the occupation. Officials and servicemen often referred to this subtle resistance as "coldness,"[76] and, much to the chagrin of Icelandic North Americans, news of Icelanders' "anything but warm"[77] treatment of the occupying forces reached the mainstream English-language media in 1941. In January, *Time* magazine published reports received from sixteen Canadian soldiers, who, "after a stint in Iceland, had deteriorated to

Class E, unfit for active service (mostly stomach ulcers)." Restrictions on food, hospitality, and female companionship made their stay unbearable, they reported to the magazine. "Soldiers were not admitted to Icelandic homes," and hungry Allied soldiers wanted for "proper" meat, but were restricted to the "narrow" diet of Icelanders, in which "mutton appeared in nearly every dish, stewed, boiled, broiled, roasted, fried."[78]

Soldiers' nutrition was a rallying point in Allied wartime campaigns, which emphasized civilian sacrifice and rationing to divert better food and resources to the fighting forces. For many North Americans, reports of Icelanders withholding food from soldiers equated resistance. As the 1941 National Film Board (NFB) film *Food: Weapon of Conquest* reminded civilians, "The modern fighting man deserves a menu twice as high in food value as that of a civilian [including] fresh meat, fresh vegetables, dairy produce, fruit and eggs.... In World War Two, as in Napoleon's time, a nation marches on its stomach."[79]

The cold reception of the Allied soldiers in Iceland created a serious public relations crisis for the Icelandic community in North America, particularly since *Time* announced that it was a thin veil for widespread Nazi sympathy. The brother of Nazi propaganda chief Joseph Goebbels, the magazine reported, had recently vacationed in Iceland, and the hostility of Icelanders towards the occupation "was the result of patiently spread German propaganda to the effect that Iceland and Germany were brother states."[80] Icelandic-immigrant leaders in North America responded that the soldiers simply did not understand local food customs and that Iceland was experiencing food shortages at the time, but the editors of *Time* published only a few of the many responses to the article.[81]

References to the soldiers' deprivation also related directly to a larger conflict over the sexualized connotations of *hospitality*. The so-called coldness of the Icelandic women towards the Allied soldiers was a particularly popular topic among servicemen, part of what *Time* described as "the soldier's greatest problem: the stubborn womankind of Iceland." Having learned the Icelandic word *stúlka* (girl), soldiers encountered only silence from women on the street when they called out "Hi, *stúlka!*" *Time* attributed the unresponsiveness of the Icelandic women to taboos against dating foreign men. "Any girl indiscreet enough to accept an Englishman," they reported, "would have all her hair shaved off."[82]

Indeed, taboos against dating Allied soldiers were strong in Icelandic society, and women who transgressed became the subject of a national crisis known as *Ástandið*, or "the Situation."[83] Women's relationships with occupying soldiers, writes Neijmann, became a symbol of the "breakdown of patriarchal authority," the corruption of "Mother Iceland."[84] Even married women who hoped to profit from providing food and domestic services, including laundry and housecleaning, faced pressure.[85] The Icelandic police monitored the contact between women and soldiers in Reykjavík, and, according to an informant in Herdís Helgadóttir's history of Iceland, "Any girls seen talking to soldiers, even if they were just asking the way, were 'Englishmen's whores.'"[86]

Few community histories have analysed the effects of the Allied occupation of Iceland on the immigrant community in North America, but in 1940, news of the occupation unleashed questions, concerns, and moments of panic among community leaders. As Icelandic North Americans well knew, the actions of their cousins at home in Iceland had the potential to affect their lives – regardless of whether they were Canadian- or American-born or had left the homeland five decades earlier. Community leaders feared that unsettling reports of Icelandic coldness and resistance to the Allied occupation would also arouse suspicions about the loyalties of Icelandic immigrants in Canada and the United States.

As many Icelanders well knew, the status and safety of established ethnic communities in North America could change quickly in wartime, especially those affiliated with anti-Allied sentiment or campaigns. As during the First World War, general intolerance of non-English languages, ethnic identities, and loyalties grew alongside fears of war and invasion. Immigrants and their children or grandchildren who identified as loyal Americans or Canadians, and had even fought for these countries during that war, could suddenly find themselves subject to surveillance, loss of property and assets, relocation, and internment during this one. The US government interned roughly 31,000 suspected "enemy aliens," and the Canadian government interned about 24,000 during the war. This included about 22,000 Japanese Canadians, some of whom had served for Canada in the First World War, as well as those with ties to Icelandic families. At the fishing settlement of Ósland, British Columbia, Icelanders watched as the Royal Canadian Mounted Police (RCMP) seized the property of their Japanese friends, neighbours, and classmates and shipped them off to internment camps – including children and the elderly. These Icelanders had lived side by side and worked with families like the Sakamotos, who ran a substantial boatbuilding business in the close-knit fishing community.[87] In a snapshot labelled "Last day as neighbours," Sigríður Einarsson and Jónína Jónsson posed with a boatbuilder's widow, Mrs. Hatsue Sakamoto, before she and her children were taken away by the RCMP for their ancestral homeland's hostility towards Allied forces[88] (Figure 4.8).

Icelandic immigrant leaders had for decades successfully portrayed their twin loyalties – to the Icelandic independence movement and their

Figure 4.8. *Last Day as Neighbours*. Japanese internment at the Osland settlement, 1942. University of British Columbia Archives, Vancouver.

new, democratic Canadian and American homelands – as compatible devotions. Icelandic immigrants, long-time vocal and visible supporters of independence, had even installed a statue of Jón Sigurðsson, the Icelandic independence leader, on the grounds of the Manitoba Legislative Building in 1921. Groups like the Icelandic National League and the Jón Sigurðsson Chapter IODE also observed these twin patriotisms and saw little contradiction among their Icelandic, Canadian, and British Empire connections and loyalties. During the Second World War, however, the strength of the Icelandic independence movement, at home and abroad, fuelled concern among North American officials. Icelandic community leaders openly supported the Allied cause in Canada, even offering to provide an all-Icelandic battalion to strengthen the occupation of their homeland and improve relations with the occupying forces, but an illtimed letter ignited a minor panic in the Canadian government about the spread of anti-occupation resistance in the immigrant community.

A few months after the Allied occupation of Iceland began, J.B. Skaptason, editor of *Heimskringla* and husband of the founder of the Jón Sigurðsson Chapter IODE, decided to write a letter of support to G.H. Lash, director of public information for the Canadian government. Skaptason was a supporter of the war effort, and he asked Lash whether he could publish the Allied forces' justification for the occupation of Iceland to help minimize opposition in the immigrant community and Iceland.[89] Skaptason asserted that his newspaper could help address the circulation of "mixed feelings both here and at home." Unbeknownst to Skaptason, his letter was one of the first English-language reports of "mixed feelings" within the immigrant community that the Departments of Public Information and External Affairs had received, and it sparked a minor panic within the federal government that Icelandic immigrants might undermine or take action against Allied operations in their homeland.

Ivana Caccia argues in her work on wartime pluralism that, by late 1939, the Canadian government was already generally anxious about potential fifth columns forming within ethnic immigrant communities and the proliferation of anti-Allied propaganda in ethnic-language newspapers and institutions.[90] But before these concerns escalated into the focused state surveillance that other migrant communities were facing, well-connected community leaders took action to protect the image of the Icelandic community, particularly member of Parliament (MP) and Minister of National War Services Joseph T. Thorson. Thorson had been a relatively low-profile MP when he was appointed to this post in 1941, a move likely fostered by his crucial role as a consultant for both Mackenzie King's government and the Allied forces, hoping to calm the waters in Iceland. Thorson quickly reassured the government that it did not need to fear interference from the immigrant community. "I have not found any trace of resentment among Canadians of Icelandic origin," he reported. "I feel quite sure that [Icelandic Canadians] perfectly understand the purpose of the occupation."[91] He also described the immigrant community's support of Icelandic sovereignty as an asset rather than a threat to Allied interests. In addition to preventing a Nazi invasion, Thorson wrote, the occupation was an opportunity to pursue "a closer relationship between Iceland and the British Commonwealth" and foster a well-positioned Icelandic North American business community in pursuit of "the severance of the relations between Iceland and Denmark."[92]

### "Hospitality Is a Tradition with the Icelanders": Producing Immigrant Propaganda

Icelandic North American leaders focused on the issue of hospitality in campaigns designed to bolster the image of the Allied occupation. While Icelandic moral regulators were concerned about too much hospitality on the part of young women, their American and Canadian counterparts attempted to contain and combat the image of too little. Thorson, as the head of National War Services and on the board of the NFB, employed popular media to actively promote a more positive image of the occupation. In 1940, the NFB began working on a film about Anglo-Icelandic compatibility and Icelandic Canadian loyalty, to be distributed both in Canada and in Iceland. Unlike the Icelandic events held during the First World War, *Iceland on the Prairies* was virtually stripped of references to the community's Viking past. Instead, it focused on picturesque community festivals, hard-working farmers, and friendly neighbours. Using the example of a thriving Icelandic Canadian immigrant community, the filmmakers cast Anglo-Icelandic "friendship" and cooperation as not only natural, but economically, socially, and politically beneficial. In addition to footage of the *Fjallkona* appearing before crowds at Gimli's Icelandic Day festival, the film provided a survey of male community members who had made significant political, economic, military, and academic contributions to Canada, including professors like Skúli Johnson and military personnel such as "Air Ace" Conrad Johannesson. Siggi Júl, the former radical and dedicated pacifist, even appeared in the film, hard at work on an Icelandic-language manual for English soldiers.

Icelandic food also enjoyed the spotlight. Icelanders were "true Canadians now," announced *Iceland on the Prairies*, but "they still retain some of the customs of their homeland, [such as] their meals, which are often Icelandic meals." Responding to reports of scarcity and the soldiers' isolation during the occupation, the film portrayed a family with smiling young women and a gracious hostess with a coffee pot in hand. Happy young men also enjoy a place at the table, which featured a meal of slowly pronounced Icelandic delicacies. "Hospitality is a tradition with the Icelanders," announces the narrator. "At the head of the table, the lady of the house ensures that her guests are well provided for. Friends are continually invited for meals or coffee."[93]

In addition to refuting rumours that Icelanders opposed the occupation, the film and other English-language campaigns targeted anti-immigrant prejudice among Allied soldiers and "the potential spread of racially founded national ideologies" too reminiscent of the Third Reich in their ranks.[94] In their English manual for soldiers, Siggi Júl and Einar Páll Jónsson instructed the Allied soldiers to cultivate friendships with local Icelandic men by inviting them for drinks, and they provided a translation for the phrase "This round is on me!"[95] They also targeted potential prejudice towards "foreign" customs and foods, instructing Allied soldiers: "Don't be prejudiced. Food is quite different in Iceland – try things before you proclaim they are no good ... [don't] jump to the conclusion that [North American] ways are invariably better. Try to understand. *Reynið að skilja*."[96]

While *Iceland on the Prairies* sought to ease tensions in Iceland with images of friendly women offering coffee to guests, another North American film about "friendly" Icelandic women released around the same time threatened the delicate situation in Iceland. In 1942, Twentieth Century Fox released its own, more sexualized tribute to Icelandic women and their soldier boyfriends in a figure skating musical simply titled *Iceland*. Film production proceeded in California with little to no reliable information about Iceland itself and was released after American forces assumed control of Iceland in 1941. The musical comedy took place in a wintery, northern land, where an American soldier (John Payne) successfully pursues "Katina," an often scantily clad Icelandic woman, played by the Norwegian Olympic figure skater and American film star, Sonja Henie. Payne out-charms the woman's Icelandic boyfriend, an effeminate weakling named Sverdrup, and is welcomed into Katina's family. References to "Eskimo love rituals" and skimpy costuming, including low-cut dresses, sheer fabrics, and short skirts, promoted an image of Icelandic women eagerly providing romantic hospitality for the soldiers. In addition to a faux wedding night that escalates into a thinly veiled rape scene, the film features a theme song, "You Can't Say No to a Soldier," which instructs the female audience that "if [a soldier is] gonna fight, he's got a right to romance." As Payne's character explains to Katina, "Honey, a soldier's not looking for a wife, he's looking for company"[97] (Figure 4.9).

Figure 4.9. Promotional photograph of Sonja Henie and John Payne in *Iceland*, 1942. Twentieth Century Fox.

News of *Iceland*'s content arrived in Reykjavík through the press and film magazines, which relayed some of the film's gross cultural inaccuracies and compounded the country's anxieties about US soldiers dating local women. Rather than encouraging the kind of local hospitality it featured, it seriously offended Icelanders and compounded an already significant public relations problem for the fledgling American occupation.[98]

### Post-war Campaigns and the Viking's Return

In spite of protests, American forces managed to remain in Iceland until the close of the Second World War and, under NATO, stayed for the duration of the Cold War, fearing a Soviet invasion of the strategically significant island. After the debacle surrounding the Twentieth Century Fox musical, *Iceland*, the United States created more sensitive and informed cultural campaigns to win support on the island, including a growing flow of translated literature, co-produced by Icelandic Americans and Icelanders who desired a closer relationship with the United States. Protests against a foreign military presence endured in Iceland, but Cold War initiatives, including US$38.7 million in Marshall Plan funding between 1948 and 1953 and strategic educational, literary, and arts exchanges between Iceland and the United States, helped American officials circumvent the linguistic and political barriers to promoting an image of a benevolent cultural "friendship" between the two countries.[99] Ideologically aligned Icelandic North American community leaders continued to play a role in the formation of this Cold War friendship, and this attitude ushered in a new period of what Helge Danielsen terms "politicized culturalism," or less conspicuous propaganda campaigns, which relied upon cultural exchange, providing new opportunities and prestige for Icelandic immigrant community leaders and institutions in North America.[100] Icelandic immigrant publications, like Thorstína Walters's *Modern Sagas*, received federal US support, while Icelandic-immigrant cultural campaigns began to enjoy impressive visibility in the post-war period.[101]

In North American Icelandic and Scandinavian communities, Viking imagery regained its popularity as political conditions changed. In addition, new Icelandic-immigrant identities and culture, showcased in Cold War forums, continued to celebrate a growing interest in Icelandic literature, culture, and food. The old currency of the Vinland voyages in North American Icelandic campaigns resumed. Following a temporary decline during the Second World War, Leifur Eiríksson began a new Cold War career, one that cast Icelanders as Cold War allies and defenders of democracy in the north. And as Viking imagery returned to favour as a symbol of North Atlantic democracy, so it resumed its place in post-war Icelandic community events and tributes.

## Conclusion

"Viking Spirits Sparkle[d]," announced the *Winnipeg Free Press*, describing the special tribute to Canada's Centennial at the Icelandic festival, *Íslendingadagurinn*, in Gimli, Manitoba, in 1967.[102] That year, the Gimli Chamber of Commerce observed the one-hundredth anniversary of Canadian Confederation by unveiling a fifteen-foot-tall sculpture of a bearded Viking wearing knee-high boots and a horned helmet (Figure 4.10). To mark that special anniversary and the unveiling, the "exceptionally beautiful and prestigious" socialite and business leader, Signy Eaton, now fifty-four years old, was chosen to serve as the *Fjallkona*, the female embodiment of the Icelandic nation (Figure 4.11).

Figure 4.10. Unveiling of the Gimli Viking statue, 1967. Collection of New Iceland Heritage Museum, Gimli, MB.

Figure 4.11. Signy Eaton as the *Fjallkona*, with Wilhelm Kristjansson, 1967. Collection of New Iceland Heritage Museum, Gimli, MB.

Dressed in the symbols of Iceland's Viking-era past, Signy rolled down Gimli's Main Street in a silver convertible, accompanied by groups of local men, "in original Viking dress," walking and riding down the parade route in homemade, Viking-themed floats.[103] In spite of their medieval dress, however, these modern-day Vikings embodied the adaptation, transformation, and endurance of a modern immigrant community in the tumultuous twentieth century.

From Signy's walk down the aisle as a Viking bride to her unveiling of Gimli's Viking statue thirty-four years later, the reoccurring figure of the Viking reveals the Icelandic immigrants' strategic deployment of a carefully crafted heritage, one designed to help them achieve upward mobility, security, and status during periods of political and social flux. The development and use of events featuring loyal, anglicized immigrants from the "Land of the Vikings" reflect the changing conditions that faced the community during periods of anti-immigrant xenophobia and war. Although the community may have appeared to outsiders as unified Viking soldiers, loyal to North America during the First World War, the Icelandic-language press concealed a much more diverse political culture, one that included pacifist campaigns and opportunities for women's political expression. As the Icelandic-language media declined, Icelanders frequently turned to ethnic festivals that maintained this focus on the Viking, in keeping with a longer trend established in Iceland and the strategies of well-established Scandinavian North American communities. This shift towards public events representing collective expression marked a temporary constriction of Icelandic women's political expression and the reinforcement of women as symbolic embodiments of the Icelandic nation. The following chapter explores some of the more complex private narratives surrounding women's place in community memory.

After the Second World War, the public identities and loyalties of North American–born descendants of immigrant Icelanders were firmly, publicly aligned with their adopted anglophone homelands. The death of much of the immigrant generation, the decline of the Icelandic language, and the galvanizing effects of two world wars shaped the emergence of an English-dominant ethnic community, whose leadership was now heavily influenced by the political and military interests of their adopted homelands.

*Chapter Five*

# Icelandic Cake Fight: A Brief History of *Vínarterta*

Say Vínarterta in a room full of the descendants of North American Icelandic immigrants and quarrels begin. In Canada, Vínarterta is in six or seven layers, flavoured with almonds, frosted with butter cream – wrong! One lady (with a Norwegian half in her family) used apricots instead of prunes between layers – wrong! Some leave out cardamom – oh-so-spicy, you know – wrong!

Bill Holm[1]

At the heart of the heart of Icelandic North American culture is not Vikings, or horses or sheep, or fishing or Black Death or language, no ... the centre of all things Icelandic North American is vinarterta.

W.D. Valgardson[2]

*Vínarterta*, a fruit torte imported to North America by Icelandic immigrants in the 1870s, can still inspire heated debates among their descendants. This little dessert emerged as a powerful symbol of Icelandic immigrant culture and history in the twentieth century, and it often appears as an essential centrepiece at major celebrations within the community. However, as Bill Holm observes above, *vínarterta* is as much a symbol of tension as unity among Icelandic North Americans. Many community members possess unusually strong opinions about the "correct" recipe for the torte and view preserving a particular recipe as a powerful symbol of both cultural integrity and family identity (Figure 5.1). Many Icelandic North Americans who produce (and consume) *vínarterta* strictly avoid any alterations to their recipe. Even small changes or variations in preparation, such as including thicker layers or icing, can incite fierce debate. But this obsession with *vínarterta* is perhaps most unusual because it has created a kind of culinary time

Figure 5.1. Nelson Gerrard, photograph of *vínarterta* prepared by Arden Jackson, 2016. EIHC.

capsule. Production of the torte declined and virtually died out in twentieth-century Iceland.[3]

This chapter explores the history of the torte and discusses its emergence as a powerful symbol of Icelandic immigrant culture in the community. Using cookbooks, immigrant memoirs, oral history interviews, and an analysis of narratives of mourning and commemoration, which help reveal some of the other meanings of this popular dessert, it begins with a discussion of the tangled origins of *vínarterta* in eighteenth-century Denmark and nineteenth-century Iceland. It then explores how and why it emerged as a public symbol of the Icelandic North American community during the 1940s and the Cold War, as anti-ethnic sentiment waned and North American interest in Iceland grew. Yet it is clear that this little dessert is more than just a prop in heritage campaigns. *Vínarterta* retains a deep meaning for community members. This final chapter explores how community members themselves have interpreted the meaning of this new public symbol as well as the role of the "striped lady" in more complex, private commemorative cultures. Although it may have appeared in public displays that promoted Canadian and American national narratives of wartime hospitality or post-war pluralism, this souvenir from the earliest days of the community often possessed very different meanings in private.

### *Wienertærte* (Vienna Torte): Danish and Continental Baking in Iceland, 1840–75

For many Icelandic North Americans, *vínarterta* is an easily accessible and edible souvenir of the late nineteenth-century Iceland their ancestors left behind. Indeed, most of the foods found in Icelandic North American kitchens and bakeries retained the imprint of the styles *en vogue* at the time of emigration as well as those of the physical conditions that shaped food culture in nineteenth-century Icelandic kitchens. For example, *rúllupylsa* (rolled spiced lamb) and *harðfiskur* (dried fish eaten with butter), still produced and consumed around New Iceland, were based on food staples more easily produced in the homeland. Other foods reflected the demands of working in traditional Icelandic kitchens. Before modern stoves were popularized in twentieth-century Iceland, most turf households relied on raised, open stone hearths that had changed relatively little over the centuries. Consequently, the culinary repertoire of the immigrant generation was dominated by baked goods that could easily be made over an open hearth in a pot or pan, fried in oil, or baked in a makeshift oven, including *pönnukökur* (pancakes), *kleinur* (knotted donuts), and the thin, baked layers of dough required to make *vínarterta*.[4]

Layered desserts like *vínarterta* and *randalín*, a similar cake-like dessert with fewer layers still found in twenty-first-century Iceland, not only reflected the conditions in nineteenth-century Icelandic kitchens but also changing economic conditions and styles particular to the period of mass emigration. Making *vínarterta* relied almost exclusively on having access to imported dried fruits and spices, rather than home-grown foods, and signalled a general improvement in Icelanders' access to international markets, goods, and disposable income in the second half of the nineteenth century. Although harsh conditions preceded emigration in the 1870s and persisted through subsequent decades, Sigurður Gylfi Magnússon reminds us that after Danish trade restrictions were lifted in 1854, some Icelanders also enjoyed a remarkable period of economic opportunity and growth. During this time, a new Icelandic merchant and entrepreneurial class emerged, and women in those families enjoyed greater access to imported goods and foods as well as the means to explore new styles of food production.[5]

The popularity of *vínarterta* among members of the North American immigrant generation signalled their origins in an Icelandic society in which Denmark, in many respects, still set the standards of style and sophistication. Fine, continental-style baking was most commonly associated with the households of Danish merchants and officials in Iceland as well as the Icelandic elite, many of whom had been educated in, or had ties to, Denmark. By the mid-nineteenth century, these fashionable continental goods and styles had become more accessible for some Icelandic households as economic conditions improved. As Carol Gold has documented, the publication of cookbooks written for housewives and households in Denmark flourished in the early nineteenth century.[6] These newly printed collections of recipes from Copenhagen's kitchens tightened the culinary links between Iceland and Denmark as they began to circulate in Iceland in the 1840s. Recipes for *Wienertærte* and other Danish favourites arrived in Iceland in several cookbooks produced by a growing number of female Danish cookbook authors, including Clara Margrethe Fristrup, Christine Rostrup, and Mathilde Roedsted Schmidt.[7]

But how did Vienna torte get to Copenhagen? The appearance of Viennese baking in the kitchens of Copenhagen reflected the uniqueness and growing popularity of new and distinctive Austrian confections in late eighteenth- and early nineteenth-century Europe. Coffee served with fashionable confections was a sign of status in Copenhagen social circles at a time when the production and baking of Viennese sweets were experiencing growing popularity in Europe. The almond flavouring in *vínarterta* reflected these roots. Viennese confectioners and shop owners often used ground almonds as a filler because pressure from local bakers' guilds prevented them from legally preparing foods using wheat flour until 1748.[8] The lifting of this restriction ushered in a new era of baking innovation in Vienna, one that blended traditions from areas around the Austro-Hungarian Empire.[9] A range of layered cakes and tortes, many of which retained the use of ground almonds and fruit preserves, became particularly popular and spread across continental Europe.

In 1795, a Danish translation of Lovise Beate Augustine Friedel's cookbook, *Nye og fuldstændige confecture*,[10] offered interested bakers in Denmark a range of fashionable and innovative recipes for delicacies like *Wienertærte*, or Vienna Torte. Such instances of international culinary exchange were not unusual, and Austrian recipes, in particular, left a major imprint on Danish baking traditions. *Wienerbrød* (Viennese bread), for example, reportedly came to be known in English as "the danish" because of its popularity among Danish American immigrant bakers.[11] But by the time *Wienerbrød* was adorning the bakery shelves and tables of the fashionable set in Copenhagen, many Danes – and potentially the subjects of the Danish Empire – had already been enjoying *Wienertærte* for half a century.

*Wienertærte* was more than a simple dessert – it was a status symbol that showcased the wealth and creativity of image-conscious Danish households. In keeping with the longer confectionery tradition in Vienna, this recipe instructed bakers how to create a layered torte using fine, preserved fruit fillings and dough made from a blend of flour and ground almonds. Unlike later Icelandic incarnations, this and other early recipes for *Wienertærte* encouraged variety and experimentation, showcasing status through access to a range of expensive ingredients. For example, Friedel's 1795 recipe recommended using different fruits between each layer, including cherry, apple, raspberry, and currant. She also instructed women to make an elaborate topping for the torte by frosting it with icing made with orange blossom water and creating a floral image on top using "flowers from black cherries, preserved rose hips, and green plums."[12] (See the first recipe in the appendix.) Clara Margrethe Fristrup's 1840 recipe reveals that Danish women were maintaining this use of multiple fillings almost half a century later because it recommended that they choose four varieties of whatever fruit preserves they preferred.[13] (See the second recipe in the appendix.) Both women also invited bakers to create innovative shapes for the finished torte by making each layer of dough smaller than the first.

### *Vínarterta* and Nineteenth-Century Icelandic Society

The very first incarnations of the torte in Iceland are difficult to trace, but it was likely that fine, continental-style baking was initially more common in the households of Danish merchants and officials or the Danish-educated Icelandic elite. By the 1850s, however, a sizeable number of Icelandic women had also gained exposure to these baking styles. In 1858, interest in European-style baking among women in Iceland was so great that it helped fuel the production of the first Icelandic-language cookbook by Þóra Andrea Nikólína Jónsdóttir. Although Icelandic nationalists may have hoped to curb Danish and other foreign influences, Icelandic women of means clearly embraced the international culinary trends and translated them into the Icelandic language, evident in the 1858 cookbook's inclusion of recipes like "Portuguese cake" and *karrí* (curry).[14]

The torte's foundational connection to early nineteenth-century Viennese baking trends through Copenhagen and Danish merchant and colonial networks was essential to its exoticism and desirability in rural and relatively isolated nineteenth-century Icelandic society. It also signalled Icelandic women's engagement with much larger transnational culinary networks. Beyond Copenhagen, similar layered cakes could be found throughout the Danish Empire. On the former Danish West Indies islands of St. Thomas, St. Croix, and St. John, for example, Crucian Vienna Cake is still revered as a symbol of their complex history and has retained its popularity despite the departure of Danish officials in 1917. The Virgin Islands' Vienna Cake is more brightly coloured than *vínarterta*, incorporates thicker layers and preserves made from fruits like guavaberry and lime, but its similarity is clear. Vienna Cake, a separate recipe that appeared alongside the *vínarterta* in early Danish cookbooks, is also always prepared in five or seven layers, and it remains an important link between the past and present at celebrations in the Virgin Islands.[15]

As they had been in Denmark, tortes like *vínarterta* were chic, edible symbols of status for image-conscious households by the middle of the nineteenth century in Iceland. Access to the resources to produce good coffee and fine desserts was a particularly powerful sign of status and class in a society bound by rigid social hierarchies. While Icelandic women engaged in newer, more elaborate dishes and baking trends during this period, the poverty, hunger, and indentured servitude that punctured the lives of many of the emigrant generation still also shaped the production of desserts. To be able to bake such foods, families needed to be able to afford imported flour, sugar, and other ingredients as well as the several hours of spare womanpower required to make the layers and filling.

More than simply copying an Austrian or Danish dessert, Icelandic women left their stamp on the recipe. First, they had to replace the elaborate fillings called for in Danish-language recipes because they were simply not available in Iceland or were far too expensive for most bakers. Instead, they turned to one of the most accessible and affordable imported fruits available in nineteenth-century Iceland: the prune. Prunes were originally a luxury item in Iceland, but they became more accessible in the last quarter of the nineteenth century.[16] Dried plums shipped and stored well, and, by the late 1880s and 1890s, had begun appearing much more frequently on the shelves of Icelandic stores, just when many emigrants were departing.[17] Although some Icelandic women may have previously turned to locally grown ingredients like berries, the intense popularity of prune filling at the time of migration is evident in recipes from the immigrant generation. The vast majority of the most commonly found recipes for *vínarterta* in North America use only prune filling (and community members often shun any experimentation with other fruits).

Many early Icelandic bakers also replaced almonds, another expensive ingredient. Friedel's 1795 recipe called for relatively expensive dough made with one pound almonds, one pound sugar, one pound flour, and six eggs. Trine Hahnemann writes that the popularity of almonds in Nordic or Scandinavian baking is rooted in the fact that they were considered a sign of prestige in the late 1700s, when almond-based delicacies offered members of the aristocracy a chance to "show off their wealth."[18] Although some Icelandic immigrant recipes maintained the use of almonds, including the acclaimed recipe of Helen Josephson of Winnipeg, by the middle of the nineteenth century, it is clear that many Icelandic women were opting to omit actual ground almonds.[19] The Icelandic immigrant generation continued to replicate the original flavour, however, with almond extract. Such alterations reflected conditions in Iceland, allowing Icelandic women to emulate continental style within a budget on an island where access to imported supplies could vary, especially in the late nineteenth century, when pack ice plagued transport in northern Icelandic harbours.

It is in this context that Icelandic *vínarterta* emerged and became popular with the emigrant generation. It was a taste of home and a symbol of status and affluence that would have been meaningful for many women as they established new homes and lives. It is these connotations (in addition to the actual taste of the dessert) that made *vínarterta* so desirable and meaningful for the emigrant generation. It became, in many respects, a familiar, nineteenth-century-Icelandic symbol of togetherness and success, representing the ambition and upward mobility of women who chose to pursue new lives and new opportunities in North America.

## *Vínarterta* Comes to North America

*Vínarterta* now has significant meaning for many Icelandic North Americans, in part because it is one of the few elements of the original culture imported by the immigrant generation that has resisted any alteration. Indeed, strictly observed recipes for this dessert reflect its role as a survivor object. While early recipes for Danish *Wienertærte* encouraged variation and experimentation, any perceived alteration to the *vínarterta* recipes used by the original immigrant generation can still inspire intense debates and sharp critiques in the Icelandic North American community. Indeed some of the earliest recorded recipes for the torte reveal that it has changed little – if at all – over the past century, while most of the other dimensions of Icelandic immigrant material culture were either abandoned or dramatically shaped and transformed by the North American context. (See the appendix.) Early Icelandic immigrant women may have worn the tasselled *skotthúfa* into North American harbours, but they quickly stopped donning it in response to the reactions of English onlookers and potential employers. Anglicization, although a necessity for Icelandic North Americans during wartime and periods of tension, ensured the decline and demise of numerous Icelandic-language presses, newspapers, and even names – but not *vínarterta*. Why?

How *vínarterta* survived in the community before its transformation into an ethnic symbol in the 1940s reveals much about the limits of assimilation and acculturation in the Icelandic North American community. Icelandic material-cultural traditions that were less publicly visible, especially food and objects associated with the home and private life, were much more likely to survive the assimilative pressures of Anglo–North American society. A survey of these material-cultural traditions in both homes and regional museums in Canadian and American Icelandic centres[20] reveals that while some Icelanders might strive to achieve a flawlessly English appearance in public, they might also continue to use a range of personally useful or emotionally meaningful cultural practices for decades in private.

Icelandic material traditions were also more likely to endure longevity in rural areas that were more isolated from commercial markets and were more densely populated with other Icelandic households. For example, dimensions of nineteenth-century Icelandic coffee culture survived well into the twenty-first century in places like Gimli, Winnipeg, and Riverton, including the traditional preparation of coffee using a *kaffi poki* (coffee bag). The people who live on the historic New Iceland site and surrounding communities continued to make, consume, and sell a range of traditional Icelandic foods such as *harðfiskur* (dried fish eaten with butter), *rúllupylsa* (rolled spiced lamb), and *pönnukökur* (crepes), in addition to *vínarterta*, which at the time of writing could still be purchased from local producers or at stores in towns such as Arborg and Gimli. Beyond New Iceland, *Þorrablót*, an annual winter feast similar to the Scottish Burns Supper, offers many Icelanders across North America an opportunity to gather and consume traditional foods.[21]

Sources also indicate that Icelandic wool and knitwear production, including the manufacture of Icelandic mitts and socks, endured into the twenty-first century in Icelandic centres like Riverton, and visitors to the homes of older generations of Icelanders might also find a *teppi*, or homemade woollen quilt, on their beds. As long as they did not interrupt or contradict the Canadian or American facade, Icelandic material traditions could enjoy longevity in private. As some interviewees recalled, many of the grandchildren of Icelandic immigrants were wearing English-style clothing to school and church in the first half of the twentieth century, but they still wore Icelandic woollen underwear underneath.[22]

Like the Icelandic coffee culture and practical textile traditions that endured, *vínarterta* has survived longer in the community because it was associated with the home and the private sphere. Material skills, or ways of producing objects, rather than objects made in Iceland and brought to North America, were also more likely to survive intergenerational shifts rather than actual objects brought from Iceland. In addition to describing assimilative pressure, Icelandic immigrant memoirs frequently reference special homeland objects, such as wooden spinning wheels, immigrant trunks, clothing, and books, that were lost in house fires, floods, and moves. While a limited number of actual objects produced in Iceland survived in the homes of Icelanders after the Second World War, it was more common for skills, styles, and knowledge from the homeland to endure, resulting in the production of homeland-style objects and foods for special occasions. Compared to other, less practical objects inherited by the descendants of immigrants, culinary knowledge was lightweight and more accessible – often passed down through the generations in Icelandic North American kitchens and recorded in the innumerable recipes written down in cookbooks, on recipe cards, and in magazines and newspapers.

Following immigration, *vínarterta* remained an integral part of more formal or special occasions in Icelandic North American enclaves, even as it began to wane in popularity at home in Iceland. By 1903, immigrant consumers could purchase *vínarterta* at Icelandic immigrant bakeries and bake sales in Winnipeg alongside other Icelandic delicacies.[23] Demand for the torte was particularly intense during the holidays, and places like the Geysir Bakery at 724 Sargent Avenue did a brisk trade in *vínarterta* and other Icelandic delicacies in the late 1930s and early 1940s.[24] By 1936, many people beyond the Icelandic community had also grown to love the little dessert, according to Madeleine Day, a food columnist with the *Winnipeg Free Press*. "The fame of Vinarterta is not confined to the Icelandic people," she asserted. "Most of us have tasted it and know just how delicious it is."[25]

## The "Striped Lady" as Ethnic Symbol

*Vínarterta* survived long enough in the kitchens of the Icelandic community to become popular in the more public ethnic-revival campaigns of the 1940s and 1950s.[26] During the First World War, many of the children and grandchildren of immigrants strove to craft a public image that was often devoid of any hint of ethnic difference, attempting to shed Icelandic accents and even changing their names to deflect some of the everyday pressures that they and many other communities faced during periods of anti-immigrant sentiment. Yet, as the Danish American immigration scholar Marcus Lee Hansen famously observed, "What the son wishes to forget the grandson wishes to remember,"[27] and, in the late 1930s and early 1940s, a resurgence of interest in the culture of the immigrant generation began to flourish among descendant generations in Icelandic North American centres. Hansen dubbed this phenomenon, or the renewed fascination of grandchildren and great-grandchildren with their immigrant grandparents' culture, "the principle of third generation interest."[28]

Echoing many of the intergenerational dynamics in Icelandic North American culture, Hansen explained that where the children of immigrants had sought to deflect the "criticisms and taunts" of Anglo–North Americans by hiding any outward marker of immigrant difference, the grandchildren and great-grandchildren of the immigrant generation could safely explore their history and culture with less risk to their status in society. Often, the grandchildren and great-grandchildren of immigrants were born into now upwardly mobile, middle-class families, which appeared fully acculturated to their North American peers, with greater access to education and higher-paying jobs. They appeared similar to their English neighbours, colleagues, classmates, and friends and generally experienced less discrimination than their parents and grandparents had.

In contrast to the English-language implications of the possible racial and social inferiority of Icelandic immigrants during New Iceland's smallpox winter of 1876–7, by 1945 many of the second-, third-, and fourth-generation descendants of those same immigrants had served in both world wars, spoke accent-less English, and increasingly had anglicized first and last names. Bonds to Anglo–North America also intensified as Icelanders increasingly married into English and other Canadian families and began to establish their own homes farther from the old Icelandic districts and neighbourhoods. These kinds of more affluent and socially secure later generations, explained Hansen, were sheltered from the class-based and xenophobic pressures that their parents had faced, and so, when choosing to reconnect with or maintain their family's culture of origin, they did not "feel any inferiority."[29]

The early pluralist campaigns of the 1930s and 1940s also often voiced an appreciation for immigrant foods and other commonplace traditions previously dismissed as "queer" or "peculiar." As discussed in the previous chapter, Icelandic food and references to friendliness and hospitality were heavily featured in the 1941 NFB film, *Iceland on the Prairies*, to respond to rumours that Icelanders had resisted the Allied occupation of their homeland by withholding food and female company. The film invited Canadian audiences to a full-colour guided tour of food in the Icelandic immigrant community, including *vínarterta*, while the narrator slowly and carefully pronounced the Icelandic name of each dish.

Beyond responding to rumours of dissent in the Icelandic community and promoting Icelandic support for the Allied occupation, such celebrations of ethnic culture appeared in other North American wartime films and reflected the strategic, larger growth of ethnic campaigns during the war. In addition to *Iceland on the Prairies*, the NFB produced several films that celebrated Ukrainian and Polish immigrant difference through ethnic food, song, and dance.[30] After they entered the war, the American government followed suit with films like *Swedes in America*, narrated by Ingrid Bergman, which featured aproned Swedish farm wives baking homemade bread, while describing Swedes' loyalty to country and devotion to freedom.[31] American discussions of Icelanders echoed this pattern of praising ethnic communities for their devotion to democracy while providing audiences with a local, tangible (and edible) bond to distant populations. As Kathleen B. Gilbert explained to readers alongside a recipe for delicious "veena terta" in 1942, Icelanders made typical, friendly American neighbours in North Dakota, and their freedom-loving relatives at home deserved American protection.[32]

### "Friendship Cake": *Vínarterta's* Cold War Career

While it was part of early celebrations of Icelandic immigrant food during the Second World War, *vínarterta* began to emerge as an ethnic symbol of the Icelandic community in its own right during the Cold War. After 1950 in some circles, the little torte began to challenge and even, at times, replace more traditional symbols in the community, including well-worn references to the Vikings and the Alþingi. As Winnipeg food columnist Clare Marcus remarked, "Iceland founded the world's first parliament and supreme court one thousand years ago, but it may be better known for Vinarterta."[33]

This shift towards ethnic food in depictions of the Icelandic immigrant community reflected a larger trend in Cold War pluralist campaigns. In both Canada and the United States, pro-pluralism campaigns endured well into the Cold War as both governments continued to monitor immigrant communities for signs of communist sympathies. Ethnic foods also assumed a more central place in Cold War ethnic festivals because of the central place of food in both Soviet and North American propaganda campaigns. As Franca Iacovetta and Valerie Korinek remind us, images of fully stocked shelves and plentiful food in modern North American grocery stores and kitchens were intensely political, pro-capitalist responses to reports of Soviet bread lines, food scarcity, and hunger.[34]

Images of inter-ethnic friendship and peaceful North American pluralism were also designed to foster alliances between a number of countries and the United States and its allies. Such images of friendship and cultural exchange were important components of Cold War militarization and defence strategies. The need for propaganda campaigns that promoted Icelandic and North American friendship only increased during the Cold War owing to fears that the Soviet Union might attempt a takeover of Iceland; this led to the 1949 announcement that NATO forces would occupy the strategically significant island. The announcement was intensely unpopular in Iceland and was met by a major riot in front of the Icelandic Parliament building in Reykjavík on March 30; thousands of Icelanders were dispersed with tear gas.[35]

Afraid that Icelandic opposition to NATO was instead possibly the product of Soviet infiltration on the island,[36] North American military and political agencies sought to develop campaigns that would encourage the Icelandic public to accept a foreign military presence. By November 1949, the US Department of State had officially launched an enhanced, top-secret Program to Decrease the Vulnerability of the Icelandic Government to Communist Seizure of Power. The program mandated the creation of initiatives and policies that would "raise the prestige of America in the eyes of Icelanders," including producing publications and organizing cultural and educational exchanges.[37] By actively encouraging an image of Icelandic American friendship and support for political and military collaboration, this more subtle propaganda campaign sought to safeguard Iceland as well as defend North Atlantic sea lanes and airspace from a potential Soviet takeover. Later campaigns would entail secret surveillance of the Icelandic Left, American university exchanges, subsidized magazines and films, and establishing American-style infrastructure that broadcast the benefits of Western capitalism and collaboration to the Icelandic public.

Food endured as a politicized symbol of hospitality during NATO's occupation of Iceland during the Cold War, and *vínarterta* emerged as a symbol of Icelandic North American friendship and cooperation during this period. As Kenneth Osgoode and Helge Danielsen reveal in their work, American embassies and the United States Information Services had begun to craft and deploy a range of cultural programs designed to promote public support and cooperation with American military campaigns in the Nordic countries.[38] It was in this context that *vínarterta* appeared in the special 1949 Christmas edition of *McCall's* magazine. While news of Icelandic protests against NATO membership reached American news outlets in the spring of that year, by December approximately 800,000 *McCall's* readers had read a very different story about Icelanders and American-style hospitality. In the special holiday edition of the magazine, well-known food columnist Miss Helen McCully invited readers to add Iceland's Christmas Cake to their baking repertoire.[39] For her column, McCully interviewed the neighbourly Mrs. Svein Peterson (Jóna S. Goodman), a 56-year-old Icelandic American welfare office caseworker in Bottineau, North Dakota (Figure 5.2 and Figure 5.3). In language that paralleled the narrative of *Iceland on the Prairies*, North American readers could expect a warm welcome in the home of the "friendly and comfortable" Mrs. Peterson, reported McCully in her profile, and "all people from that shining land [Iceland]." Guests in Mrs. Peterson's Bottineau kitchen would always "find a pot of coffee brewing on [her] old fashioned range and, almost certainly, a fabulous Vinarterta, ripe and ready for slicing."[40]

I argue that it was the appearance of *vínarterta*, rather than other Icelandic foods, in this major American magazine and other publications that began to cement its status as a symbol within the community itself after the Second World War. For the Icelandic immigrant community on both sides of the Canadian-American border, this special tribute to an Icelandic food created a stir. Icelandic Canadians celebrated *vínarterta's* new-found fame and a profile on Peterson in *Lögberg's* women's column, *Áhugamál kvenna* (Women's interests). The column celebrated the magazine's praise of Icelandic food, reporting that Helen McCully, "who travels far and wide to find the best cooks in the United States," had found *vínarterta* "so light and delicious compared to other cakes."[41] The story was so popular that *Áhugamál kvenna* reprinted the "famous *vínarterta* recipe" the following Christmas, in 1950.

Before the release of *Iceland on the Prairies* in 1941, few beyond the Icelandic community and their neighbours had heard of *vínarterta*. Moreover, the torte had appeared in only a brief flash on the wartime screen and as only one among many other Icelandic foods, including

Figure 5.2. Jóna Goodman (Mrs. Svein Peterson). Reprinted from "The Best Cook in Our Town," *McCall's*, December 1949, 72.

Icelandic Cake Fight 149

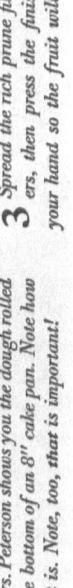
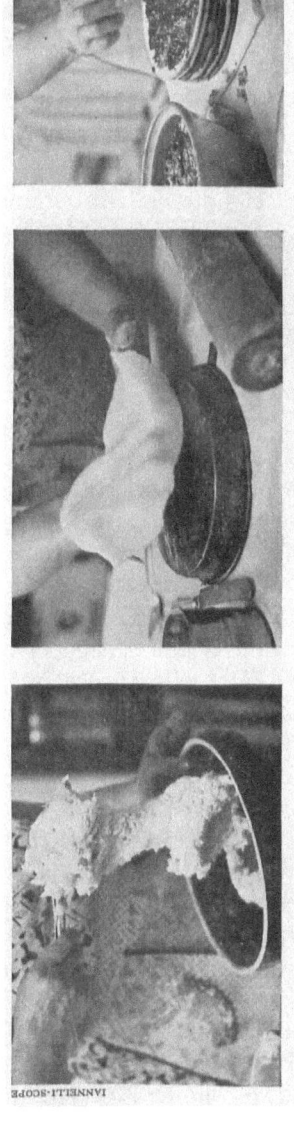

1 The dough, you can see, is firm but not stiff. At this point chill it in the refrigerator, so it will handle more easily when you roll it

2 Here Mrs. Peterson shows you the dough rolled to fit the bottom of an 8" cake pan. Note how very thin it is. Note, too, that is important!

3 Spread the rich prune filling between the layers, then press the finished Vinarterta with your hand so the fruit will blend with the cake

Figure 5.3. Step-by-step *vínarterta* preparation instructions. Reprinted from *McCall's*, December 1949, 73.

rúllupylsa and *skyr*, in the large Icelandic buffet that might await guests in an Icelandic immigrant home. Following the *McCall's* profile, however, Icelandic American media and celebrations began to focus intensively on *vínarterta* as *the* consummate Icelandic food. In her 1953 description of the community's early days in Dakota Territory, for example, Thorstína Walters explained to American readers that *vínarterta* was the Icelandic American *pièce de résistance*. North of the border, Miss Canada, Margaret Sigvaldason, asked attendees at the 1951 Canada Day celebration in Hnausa, Manitoba, "Who can deny that Icelandic coffee ... and vínarterta, have not added to our Canadian way of life?"[42]

### "Icelandic Bannock": *Vínarterta* as North American Phenomenon

As it declined in popularity in Iceland, *vínarterta* became famous as a consummate Icelandic food in North America, and Jón Karl Helgason contends in his compelling analysis that the *vínarterta* "obsession" should be understood as a distinctly Icelandic North American tradition.[43] By the middle of the twentieth century, this popular, labour-intensive dessert could be found at almost every major Icelandic social event in North America, while in Iceland, it was being replaced with desserts that required less time to make. Nanna Rögnvaldardóttir, renowned Icelandic food author, writes that this shift also stemmed from a flood of new baking options that women in Iceland embraced as manufactured ovens began to appear in modernizing Icelandic homes.[44] Geir H. Gunnarsson similarly noted that the appearance of new foods on the island, popularized through the international military presence, also aided the decline of old nineteenth-century favourites. *Vínarterta's* virtual disappearance in Iceland was a source of confusion among Icelandic North Americans who travelled to Iceland in the late twentieth century with out-of-date, nineteenth-century notions of Icelandic culture inherited from their grandparents and great-grandparents. As Icelandic homeland tourism increased in the 1970s, many Icelandic North Americans who visited the island noted with disappointment that not only did Icelanders not have any *vínarterta* but also many of them had not even heard of the dessert so popular on the island a century before.[45] As Gunnarsson explained to disappointed readers of *Lögberg-Heimskringla*, *vínarterta* and many of the other foods popular in the Icelandic North American community had long since passed out of fashion. "Icelandic eating habits have drastically changed since the last century, especially since World War II when Iceland actually became de-isolated and new foreign habits were introduced, like fish and chips when the British invaded in 1940," he wrote.[46] Hot dogs, hamburgers, and milkshakes, he reported, "have become to modern-day Icelanders what *rúllupylsa* was to their grandfathers." While visitors to Iceland still might find *randalín*, a layered cake made with fewer layers and featuring store-bought strawberry jam, "The old vínarterta is therefore no longer existent in Iceland as such."[47]

*Vínarterta* represented, in many respects, a living link to nineteenth-century Iceland that had been preserved in the immigrant community, but numerous factors in the post-war North American context actively fostered the rise of the torte as an ethnic symbol. How did a cake that had almost totally disappeared at home in Iceland not only remain popular in North America but also continue to operate as such a popular (and somewhat intense) symbol of endurance and identity? Helgason asserts that the *vínarterta* tradition offers scholars a key to understanding the endurance of Icelandic identity in a community that appears so seamlessly North American in public. Quoting Erla Simundsson, he writes that *vínarterta* is perhaps best understood as part of a widespread *einstaklingur* (individual) attitude in the Icelandic North American community, which has a popular reputation for eccentricity, intense individuality, and stubbornness, all of which arguably also shaped the boundaries of assimilation in North America.[48]

## Memory and the *Vínarterta* Obsession

The immigrant generation may have imported the torte and twentieth-century cultural and political conditions transformed it into a public symbol, but we must also examine the personal attitudes and beliefs of the migrants' descendants to truly understand the *vínarterta* tradition – even obsession – in Icelandic North America. It is clear that the dessert's symbolism represents more than its survival in the private sphere or external validation from mainstream media outlets from the 1940s onward. It is also the product of a home-grown, deeply conservative baking tradition, which encourages community members to resist any change to the "original" recipe (or whichever recipe is perceived to be the original).

As Minnesota poet and writer Bill Holm attests (in his quote at the start of this chapter), discussions about the "correct" recipe for *vínarterta* still inspire intense conflict and heated debate in the community. Oral history interviews and discussions of the dessert in the Icelandic immigrant press reveal a seemingly endless supply of strong opinions among community members – about the correct number of layers, the inclusion or exclusion of icing, and the use (or abuse) of spices and flavourings like cardamom and almond extract. The intensity of this debate and the reasons for the popularity of *vínarterta* have been sources of curiosity and confusion for scholars and popular media alike. As Matt Kwong's 2012 article in *Maclean's* simply warned: "Don't ask Icelanders how to make their traditional Christmas cake."[49]

Most twentieth-century recipes for *vínarterta* focus on a particular version of the torte commonly found in late nineteenth-century Iceland – namely, a five- or seven-layer torte featuring prune filling flavoured with ground cardamom and aged for a period of time to create a dense, moist consistency. Variations of *vínarterta* appeared in old country kitchens and cookbooks, including versions that used more affordable, local blueberry and rhubarb jams for filling. Almost all North American *vínarterta* recipes, however, specify a prune filling, possibly because imported prunes were exotic and considered by nineteenth-century homemakers more appropriate for formal occasions. The "correct" number of layers and other variations – including the use of cardamom, icing, sprinkles, and almond extract – can also instigate fierce debate among twentieth-century community members. Their ability to produce one of these labour-intensive tortes, as well as their faithfulness to original recipes, is part of a larger debate over the authenticity of their claims to an Icelandic identity and resistance on the part of some makers to the rigidity of the *vínarterta* tradition. As Louise Kahler explained, "Vínarterta is like a religion in our house. You don't mess with vínarterta, and it is served with an expectant hush. We keep our family recipe closely guarded."[50]

The production of the torte has become a ritual in the Icelandic North American community, evident in the intense debates over the correct recipe and the special place occupied by *vínarterta* at major events, including weddings and funerals. In spite of the rigidity with which some community members view *vínarterta* production, some makers enjoy adding their own ornamental flare to the finished product. Their individual stamp might incite criticism from other community members, but many *vínarterta* aficionados consider it important to replicate their own particular version of the torte. Some makers have added flare to the top of the torte with round, multi-coloured sprinkles (nonpareils), while others, like Halldora Sigurdson of Steep Rock, Manitoba, enjoyed using maraschino cherry juice to turn the icing pink.[51] For many, however, aesthetic simplicity or a strong position on the inclusion or exclusion of certain ingredients, especially cardamom, almond extract, and icing, are invoked as proof of the strength of a family's Icelandic cultural identity. Real or imagined deviations from the so-called original recipe are taken as a sign of cultural degeneracy. As W.D. Valgardson joked,

> There are sides [in the Icelandic community] ... like Irish catholics and protestants, but the sides aren't political or religious, they're whether you

eat your vinarterta iced or not iced. No icer has ever been known to convert to being a non-icer, although there have been rumours that a non-icer has been known to convert to being an icer.[52]

In Gimli, Manitoba, some entrepreneurs decided to branch out and sell *vínarterta* with a range of fillings, including blueberry and raspberry, but, asserted one interviewee, "I just think it's wrong."[53] Echoing this sentiment, Jennifer Miller recalled that the slight variations in *vínarterta* produced by different family members caused more disruption than unity at family gatherings.

> One Auntie's layers were thicker than Amma's. One had too much almond extract in the icing. Another used a lot of cardamom. Yet another produced cake layers that were more brown than white.... It was always a big deal to see a plate put out with coffee, but it was always a bit unsettling too.[54]

Encounters with *vínarterta* facsimiles in twenty-first-century Iceland, like the simpler, jam-filled torte, *randalín*, inspired numerous stories. Brett Lamoureux recalled being served *randalín* at a reception for Icelandic Canadians in Iceland. "We were served a layered vínarterta-like cake at a reception a bank put on for us – except it had strawberry filling! When the server put the tray on the table in front of us thirteen Western-Icelanders, we all gasped!"[55] In particular, the number of layers a *vínarterta* possesses is often taken as a sign of authenticity. Although established *vínarterta* recipes might call for five or eight layers, the seven-layered version is most common. Maxine Ingalls of Hecla Island, Manitoba, similarly recalled her father's firm stance on seven layers as the most authentic "Icelandic" number of layers. "He used to say, 'If it hasn't got seven layers, then it's just Viennese torte!'"[56]

*Vínarterta* has become an immensely popular dessert in Manitoba, where it functions as both a symbol of Icelandic-ness and a broader representation of regional memory and status. Numerous *vínarterta* makers may not have an Icelandic family connection, but they have adopted the tradition because they grew up in and around Icelandic communities. For example, the torte can be found in Mennonite cookbooks and bakeries in Winnipeg as well as in several Interlake First Nations and Métis communities like Fisher River, Matheson Island, and Peguis First Nation, where it is served at special occasions such as band elections.[57] Inside and outside the Icelandic community, the dessert functions as a representation of skill and (often female) authority.

As many inexperienced and disappointed North American bakers may have discovered after experimenting with the *McCall's* recipe for

Iceland's Christmas Cake in 1949, *vínarterta* preparation usually takes years to perfect and requires perseverance and many attempts. For example, Elizabeth Dorey noted of her own experiences learning how to perfect the torte, "My first few times I was overly generous with the filling and the cakes slipped, slid and slithered when I was trying to cut the 'tower.'"[58] Indeed, many of the best-known *vínarterta* makers have been older women who have spent decades perfecting their techniques. Aðalbjörg Benediktsdóttir Brandson, who immigrated to Canada at the age of four in 1878, was a widely renowned *vínarterta* maker in the Icelandic Winnipeg community. She grew up immersed in an image-conscious society and, by the early 1930s, had won recognition for her recipe, both in the *Winnipeg Free Press* and in an influential cookbook published by the Ladies' Aid of the Icelandic First Lutheran Church in the city's West End.[59]

Family or community members like Brandson, who produce excellent *vínarterta*, have often enjoyed special status in their community. Some protectively guard their "authentic," time-honoured versions of the recipe (as several futile calls for recipe submissions for this book can attest). Personalized obituaries of Icelandic North Americans who were skilled *vínarterta* makers regularly mention this as a special accomplishment. For example, when Kristín Gunnlaugson died in Winnipeg in 1983, a special tribute to her in *Lögberg-Heimskringla* described her expertise in producing the torte. Kristín, who was born in Akureyri, Iceland, in 1893, produced exceptional *vínarterta* "that was recognized as a form of art." According to the tribute, her friends and family referred to Kristín as "Queen of the Tertas."[60]

While several accomplished bakers are men, this frequent association with older women, and especially the *amma*, or grandmother, has made the torte an important symbol for commemorating female generations in Icelandic families, while also creating a point of contact with seemingly abstract and distant roots in nineteenth-century Iceland. As an embodiment of both absent female generations and a distant place and time of origin, preserving *vínarterta* recipes performs a kind of genealogical function, reminding descendants of the earlier generations.

It is clear that Icelandic North Americans use *vínarterta* to preserve and transmit intergenerational memory, but the often family-centred stories told through this baking tradition can appear out of step with the depictions of the dessert in Cold War and multicultural-era pluralism campaigns. As Donna Gabaccia argues, ethnic food acted as a medium through which immigrant communities could speak about histories that might stray from the narratives proclaimed in American and Canadian post-war celebrations.[61] Similarly, Marlene Epp and S.

Holyk Hunchuk make clear in their work on Mennonite and Ukrainian immigrant food that certain dishes might appear in public as a quaint symbol of immigrant origins, or even in cookbooks that celebrate the multicultural nation, but they might also preserve and transmit more complex, personal, and problematic histories of tragedy and loss within the community and families.[62]

In many Icelandic North American families, *vínarterta* has come to represent past generations of female bakers, imbuing the making, consumption, and passing down of recipes with a strong genealogical function. Genealogy, according to a well-known saying, is Iceland's "national sport."[63] This claim is reinforced by a wealth of extensive genealogical texts, centres, and databases on both sides of the Atlantic, all reflecting the value that Icelandic society has historically placed on preserving, observing, and valuing both maternal and paternal lineages. Richard M. Rice, in a 1971 study, asserted that a "matrilineal bias" existed in the Icelandic community. By surveying family ties separated according to maternal and paternal lines, Rice contended that, in the Icelandic Canadian community, family bonds tended to be more focused on female relations.[64] The existence and precise extent of such a bias in the larger community is difficult to determine, but the significance of *vínarterta* to many community members can be understood as part of a popular commemorative tradition that clearly observes and seeks to preserve the history of grandmothers and other female relatives.

Indeed, oral histories, popular lore, and commemorative practices in the community clearly attest to the important role that the grandmother, or *amma*, plays in family commemoration. As "Sunna" Pam Furstenau of Mountain, North Dakota, writes, her identity and connections to Iceland come from many places, "but the heart of it is my Amma."[65] The *amma* has also, to some extent, emerged as a popular public symbol in community celebrations and histories. Since the 1990s, the production of community biographies has been characterized by multiple family publications of *amma*-themed biographies,[66] and in 2004, local women in Gimli began selling "amma dolls" (grey-haired women dressed in traditional Icelandic clothing) at the newly opened Amma's Teahouse, to raise money for heritage projects.[67] Since the 1980s, Icelandic food stands and restaurants have also used the image of the *amma* to attract customers in search of *vínarterta*, including Amma's Kitchen, the food stand at Gimli's annual Icelandic Festival. The very endurance of the Icelandic word for grandmother within the anglicized post-war community speaks volumes about her exceptional role.

The frequent appearance of *vínarterta* at major Icelandic North American life celebrations, such as funerals, weddings, and baby showers, further reveals its role as a tangible link among generations. As baker Alice Gudmundson explained to a *Winnipeg Tribune* reporter in 1978, *vínarterta* reinforced these bonds, in part, because it usually appeared when children listened to stories from their grandparents at celebrations like Christmas.[68] Although initially a symbol of bourgeoisie sophistication in nineteenth-century Iceland, *vínarterta* became a reminder to community members of the sacred nature of food, a reference to earlier scarcity and deprivation. As Hunchuk argues in her work on culinary symbols of plenty in Ukrainian immigrant culture, wheat sheaves have a double meaning: they remind diners of both the feasts of the present and the famines of the past.[69] Such symbols act as intergenerational binding agents that feed living generations, while reminding them, often in a very personal way, of past generations.

In one of many meditations on Icelandic North American culture and memory, Bill Holm writes that immigrant food possesses transformative power capable of forging a personal, physical link between the diner and his or her ancestors. *Vínarterta* and other foods are a sort of "historical Eucharist," he contends, one that community members eat "whether consciously or not, to honor their ancestors, the poverty, grief, and uprooting in their own history."[70] In her analysis of Mennonite foods, Marlene Epp contends that certain immigrant foods, including the Mennonite bread *zwieback* – a dish associated with an absent loved one – offer community members a way of representing histories of trauma or loss that can be difficult to articulate. Stories about food, she argues, can act as anchors for organizing and speaking about otherwise large, complex, and difficult histories of the immigrant experience.[71]

In some Icelandic North American families, *vínarterta* is also used to represent and transmit stories of the family that might fit poorly into, or are too private for, public celebrations of Icelandic, Canadian, or American society. Genealogical narratives that more carefully observe the experiences of women in the community, for example, often frequently discuss the issue of infant mortality and premature death in the immigrant generation.[72] When asked about family traditions and memories of Iceland, Ken Melsted of Wynyard, Saskatchewan, turned to the story of his great-grandmother to carefully acknowledge the pitfalls of life in both Iceland and Canada. "I may remember the past, the nineteenth century in northern Iceland with its poverty and near starvation, but that is not 'special,' nor is it a fond memory," he wrote. "My great-grandmother had six small children when her husband was lost in a fishing accident in the North Atlantic." He remembered that "they virtually starved in Iceland, [before] they emigrated and settled on a farm about three miles out of Gimli, which was rock, gravel, and bush.

Again they virtually starved until they moved to the Mountain district of North Dakota, where everyone began to prosper."[73]

Here, the differences between the popular public and private meanings of *vínarterta* become most evident. While post-war heritage campaigns may have used it in the service of national campaigns promoting Cold War hospitality and multicultural unity, many Icelandic North Americans viewed *vínarterta* as an embodiment of familial, rather than national, identities and histories. These versions of the past could differ radically in public heritage celebrations. Public representations of immigrant motherhood, in particular, often downplay or erase histories of tragedy, which offer a more unsettling image of migration. An example of this tendency is associated with Gimli's White Rock, a symbolic monument commemorating the historic landing of the first Icelandic settlers on Willow Point on 21 October 1875 and the legendary birth of an Icelandic baby next to the rock – ostensibly on the night of the landing. As the site of this foundational landing (not unlike the arrival of the Pilgrims at Plymouth Rock), Willow Point has been the focus of several commemorative campaigns, many of which describe the birth of a child shortly after the arrival of the Icelandic settlers.[74]

All his life, Jón Ólafur Jóhannsson enjoyed a certain degree of status as the Willow Point baby, or "the first Icelander born in Western Canada," including special mention in local history books and on the commemorative plaque at the white rock – ostensibly the same boulder beside which Jóhannsson's mother gave birth. Yet as the parish records of Rev. Jón Bjarnason (pastor to New Iceland) show, Jóhannsson was actually born on 6 November 1875 – not on 21 October. A document discovered by local historian Nelson Gerrard reveals that, in fact, the landing story recalled the birth of Jónas Friðrik Bjarnason. A female child named Steinvör Wilhelmína Pálsdóttir was subsequently born on 1 November, also before Jóhannsson. Unfortunately, both children died in their first year, in 1876 – Bjarnason of smallpox and Pálsdóttir of "cramps."[75] These children died young, but both lived well into their first year and should, therefore, not be confused with miscarriages or stillbirths. While their lives and deaths would be important components of a family's experience of migration, their stories tarnished the image of the immigration and settlement of New Iceland as a successful venture. In contrast, Jóhannsson's survival into adulthood marked his birth as the only publicly legitimate and "memorable" of the three.

When it is placed into the context of these larger, post-war commemorative traditions, *vínarterta* can be understood as a strategy for creating and reiterating narratives about the past that might differ markedly from those set forth in public. Rather than "loud" public events or formal ways of transmitting knowledge, David Sutton argues, memories attached to the senses can be some of the most powerful and enduring.[76] Recalling and preparing food ritualistically, he writes, instructs younger generations in how to mentally store and recall narratives, mental landmarks, past meals, and past generations, while creating "future memories" for the next generation.[77] In other words, *vínarterta* does not simply represent Iceland or the Icelandic immigrant community. It has become a means of creating and maintaining intergenerational bonds and preserving stories that might be lost or downplayed in more formal community histories. The preservation of the torte, or specific recipes associated with certain women, makes it an embodiment of absent generations and a powerful point of contact between the past and the present.

The torte continues to be a mainstay of Icelandic North American funerals, but is also prepared as a tribute to departed family members during special occasions like Christmas. Doreen-Dawne Trach wrote to the *Winnipeg Free Press* of how the torte represented her late mother, who was previously responsible for making it at Christmas. After her mother passed away, she recalled, she "wept into the dough as I started the annual *vínarterta*," noting that now her mother "is always present every year when I make this."[78] Similarly, Jennifer Miller wrote of the last *vínarterta* made by her amma that its importance stemmed, in part, from its ability to stand in, sometimes in profoundly personal ways, for the older generations of women who had made and perfected the recipe. Her amma had always provided her family with a whole *vínarterta* each year, but in 2009,

> it was clear that her health was declining rapidly. She managed one last *vínarterta* for the reunion, but there weren't any extras, and we all knew no more were coming. I had *vínarterta* at breakfast, lunch and dinner that week, but I've had none since. Amma passed away in fall. I'm down to half a cake in my freezer, and I just can't make myself cut it. I need to eat it soon, or it won't be good any more (and Amma wouldn't like that, either), but I just can't let it be gone.[79]

## Conclusion

Understanding the origins and meanings of *vínarterta* culture in the North American Icelandic community is complex, but the ability of one torte to represent so many, often radically different chapters in the immigrant past makes it arguably one of the most effective representations of the layered personalities, historical forces, and ideas that have shaped this community's identity. From its origins in early nineteenth-century Iceland as a symbol of refinement and engagement with Danish and international culinary trends, *vínarterta* had become entrenched in the Icelandic baking repertoire by the 1850s. An appetite for the torte arrived along with Icelandic immigrants to North America in the 1870s, and, as immigrant families re-established their households in the new land, they began to replicate it, alongside a range of other homeland favourites. While *vínarterta* was simply one of many Icelandic foods produced in the community until the 1940s, it emerged as a symbol of Icelandic culture in wartime and later Cold War festivals that celebrated Icelandic hospitality amid protests against the Allied occupation of Iceland. It also became a representation of quintessential Icelandic food during a period of linguistic decline and anglicization, and, as a result, many consumers missed the reference to Vienna in its name. In many respects, however, *vínarterta* had become distinct to the Icelandic community by this time, with very particular versions being produced based on the styles most popular with the immigrant generation.

Although the making of *vínarterta* declined and virtually disappeared in Iceland over the course of the twentieth century, its popularity actually increased in the immigrant community in North America as an increasingly conservative baking tradition began to shun any alteration to the recipe. In many respects, *vínarterta* became a culinary time capsule of nineteenth-century Iceland and the migration era, one that was rigorously preserved within a community that had undergone a series of radical cultural changes since the 1870s. As one of several material-cultural traditions that survived the pressure of anglicization in Icelandic immigrant homes, *vínarterta* thrived, in part, because it could act both as a positive symbol of Icelandic immigrant culture in public and as a memento of immigrant family histories in private.

While *vínarterta* emerged as a public symbol of Icelandic culture in nationalist celebrations in the post-war era, its meaning could differ significantly within families. As Daisy Neijmann argues, the multicultural and centennial celebrations of the 1960s and 1970s often demanded a display of anachronistic and artificial symbols of Icelandic-ness, but "That which is experienced as being Icelandic is private, largely invisible to outsiders, and not what is publicly expected to be authentically Icelandic."[80] Preserving family stories about migration might also directly contradict or criticize the celebration of nations, including both early conditions in North America and an assumed Icelandic nationalism among immigrants' descendants. The assumption that *vínarterta* represents simply a celebration of the Icelandic nation that immigrants left behind, or the Canadian or American multicultural state, misses the complexity with which some Icelandic North Americans view their history or identity. While the torte appears at celebrations like Canada Day and Icelandic state visits to North America, scholars must also attend to the power of local and family-based identities and loyalties in the community, rather than national ones.

The powerful connection between particular versions of *vínarterta* and family commemoration speaks to the power of kin-based identities in the community. Respected *vínarterta* makers – most frequently older, more experienced female bakers – have enjoyed special status within the Icelandic community, and the torte has emerged both as a symbol for the grandmother, or *amma*, and for the intergenerational bonds within particular families and the community at large. Discussions about *vínarterta* can quickly spark the telling of family narratives of origin, some of which can be deeply critical of immigrants' treatment in Iceland, Canada, and the United States. For the many Icelanders who frequently crossed the forty-ninth parallel in pursuit of better deals and better living conditions, neither Canada nor the United States was a singular promised land. Stories about women's migration experiences presented in public, including the story of the birth on Willow Point, could radically alter or erase chapters considered important, and even central, to stories that families told about their origins. In this context, the preservation of *vínarterta* within families as a representation of absent generations reflects Bill Holm's assertion that such foods act as a kind of immigrant Eucharist, a way of observing loss, while physically manifesting the bonds between past and present generations. Rather than being a singular symbol, *vínarterta* – with its many meanings – serves as a road map for understanding how different generations of North American Icelanders have connected their pasts and presents across three centuries.

# Conclusion

Though the pioneer's course is neither shown by burning beacons nor lavishly praised in writing, the axe-marks on the birch trees show us the way.
Stephan G. Stephansson[1]

Stephan G. Stephansson was one of thousands of Icelanders who sought opportunity and a new life in North America between 1870 and 1914. Considered the most important Icelandic immigrant poet in his lifetime, he travelled a familiar journey between multiple Icelandic settlements on both sides of the border, including Dakota Territory and Alberta, after he left Skagafjörður in Northern Iceland in 1873. The verse above was written in 1914, the year that the First World War ended the mass immigration of Icelanders to North America. It is a meditation on history that arguably also reflected Stephansson's own experiences, both as an immigrant and as a one-time lumberjack.[2] These words could also be taken as a larger invitation – and a warning – about the pitfalls of relying only on written texts when examining the historical experience of immigrants. More than writing, argues Stephansson, "the axe-marks on the birch trees," or the physical imprints of everyday life and labour, offer us an essential vantage point for understanding their lives.

Existing works in Icelandic migration scholarship have provided solid coverage of the political, economic, and religious events, institutions, and personalities that have shaped the community's public life. However, such vantage points can privilege the voices of a smaller minority of influential Icelanders, including politicians, church leaders, members of formal Icelandic organizations, and business owners. Thus, they can often still omit women's experiences as well as what might be termed the "goolie" component of Icelandic immigrant culture – popular, often working-class practices considered kitschy, mundane, or hybrid, exhibiting a tangled blend of North American and Icelandic elements. To better understand this side of immigrant life and culture, we must focus on the alternative media through which so many Icelandic immigrants expressed themselves. In addition to the religious and political schisms expressed in sermons, speeches, and print, Icelanders experienced life and crafted new identities in North America in more immediate and multi-sensory ways.

Immigration was a three-dimensional experience. Migrant narratives frequently reference sensations other than sight and sound in their descriptions of life in North America, and these perspectives reveal valuable and compelling information about the interplay among the body, space, and material world in ethnic history. From the feel of woollen cloth to the smell of fresh-roasting coffee or the intense feeling of winter cold around Lake Winnipeg, migrants encountered North America through a range of senses, which shaped how they responded to their new environment.

Bodies, especially women's bodies, were also the focus of conflict and tension in the community. As the "bald women epidemic" of 1924 and the *Time* scandal about the "coldness" of Icelandic women in 1940 demonstrate, the female body became a highly politicized cornerstone of twentieth-century representations of the community. Yet depictions of the female body during this period were never uniformly conservative. Women such as the *Fjallkona* Sigrún Lindal and editor Margrét Benedictsson played with gender norms and cultural symbolism to create more radical or relevant images of Icelandic womanhood that spoke to their own political views and aesthetic tastes. Moreover, the *vínarterta* tradition in the community acts as a kind of immigrant Eucharist. Rather than being a simple symbol of Cold War friendliness or a cheerful dessert for the post-war multicultural buffet, this powerful little recipe has come to embody past generations of female makers, loss, and the bonds between generations.

Media closely connected to the body, like clothing and fashion, shaped Icelandic experiences in the new geographical and cultural terrain of the Prairies. From the short lifespan of mitts worn by men clearing the bush to the homeland dresses that were altered and replaced for life in North America, a focus on cloth can help us retrace the contours of migrant bodies and labour in relation to early lived experiences of poverty, marginalization, disease, and cold. Rather than simply accepting the abandonment of Icelandic nationalist dress as a sign of assimilation and cultural loss, the first chapter in this book shows that the tremendous amount of time, energy, labour, and attention that migrants invested in dress is evidence of both transformation and cultural production and innovation. The long-standing adoption of Indigenous clothing by Icelandic men around Lake Winnipeg and the central role of domestic service and urban life in the adoption of Anglo-Victorian dress also illuminate the relationship between clothing and networks of intercultural exchange.

Clothing became an alterable skin, one that migrants could change to achieve upward mobility by downplaying ethnic difference in an often xenophobic society. Indeed, Icelanders experienced the alternating demands for assimilation and ethnic performance through clothing since Anglo–North Americans often used clothing as a kind of shorthand to assess the character of new arrivals. Even the poorest immigrants, those who could not really afford a new dress or pair of boots, actively pursued anglophone style because of the upward mobility and accompanying respectability they believed such fashions brought.

Rapid changes in clothing stand in stark contrast to the conservatism of Icelandic North American kitchens, especially when it came to coffee culture. Although many Icelandic women abandoned their "peculiar" headgear, or *skotthúfa*, within days or even hours of arriving in North America, some of their descendants (including several women interviewed for this book) are still preparing coffee in nineteenth-century Icelandic fashion – using a *kaffi poki* (coffee bag). The book's second chapter traces the history of both coffee and alcohol since these were the two beverages that left the biggest imprint on nineteenth-century Icelandic North American culture. More than simple beverages, coffee and alcohol were sources of desire through which Icelanders pursued pleasure, mediated relations, and constructed or challenged gender, class, and ethnic identities. As migrants who complained of the "inferior" beans that they could only occasionally access in North America, they also reveal some of the shortcomings and discomfort resulting from immersion in Anglo–North American society.

As much as coffee culture brought Icelanders together, alcohol divided, sparking fierce debates, prohibition campaigns, and household bans. From the mid-1880s onward, an increasingly organized Icelandic temperance movement targeted the "unhealthy" drinking habits of Icelandic men, which some feared could seriously undermine the community's reputation. Debates over the boozy reign of King *Bakkús* in North America also offered Icelandic women new venues for public activism and leadership through the popular Icelandic temperance movement. Indeed, temperance became part of the coded language through which Icelanders campaigned against homeland inequalities and abuses. Many Icelandic male labourers, however, found the culture of alcohol a significant part of male sociability in North America, and tensions between dry and wet Icelanders endured well into the twentieth century. Still, Icelandic beverage cultures seemed to bind the community together, whether it was in pursuit of a good cup of coffee in a tea-centric society, in the temperance lodges that sprung up in Icelandic settlements, or at the bars, fishing camps, and even outhouses where men gathered to drink and socialize.

While the spectre of the "drunken foreigner" haunted the ambitions of the upwardly mobile immigrant classes, he was only one of many in a larger pantheon of more literal ghosts in the Icelandic community. The third chapter's exploration of superstitious, or *hjátrú*, narratives reveals a rich ghost-story tradition, which reflected unique ways of discussing history, power, and space in Icelandic districts. Widespread stories about a range of ghosts and other supernatural figures in settlements like Riverton offer a reminder of the popularity of this narrative tradition, which blended older storytelling traditions imported from Iceland with the populations, landscapes, and concerns the immigrants met in North America. More than simple ghost stories, narratives involving powerful beings that appeared in the form of a child or an Indigenous follower, or *fylgja*, offer compelling critiques of race, gender, and class-based hierarchies in Christian settler society.

This is not to imbue *hjátrú* narratives with a sense of altruism, particularly since many of them promote the notion of malevolent retribution. Rather, these narratives provided Icelanders with an adaptable venue for understanding and analysing the past. Indeed, *hjátrú* stories relating to Indigenous ghosts reveal some of the ways that Icelanders understood their everyday proximity to colonial violence – as an unsettling, and potentially harmful, intergenerational inheritance capable of establishing powerful competing claims to land. These and many other understudied narratives in the community offer rich and complex insight into otherwise undocumented collective concerns.

The fourth chapter explores a figure that came to define the public image of the twentieth-century community: the Viking. While Viking-era literature was an important part of immigrant culture imported from the homeland, this chapter argues that Viking-themed displays and celebrations emerged in response to pressures and conditions in twentieth-century North America. Viking parades and other Viking-themed campaigns grew as the community anglicized. This shift not only signalled the attempts of community leaders to reach out to the increasingly English-speaking children of immigrants, it also partially reflected the larger xenophobic, anti-immigrant sentiment that encouraged anglicization. Generally speaking, the image of the Viking became a tool for securing upward community mobility in the early twentieth century by cementing Icelanders' status as white "cousins to the English" with a pre-Columbian claim that justified their presence in North America.

The popularity of the Viking image during times of significant anti-immigrant sentiment in North America reflects the defensive function of this picturesque icon. Frequent references to modern Icelanders as Vikings over time, from longboat parade floats to Viking-themed battalions, were part of a larger response to the continued barriers that immigrants faced as non-anglophone, racially ambiguous arrivals from the far north. While other scholars have quite rightly identified the Icelandic immigrant community as a privileged one, oral history accounts, memoirs, and the records surrounding community campaigns contend that its status and acceptance in North America was secured over a much longer period of time. Icelandic upward mobility, individually and collectively, was not a given but rather the product of continual effort and strategy in first half of the twentieth century.

This book closes intentionally with a discussion of *vínarterta*. Slices of this little brown- or black-and-white torte often appear at the end of a special occasion in the community – from weddings to funerals (alongside strong coffee) – and their presence usually inspires conversation, storytelling, reflection, and a sense of connectedness to the past. Although *vínarterta* is best understood by community members as an unaltered culinary memento from the nineteenth-century Icelandic society from which they emerged, the torte's rise as a symbol of the community was fostered by events in the middle of the twentieth century. Indeed, *vínarterta* is one of many foods that Icelandic immigrants produced and consumed, so its place as an almost sacred representation of Icelandic immigrant identity is compelling and somewhat unexpected, particularly given its roots in the kitchens of Denmark and Vienna.

That chapter focuses on two issues. First, it reveals the history of the evolution of *vínarterta* as a symbol, describing its arrival in Iceland and North America and its celebration as a politicized American representation of Icelandic "friendliness" and "hospitality" meant to help neutralize protests against the Cold War occupation of the island. Second, it argues that *vínarterta* has come to mean something different – or at least something more – to Icelandic North Americans in practice. The torte's immense commemorative significance is perhaps most evident in the amount of energy (and rigidity) with which so many *vínarterta* producers still protect their particular, "correct" recipe. Oral narratives surrounding the torte reveal that community members imbue the production and consumption of *vínarterta* with deeply meaningful commemorative qualities, particularly related to the identification with the *amma* or other past generations of *vínarterta* makers. Oral history interviews, accounts, and recipes reveal that the torte has become more than a symbol of Iceland or Icelandic North American culture in popular practice – instead, it acts as a kind of Eucharist that binds together past and present generations.

Beyond a seamless image of progress, assimilation, or patriotism, the cultural history of Icelandic North America reveals a more complicated process of adaptation, one that involved everyday forms of expression. Engaging with these everyday forms reveals the subtleties of that process. Continual contests over Icelandic cultural degeneracy and "authenticity," and the adoption of Anglo–North American styles and allegiances, reveal that the formation of migrant culture was often a very physical project, one that involved the senses and the body. For ethnic leaders, government officials, and Anglo–North American neighbours, migrant bodies were to some extent unknown quantities that could pose a potential threat. As Icelanders quickly learned, migrants perceived as racially ambiguous or peculiar, and those associated with disease, disloyalty, or poverty, could be quickly rejected in the white, Anglo-centric project of western Canadian and American settlement. Collectively and in everyday actions, then, many Icelanders strove to create an image of their community as hospitable, literate, "loyal pioneers from the land of the Vikings" who belonged in North America.

Attention to the changing public image and private culture and identities within the Icelandic community are important to moving beyond arbitrary declarations of its death or final assimilation. Beyond official Icelandic institutions and channels, it is clear that many community members expressed themselves in a much larger range of vibrant popular forums – from the kitchen to the fishing camp – when they thought about and expressed their identities and culture. It is this culture that arguably reveals the most about a community otherwise outwardly marked by internal divisions, language loss, and continual reinvention. While some Icelandic forms, such as food and *hjátrú* narrative traditions, endured relatively intact for more than a century in the homes and private lives of community members, Icelandic North American culture is perhaps best understood as the product of a constant interplay between personal and public expectations, ideas, and desires. It is this fluidity, coupled with the cultural innovation of everyday community members, that fostered the growth of Icelandic identities in North America a century and a half after arrival.

# Appendix: Historical *Vínarterta* Recipes

### Lovise Beate Augustine Friedel, *Wienertærte*, 1795[1]

This is the oldest recipe located for this study and comes from the first Danish edition of a manual produced for women, including housewives and cooks, rather than professional bakers. It circulated widely in Europe and was translated into a number of languages, including German and French. Expensive ingredients, including almonds and orange blossom water, made this particular recipe a marker of sophistication and wealth in eighteenth-century Copenhagen.

*Cake*

Take one pound of sweet almonds and remove their skins. Pound them to a fine paste along with a pound of sugar and six whole eggs. Take a pound of lightly salted butter and use cold water to wash the salt out of the butter. Add one pound fine wheat flour to the butter. Knead the butter, almonds, and flour together to make a dough. Add a half ounce of mace and roll out the dough until it is as thick as the back of a knife. Cut it into the shape of a round serving dish, lay it on a piece of parchment paper, and bake it at high heat until it is golden.

Make more of these cake layers from the remaining dough so that each is a half-finger width smaller than the previous, and bake them just like the first one. When they have all been baked, take some fruit preserves, as many different kinds as you have, first cherry preserves, and cover the first cake layer with them. Lay the next cake layer on top, cover it with raspberry preserves, and after that, a layer covered with apple jam, and on top of that, a layer covered with red currant preserves, but don't put any preserves on the top layer.

Make a white icing in the following way: Take two egg whites and a quarter-pound fine icing sugar. Mix them together with a wooden spoon for at least fifteen minutes until it turns white. Then take a half eggshell-ful of orange blossom water and add it. If it becomes too thin, more sugar can be added. Add a few drops of lemon juice and stir well until the icing becomes completely white. After that, cover the cake with the icing, the top layer, and the sides.

Cut small, thin strips from bitter orange peel. Make vines from these and lay them on the top and around the sides of the cake. After that, take candied lemon peel and cut it into small diamond shapes and use it as leaves on the vines. After that, make flowers from black cherries, preserved rose hips, and green plums. When the cake has been decorated in this way, put it in a warm oven to dry. It is finished when the icing is shiny.

500 g butter
500 g wheat flour
500 g sugar
450 g almonds (including a few bitter almonds)
1 lemon, only the finely grated peel

*Filling*

red jam or jelly

*Icing*

250 g icing sugar
30 g (1) egg white
a little orange blossom water
a little lemon juice

The dough is mixed and left to chill. It is rolled out on parchment paper in the right shapes in four thin layers and baked until it is light brown. Cool the layers, cover three layers with jam, and assemble the four layers. Let it sit and settle before cutting it into nice slices, which are decorated with icing mixed thoroughly from icing sugar, egg white, orange blossom water, and lemon juice. Finally, dry the icing in an oven at a low temperature.

### Clara Margrethe Fristrup, *Wienertærte*, 1840[2]

This later Danish recipe for *Wienertærte* appears in Clara Margrethe Fristrup's 1840 cookbook. It reveals that the torte had endured in popularity among Danish women since 1795, but infers that they increasingly experimented with different fillings. Initially, Icelandic women of means would have used these kinds of Danish recipes to demonstrate their skill, access to more expensive ingredients, and engagement with fashionable trends in baking recipes. Over time, however, their preferences and practice transformed these kinds of recipes, evident in the difference between such Danish versions of *Wienertærte* and the Icelandic *vínarterta* that became so popular in the immigrant community.

"For this dish you make a butter dough, from which a round sheet is cut that fits the platter on which the cake will be served. Cover the edge of this piece of dough with another piece of dough a good finger-width wide, and then bake it in a pie pan. In this fashion, four to six additional pieces are cut out, to the size you want your cake to be. Spread jam on each of these pieces and then place them on top of each other on the serving platter, after which you trim off the edges so that the cake is smooth, and then glaze it. After the cake has been in a baking oven or pie pan, it is garnished on the top with four varieties of jam and served in this manner. This cake can be given a different shape if you bake one sheet of butter pastry smaller than the next, and then, when the cake has been glazed, you decorate these steps with jam and serve it in this way."[3]

### Aðalbjörg Benediktsdóttir Brandson, Icelandic Cake, 1936[4]

This 1936 recipe is attributed to Aðalbjörg Benediktsdóttir Brandson (Mrs. B.J. Brandson), who immigrated to Canada as a child and grew up in Winnipeg. It is notable for its use of only five layers and the inclusion of cardamom in the dough and cinnamon in the filling. This may have been more common in the immigrant generation. Although many later bakers added cardamom only to their fruit filling and omitted cinnamon, Brandson's practice was also used by Elísabet Polson, who learned the recipe in Skagafjörður before she left with her parents in 1876. Brandson's recipe also includes icing, another point of contention. As the baker explained to *Winnipeg Free Press* reporter Madeleine Day, "On very special occasions this cake is iced." This is one of the earliest North American versions of the recipe located for this study. Few recipes found in the immigrant community deviate substantially from what had become a common recipe by this point, notably the use of prunes and cardamom as opposed to the far more varied fillings originally found in Danish *Wienertærte*.

### Icelandic Cake

The fame of Vinarterta is not confined to the Icelandic people; most of us have tasted it and know just how delicious it is, so the opportunity of seeing Mrs. B. J. Branson actually make one right here was a real privilege. Too bad you couldn't have been here also, but since you weren't, I'll describe it to you as carefully as I know how.

#### Vinarterta

1 cup butter
1½ cups fine fruit sugar
2 eggs
3 tablespoons cream
1 tablespoon almond extract
1 teaspoon cardamon seed, shelled and ground
1 teaspoon baking powder
4 cups flour

Method: Cream the butter well and add the sugar gradually, then add the eggs, one at a time and beat hard after each addition. Sift the flour and baking powder and add a little of it to the creamed mixture. Then add the flavoring and the cream and work in as much of the flour as possible. Turn out onto a pastry cloth and knead in the rest of the flour.

Divide the dough into 5 equal parts and pat each one into a 9-inch, greased layer pan. Bake in a moderate, 375 deg. F. oven until each layer is a delicate brown. Then put together with the prune filling.

#### Prune Filling

1-lb. prunes
¾ cup sugar
½ cup prune juice
1 tablespoon cinnamon
1 tablespoon vanilla

Method: Soak the prunes and cook until they are tender. Remove the stones and put them through the food chopper. Add the sugar and ½ cup of the water in which they were cooked, and the cinnamon. Bring this to a boil and cook until it thickens a little. Remove from the fire and add the vanilla. Let the filling cool before spreading between the layers.

Mrs. Branson says that on very special occasions this cake is iced, but I think you'll agree that that isn't necessary as it is awfully rich anyway. Also this same dough is often baked as cookies. In fact, I don't see why you couldn't do that and then spread 5 of them with the filling and make individual vinartertas. Perhaps I've invented something there that even the Icelanders haven't thought of!

Danish Recipes and Customs

Figure A.1. Aðalbjörg Benediktsdóttir Brandson's Icelandic Cake, from her 1936 recipe.

### Mrs. F.J. Bergmann, *Vínarterta*, 1938[5]

Although most *vínarterta* were made with prunes, some Icelandic women like Guðrún Ólöf Magnúsdóttir (Mrs. F.J. Bergmann) continued to prepare varied fillings that more closely reflected the earlier Danish recipes for *Wienertærte*, including raspberry jam, and include actual almonds (rather than almond extract) in the batter. Such variation was much rarer in the second half of the twentieth century.

3 eggs.
1 cup sugar.
1 heaping teaspoon cardamom seed (ground).
1 lb. butter.
1/2 cup finely chopped almonds.
4 1/2 cups flour.
Raspberry jam.

Beat eggs well, add sugar, cardamoms, and almonds. Sift in two cups flour and mix. Turn out on board and knead in butter and balance of flour. Divide dough into five equal parts. Roll out and cut with 9-inch plate. Bake in moderate oven until golden brown. Spread raspberry jam between layers and ice with almond icing.

### Jóna Peterson, *Vínarterta*, 1949[6]

The recipe on page 172 for a seven-layer *vínarterta* by Jóna Peterson of Bottineau, North Dakota, along with photographs of her demonstrating the required steps, reached approximately 800,000 North American readers in the 1949 Christmas edition of *McCall's*.

### Helen Josephson, Icelandic *Vínarterta*, 1962[7]

Helen Josephson's famous six-layer *vínarterta*, page 173, was known in some circles as *the* Winnipeg *vínarterta*, especially in the city's West End Icelandic neighbourhood.[8] Josephson is one of a number of North American bakers who included ground almonds in their dough, like Mrs. F.J. Bergmann, a practice that extends to some of the earliest *Wienertærte* recipes. The recipe for the filling on page 174 was omitted from the original article in the *Winnipeg Free Press*, but printed in a later edition.[9]

### MRS. PETERSON'S VINARTERTA, ICELAND'S CHRISTMAS CAKE

2 lb dried prunes, cooked
½ cup prune liquid
1 cup sugar
½ teaspoon cardamom seeds
1 teaspoon vanilla extract
¼ teaspoon salt
1 cup butter

1 cup sugar
2 eggs
1 teaspoon vanilla extract
4 cups sifted all-purpose flour
2 teaspoons baking powder
½ teaspoon salt
¼ cup milk

Best to make up prune filling first. Wash prunes (if you use bulk or untenderized ones, soak fruit for 2 hours. With packaged tenderized prunes, soaking is not necessary). Cover fruit with water and cook *slowly* for about 45 minutes or until tender when tested with a fork. Drain prunes, *saving the liquid*. Cool, remove pits, put prunes through a food grinder or cut them into fine pieces with scissors.

Now add prune liquid, sugar and cardamom seeds, split in half, to prunes and cook until filling is about as thick as jam. Cool, add vanilla extract (many Icelanders use wine, rum or whiskey) and salt. Set aside until all cake layers are baked.

Now comes the cake-making time. Work or cream butter until soft. Add sugar gradually and continue mixing until very creamy. Beat eggs slightly, then stir eggs and vanilla extract into creamed sugar. Sift flour, baking powder, salt together. Add alternately with milk to butter mixture. The dough should be firm but not stiff. Mrs. Peterson suggests you chill Vinarterta dough in the refrigerator so it will handle more easily.

Start your oven at 350F or moderate.

When dough has chilled enough to be manageable, divide into 7 equal portions. Roll out each portion *very thin* on a lightly floured bread board to fit an 8" cake pan. Turn cake pan upside down, place dough on ungreased top of pan and trim the edges tidily. Bake 20 minutes or until edges turn a delicate brown. Remove from oven and slide cake off bottom of pan with the help of a spatula and cool on a wire rack until all 7 layers are baked. Of course, bake as many layers at a time as you have 8" cake pans and oven space. The baked layers should not be more than ¼" in thickness and will be very hard.

When all 7 layers of dough have been rolled and baked and cooled, spread a generous amount of prune filling between the layers and pat the Vinarterta with the palm of your hand to make the many thin layers of cake blend with the fruity filling.

Mrs. Peterson wraps her handsome holiday cake rather tightly in a dry cloth so moisture from the filling mellows the cake, then *lets it stand at least overnight before cutting*. "Better yet," says Mrs. Peterson, "let it age several days."

Figure A.2. Jóna Peterson's recipe for her seven-layer *vínarterta*, 1949.

**'COOKING IS FUN'** by CLARE MARCUS

## Tasty Icelandic Dishes

Traditional Icelandic dishes are featured attractions at Islendingadagurinn celebrations held in Gimli every summer. Visitors to the 73rd festival on Monday certainly will enjoy better fare than the first group of Icelandic settlers had when they arrived at Lake Winnipeg in the fall of 1875.

Many of the pioneers perished that winter but despite the cold, trees were felled for cabin building and fish caught for food. The second winter a larger group joined the colony but a small-pox epidemic took a heavy toll of their number. Their courageous struggle is remembered on Icelandic Day when the Maid of the Mountain lays a memorial wreath in their honor at the cairn in Gimli.

The settlers brought a love of democracy and good cooking with them to North America. Iceland founded the world's first parliament and supreme court more than a thousand years ago, but may be better known for Vinarterta.

**MISS HELEN JOSEPHSON** learned how to bake this cake from her mother in Winnipeg and improved her baking skills on trips back to Iceland. Her family emigrated to Canada 50 years ago but she still has more than 100 relatives to visit in her native land. The tiered Vinarterta, she said, will keep well in a cake tin for a month. However, having sampled Miss Josephson's cake we know it would not last more than two days at our house.

"I always make two and freeze one for later use," she said. "You have to grind the cardomoms yourself, and you should have them to make this cake."

**ICELANDIC VINARTERTA**
¾ cup butter
2 cups sugar
4 eggs
1 cup ground almonds
1 tsp. ground cardomoms
½ tsp. vanilla
4 cups flour
3 tsp. baking powder
1 tbsp. cold water

Cream butter and sugar. Beat eggs and add to mixture. Add cardomoms, vanilla, almonds, water and dry ingredients. Turn out on board and knead. Divide in six portions and bake on buttered cookie sheet 10 by 12 inches at 400 degrees for 12 minutes.

Helen Josephson

**ICELANDIC PANCAKES**
⅓ cup sugar
4 eggs
¼ tsp. salt
½ tsp. soda
1 tsp. baking powder
½ cup sour cream
1½ cups flour
2 cups milk
4 tbsp. melted butter
1 tsp. caraway seeds

Beat eggs, sugar and butter, salt and caraway seed. Dissolve soda in a little boiling water and mix with sour cream. Add to mixture. Add flour and baking powder. Beat well. Gradually stir in the milk. To bake use a fairly heavy griddle, pouring on about two tablespoons of batter at a time. Tip griddle around until entire bottom is covered. Set back on stove as quickly as possible, turn pancake and bake other side. Sour cream may be omitted by adding more milk. When all pancakes are baked sprinkle each one with a teaspoon of fruit sugar and roll. Cut in half.

Miss Josephson often bakes a box of treats for the Icelandic patients at Princess Elizabeth hospital, a habit she began while serving on the board of deacons of first Lutheran Church here.

Figure A.3. Helen Josephson's 1962 recipe for her famous six-layer *vínarterta*, known as *the* Winnipeg *vínarterta*.

*Filling*

Boil two pounds prunes until soft and almost all water has been absorbed. Cool and stone. Run through meat grinder. Add 2 1/2 cups sugar, a teaspoon of cardamoms, rind and juice of one lemon. Heat on stove and place between layers of cake when cooled.

# Notes

### Introduction

1 The number of respondents who identified as Icelandic or partially Icelandic increased from 70,685 in 1996 to 88,875 in 2006 and 101,795 in 2016. Statistics Canada, 2006 Census of Canada: Ethnic Origins of Canadians, Icelandic, accessed 28 February 2010, http://www12.statcan.ca/english/census06/data/highlights/ethnic/; Statistics Canada, 2016 Census of Canada: Data Tables, Icelandic.
2 Arjun Appadurai, *Modernity at Large: Cultural Dimensions of Globalization* (Minneapolis: University of Minnesota Press, 1996), 33, 48; Matthew Frye Jacobson, *Special Sorrows: The Diasporic Imagination of Irish, Polish and Jewish Immigrants in the United States* (Berkeley: University of California Press, 2002), 8.
3 "Goolie," the slang term for an Icelandic immigrant, likely emerged in Winnipeg at the turn of the century. For more, see pages 33, 110.
4 Here I draw from the innovative methodologies set out by scholars of a range of communities, immigrant and otherwise, and the ways in which they define cultural production and the making of categories of belonging. These include George Chauncey, *Gay New York: Gender, Urban Culture, and the Making of the Gay Male World, 1890–1940* (London: Hachette, 2008); Franca Iacovetta, *Gatekeepers: Reshaping Immigrant Lives in Cold War Canada* (Toronto: Between the Lines, 2006); Matthew Frye Jacobson, *Roots Too: White Ethnic Revival in Post–Civil Rights America* (Cambridge, MA: Harvard University Press, 2008); Monica L. Miller, *Slaves to Fashion: Black Dandyism and the Styling of Black Diasporic Identity* (Durham, NC: Duke University Press, 2009); Ruth B. Phillips, *Trading Identities: The Souvenir in Native North American Art from the Northeast, 1700–1900* (Montreal: McGill-Queen's University Press, 1999); Laurel Thatcher Ulrich, *The Age of Homespun: Objects and Stories in the Creation of*

*an American Myth* (New York: Vintage, 2009); Erica Rand, *The Ellis Island Snow Globe* (Durham, NC: Duke University Press, 2005). For a more in-depth historiography of the methodologies used throughout the book, please see the respective chapters.

5 In particular, this project was initially modelled to create an Icelandic contribution to critical ethnic-community historiography, which includes the work of Marlene Epp, *Mennonite Women in Canada: A History* (Winnipeg: University of Manitoba Press, 2008); Ruth Frager, *Sweatshop Strife: Class, Ethnicity and Gender in the Jewish Labour Movement of Toronto, 1900–39* (Toronto: University of Toronto Press, 1992); Oscar Handlin, *The Uprooted: The Epic Story of the Great Migrations That Made the American People* (Philadelphia: University of Pennsylvania Press, 2002); Franca Iacovetta, *Such Hardworking People: Italian Immigrants in Postwar Toronto* (Montreal and Kingston: McGill-Queen's University Press, 1993); Royden Loewen, *Family, Church and Market: A Mennonite Community in the Old and New Worlds* (Chicago: University of Illinois Press, 1993); Frances Swyripa, *Wedded to the Cause: Ukrainian-Canadian Women and Ethnic Identity, 1891–1991* (Toronto: University of Toronto Press, 1993).

6 For example, the subject is still all but completely ignored in official narratives created by institutions like Þjóðminjasafn, the National Museum of Iceland. The lone reference to migration in the museum's "Story of a Nation" permanent exhibit remains a laminated pamphlet stored in the pocket of a seat in the gallery. Visitors are invited to practically sit on the text rather than read it – a compelling illustration of the challenges that emigration poses to narratives of Icelandic national progress.

7 See, e.g., Guðjón Arngrímsson, *Nýja Ísland: Saga of the Journey to New Iceland* (Winnipeg: Turnstone, 1997); Anne Brydon, "Mother to Her Distant Children: The Icelandic Fjallkona in Canada," in *Undisciplined Women: Tradition and Culture in Canada*, ed. Pauline Greenhill and Diane Tye (Montreal and Kingston: McGill-Queen's University Press, 1997), 87–100; Ryan Eyford, *White Settler Reserve: New Iceland and the Colonization of the Canadian West* (Vancouver: UBC Press, 2016); Jónas Thor, *Icelanders in North America: The First Settlers* (Winnipeg: University of Manitoba Press, 2002); Kirsten Wolf, "Emigration and Mythmaking: The Case of the Icelanders in Canada," *Canadian Ethnic Studies* 33, no. 2 (2001): 1–15; Daisy Neijmann, *The Icelandic Voice in Canadian Letters* (Ottawa: Carleton University Press, 1997); Böðvar Guðmundsson, ed., *Bréf Vestur-Íslendinga* (Letters of Western Icelanders), 2 vols. (Reykjavík: Mál og Menning, 2001–2).

8 See, e.g., Birna Bjarnadóttir and Finnbogi Guðmundsson, eds., *My Parents: Memoirs of New World Icelanders* (Winnipeg: University of Manitoba Press, 2007); Neijmann; Víðar Hreinsson, *Wakeful Nights:*

*Stephan G. Stephansson, Icelandic-Canadian Poet* (Calgary: Benson Ranch, 2012); Wolf; Kirsten Wolf, ed., *Western-Icelandic Short Stories* (Winnipeg: University of Manitoba Press, 1992); Kirsten Wolf, ed., *Writings by Western Icelandic Women* (Winnipeg: University of Manitoba Press, 1997).

9 For some important existing contributions to this area, see Anne Brydon, "Dreams and Claims: Icelandic-Saulteaux Interactions in the Manitoba Interlake," *Journal of Canadian Studies* 36, no. 2 (2001): 164–90; Eyford, *White Settler Reserve*; Nelson Gerrard, *Icelandic River Saga* (Arborg, MB: Saga Publications, 1985) (although not published by an academic press, Gerrard is considered to be the foremost expert in this field, and *Icelandic River Saga* is cited as a central text in all scholarship on the community); Thor, *Icelanders in North America*.

10 Jónas Thor, *A Monument in Manitoba*, trans. Daniel Teague (Winnipeg: Heartland Associates, 2011); Frances Swyripa, *Storied Landscapes: Ethno-religious Identity and the Canadian Prairies* (Winnipeg: University of Manitoba Press, 2010); Tinna Grétarsdóttir, "'Art Is in Our Heart': Transnational Complexities of Art Projects and Neoliberal Governmentality" (PhD diss., Temple University, 2010).

11 See, e.g., John Matthiasson, "The Icelandic Canadians: The Paradox of an Assimilated Ethnic Group," in *Two Nations, Many Cultures: Ethnic Groups in Canada*, ed. Jean L. Elliott (Scarborough, ON: Prentice Hall, 1979), 195–205; Birna Arnbjörnsdóttir, *North American Icelandic: The Life of a Language* (Winnipeg: University of Manitoba Press, 2006, 15); Brydon, "Dreams and Claims," 183.

12 Percentage based on average recorded national population of 75,361 between 1870 and 1914. Hagstofa Íslands (Statistics Iceland), Population Development in Iceland, 1870–1914, http://px.hagstofa.is/pxen/pxweb/en/Ibuar/Ibuar__mannfjoldi__1_yfirlit__yfirlit_mannfjolda/MAN00109.px/table/tableViewLayout1/?rxid=3d0364df-3c58-4464-a072-f67eb0091007.

13 The number of departures is likely much higher as the 14,268 figure from Júníus H. Kristinsson's study accounts only for confirmed, officially documented immigrants and not those who departed without "reliable documentary evidence." Sveinbjörn Rafnsson reports in his introduction to Kristinsson's seminal survey that the existing "record is certainly far from complete and the number of those lacking may run into the thousands." See Júníus H. Kristinsson, *Vesturfaraskrá 1870–1914* (Reykjavík: Sagnfræðistofnun Háskóla Íslands, 1983), xvi.

14 When a particularly devastating volcano, Laki, erupted in 1783, e.g., poisonous gases, starvation, and pestilence killed approximately one-quarter of the population over a three-year period known as the "Mist Famine" (*Móðuharðindi*). In the decade preceding nineteenth-century immigration, however, it was ice rather than fire that caused the greatest hardship.

Pack ice frequently visited Icelandic fjords in the late 1860s and early 1870s, lowering the surrounding temperatures, cutting off access to the outside world, and thwarting fishing, farming, and trade.

15 Guðmundur Hálfdánarson, "Social Distinctions and National Unity: On Politics of Nationalism in Nineteenth-Century Iceland," *Journal of European Ideas* 21, no. 6 (1995): 770.

16 Hagstofa Íslands, Population Development in Iceland, 1870–1914. http://px.hagstofa.is/pxen/pxweb/en/Ibuar/Ibuar__mannfjoldi__1_yfirlit__yfirlit_mannfjolda/MAN00109.px/table/tableViewLayout1/?rxid=b9b23f1b-35ca-45e1-a646-8199a9f3e03a.

17 Sigurður Gylfi Magnússon, *Wasteland with Words: A Social History of Iceland* (London: Reaktion, 2010), 48–50.

18 The emigration movement was particularly popular with poor and working-class people; among their ranks were thousands of *vinnumenn* and *vinnukonur* (male and female farm servants) and individuals from the lowest rungs of Icelandic society, including single mothers, foster children, welfare wards, and other vulnerable people living on the margins of Icelandic society. Skilled Icelanders, such as carpenters, saddlers, blacksmiths, goldsmiths, printers, midwives, shoemakers, and seamstresses, as well as some professionals and wealthy Icelanders, also appear, although they were outnumbered. More than a few Icelanders resorted to emigration to escape quarrels, financial woes, and complicated personal lives. For the unhappily married, migration could serve as a form of informal divorce, enabling those who sought to, to build a new life elsewhere. Migration also provided an escape from legal troubles and personal prosecution, as in the case of those who offended the political and religious establishments. Two well-known examples were Jón Ólafsson, *ritstjóri* (editor), and Sigurður Júlíus Jóhannesson ("Siggi Júl"). For the most comprehensive listings of emigrant occupations, see Kristinsson, *Vesturfaraskrá, 1870–1914*, 1–361.

19 Kristján's story is an excellent example of the upward mobility that migration could offer to Icelanders on the margins. The young boy grew up to become a successful contractor in Winnipeg and was the co-founder of the Stefansson political family in Canada. His descendants, including a former provincial minister of finance, Eric Stefanson, have held a number of positions in the Canadian federal and Manitoba provincial governments. Nelson Gerrard, personal communication with author, 13 December 2018.

20 See references to priests discouraging parishioners from departing and the spread of cannibalism rumours in Jón Jónsson frá Vogum við Mývatn, *"Útflutnings-undirbúningur,"* handwritten booklet, 1865, collection of Landsbókasafn Íslands, Lbs. 2415 8, vol. 25.

21 Wolf, "Emigration and Mythmaking," 6–7.
22 Wolf, 1, 6–7.
23 Thor, *Icelanders in North America*, 13.
24 See, e.g., Þórsteinn Jónsson to Jón Jónsson Borgfirðingur, 4 November 1883, in *Fire on Ice: The Story of Icelandic Latter-day Saints at Home and Abroad*, by Fred E. Woods (Provo, UT: Brigham Young University), 51.
25 Some medieval Icelanders had lived in Greenland for over 400 years, and the large, neighbouring island seemed a geographically similar region where Icelanders might re-establish fisheries and settlements.
26 Sigurður Sigurðsson frá Fagranesi, *"Brasilíuferðir Íslendinga"* (Icelandic emigration to Brazil), ed. Júlíana Guðmundsdóttir; repr., *Ingólfur*, 31 December 1914, 203.
27 Thor, *Icelanders in North America*, 16; Þorsteinn Þ. Þorsteinsson, *Saga Íslendinga í Vesturheimi* (Saga of Icelanders in North America) (Reykjavík: Þjóðræknisfélag Íslendinga í Vesturheimi, 1940), 2:37.
28 Árni Guðmundsen, *"Landnám Íslendinga á Washington eyjunni"* (The Icelandic settlement on Washington Island), *Almanak Ólafs S. Thorgeirssonar*, vol. 6 (1900): 27.
29 This book often uses the term *migrant* as opposed to *immigrant* to reflect the larger significance of Icelanders' frequent journeys across national borders and into new territories – and sometimes back again – after they arrived in North America.
30 Thor, *Icelanders in North America*, 43.
31 George J. Houser, *Pioneer Icelandic Pastor: The Life of the Reverend Paul Thorlaksson*, ed. Paul A. Sigurdson (Winnipeg: Manitoba Historical Society, 1990), 45.
32 Houser, 46.
33 Þorsteinsson, *Saga Íslendinga í Vesturheimi*, 2:321–2.
34 Wilhelm Kristjanson, *The Icelandic People in Manitoba: A Manitoba Saga* (Winnipeg: Wallingford Press, 1965), 26–7.
35 Lord Dufferin [Frederick Temple Blackwood], *Letters from High Latitudes: Being Some Account of a Voyage in the Schooner Yacht "Foam"* (London: John Murray, 1856); Kristjanson.
36 Dufferin's book recounting the journey became immensely popular and earned him considerable success as an author. See also "Travelling in Iceland," *Literary World* (London) 10, no. 255 (18 September 1874): 177–9; Samuel Edmund Waller, *Six Weeks in the Saddle: A Painter's Journal in Iceland* (London: Macmillan, 1874); Frank Ponzi, *Ísland fyrir aldamót / Iceland: The Dire Years 1880–1888* (Reykjavík: Brennholt, 1995); Dufferin; Heidi Hansson, "The Gentleman's North: Lord Dufferin and the Beginnings of Arctic Tourism," *Studies in Travel Writing* 13, no. 1 (2009): 62.

37 For an analysis of the origins of this misrepresentation, see Eyford, *White Settler Reserve*, 142–3.
38 Kristjanson, *Icelandic People in Manitoba*, 98.
39 See Erla Louise Colvil Anderson, "Tolerance, Intolerance, and Fanaticism: W. D. Valgardson's Reaction to the Religious Debate in New Iceland" (master's thesis, University of Manitoba, 2000); Houser, *Pioneer Icelandic Pastor*; Jónas Thor, "A Religious Controversy among Icelandic Immigrants in North America, 1874–1880" (master's thesis, University of Manitoba, 1980).
40 Daniel Odess, William Loring, and William W. Fitzhugh, "First Peoples of Helluland, Markland and Vinland," in *Vikings: The North Atlantic Saga*, ed. William W. Fitzhugh and Elisabeth I. Ward (Washington, DC: Smithsonian Institution Press, 2000).
41 Gwyn Jones, ed., *Eirik the Red and Other Icelandic Sagas* (Oxford: Oxford University Press, 2008), 151–3; Kirsten Thisted, "On Narrative Expectations: Greenlandic Oral Traditions about the Cultural Encounter between Inuit and Norsemen," *Scandinavian Studies* 73, no. 3 (2001): 253–96.
42 Magnús Eliasson, *"Kona verður hissa þegar indjáninn Ramsay heilsar á íslensku"*(Woman surprised when the Indian Ramsay greets her in Icelandic), in *Sögur úr vesturheimi* (Stories from the New World), by Hallfreður Örn Eiríksson and Olga María Franzdóttir (Reykjavík: Stofnun Árna Magnússonar, 2012), 275. Although Ramsay's Icelandic skills have not been recorded in many other sources, this narrative is very likely true given his close business and personal relationships with numerous Icelanders, including Friðjón Friðriksson, and the many stories that describe the popularity of Icelandic with Indigenous neighbours and colleagues, who needed the language for work, business, and socializing.
43 For a more thorough discussion, see Laurie K. Bertram, "'Eskimo' Immigrants and Colonial Soldiers: Icelandic Immigrants and the North-West Resistance, 1885," *Canadian Historical Review* 99, no. 1 (2018): 63–97.
44 Eyford, *White Settler Reserve*, 47.
45 For a more detailed discussion of Métis claims on Mennonite land, see Donovan Giesbrecht, "Metis, Mennonites and the 'Unsettled Prairie,' 1874–1896," *Journal of Mennonite Studies* 19 (2001): 103–11.
46 Dr. James Spencer Lynch, "Report about Trouble with the Icelanders and a Smallpox Epidemic among the Indians of Lake Winnipeg, Especially at Sandy Bar," Indian Affairs, RG 10, vol. 3626, file 8064, 18, Library and Archives Canada, Ottawa. John Ramsay was well known as a leader and businessman by those outside his community and was referred to colloquially within the Icelandic community at times as "chief."
47 As Eyford writes, government negotiators refused to negotiate a treaty deal with the Sandy Bar Band, instead insisting that it sign along with

four other bands, all of whom would be required to elect a single chief and council; Eyford, *White Settler Reserve*, 105–6. For a more detailed discussion of the Icelandic land grant and the rejection of Ramsay's land claim, see Ryan Eyford, "Quarantined within a New Colonial Order: The 1876–77 Lake Winnipeg Smallpox Epidemic," *Journal of the Canadian Historical Association* 17, no. 1 (2006): 55–78.

48 Brydon, "Dreams and Claims," 171.
49 Friðrik Sveinsson, quoted in *"Endurminningar frá Landnámstímanum"* (Memories from the time of settlement), in *Brot af Landnámssögu Nýja Íslands* (Fragments of the settlement history of New Iceland), by Thorleifur Jóakimsson Jackson, trans. courtesy Nelson Gerrard (Winnipeg: Columbia Press, 1919), 33.
50 Thorstína Walters, *Modern Sagas: The Story of the Icelanders in North America* (Fargo: North Dakota Institute for Regional Studies, 1953), 63.
51 Franca Iacovetta, "Manly Militants, Cohesive Communities, and Defiant Domestics: Writing about Immigrants in Canadian Historical Scholarship," *Labour/Le Travail* 36 (Fall 1995): 237.
52 Phillips, *Trading Identities*, x.
53 Bruno Latour, "The Berlin Key or How to Do Words with Things," in *Matter, Materiality and Modern Culture*, ed. P.M. Graves-Brown (London: Routledge, 2000), 10.
54 This includes the well-established tradition of popular historical scholarship, which consists of unique and often well-documented insights into the community's history and cultural values. Scholars and community members alike have produced a considerable number of historical works, often engaging in a range of revealing historiographical debates. Early, multi-volume, Icelandic-language publications provided comprehensive retrospectives on community events and personalities for Icelandic and Icelandic North American readership during the first half of the twentieth century. See, e.g., Thorleifur Jóakimsson Jackson, *Framhald á Landnámssögu Nýja Íslands* (From east to west: Continuation of the settlement history of New Iceland) (Winnipeg: Columbia Press, 1923); Þorsteinn Þ. Þorsteinsson, *Vestmenn: Landnám Íslendinga í Vesturheimi* (Reykjavík: Ísafoldarprentsmiðju, 1935); Þorsteinsson, *Saga Íslendinga í Vesturheimi*. These works reflect the enduring importance of the biographical and autobiographical tradition in immigrant culture. The popularity of autobiographical writing by farmers and fishermen also reflects a larger tradition in which Icelanders – from the working class to the wealthy – placed significant value on recording personal experience. See, e.g., Helgi Einarsson, *Helgi Einarsson: A Manitoba Fisherman*, trans. George Houser (Winnipeg: Queenston House, 1982); Magnús Guðlaugson, *Three Times a Pioneer* (Winnipeg: s.n. 1958); Glenn Sigurdson,

*Vikings on a Prairie Ocean: The Saga of a Lake, a People, a Family and a Man* (Winnipeg: Great Plains Publications, 2014).

55 Daisy Neijmann and Kirsten Wolf have discussed several of the relatively prolific female authors in the nineteenth- and early twentieth-century community, including those whose work was translated for the 1997 anthology edited by Wolf, *Writings by Western Icelandic Women*. Middle-class and educated Thorstína Walters, an accomplished writer who lived in the Icelandic community in North Dakota, also published several well-received texts and translations, including *Modern Sagas* (1953), an English-language history of the community produced as a result of her fellowship at the University of Minnesota. More often, however, female community historians contributed to historical texts uncredited. Working with other members of the Gimli Women's Institute, schoolteacher-turned-historian Sigurbjörg "Bogga" Stefansson invested innumerable hours translating and researching *Gimli Saga*, an almost eight-hundred-page community history published in 1973. Conversely, many nineteenth-century Icelandic immigrant women remained proportionately under-represented in published community histories; this is particularly evident in the fewer autobiographies produced by first- and second-generation Icelandic North American women. The memoirs of award-winning author Laura Goodman Salverson help illuminate the uphill battle that gifted working-class women of her generation faced if they wished to join the ranks of published authors in the Icelandic community. Salverson worked as a domestic to help support her parents, immigrants from Bolungarvík, and described the many hours of unrecorded, often unacknowledged labour that could keep exhausted, working-class Icelandic domestics and laundresses away from writing more than the obligatory letters home. "For girls like us the dice were loaded from the start," she wrote. "The ensign of the mop and the dustbin hung over our cradles.... Just eat and sleep, propagate your misery and die!" See Wolf, *Writings by Western Icelandic Women*; Walters, *Modern Sagas*; and Gimli Women's Institute, *Gimli Saga: The History of Gimli Manitoba* (Gimli: s.n., 1975); Laura Goodman Salverson, *Confessions of an Immigrant's Daughter* (London: Faber, 1939), 323.

56 These include interviews conducted by the author as well as extensive pre-existing collections created mostly in the 1960s and 1970s, such as the three-volume set produced by the Canadian Museum of Civilization: Magnús Einarsson, ed., *Icelandic-Canadian Oral Narratives* (Hull, QC: Canadian Museum of Civilization, 1991); Magnús Einarsson, ed., *Icelandic-Canadian Memory Lore* (Hull, QC: Canadian Museum of Civilization, 1992); Magnús Einarsson, ed., *Icelandic-Canadian Popular Verse* (Hull, QC: Canadian Museum of Civilization, 1994); also Hallfreður

Örn Eiríksson and Olga María Franzdóttir, *Sögur úr vesturheimi* (Stories from the New World) (Reykjavík: Stofnun Árna Magnússonar, 2012).
57 These include the excellent collections in North Dakota, specifically at the Icelandic State Park and Pembina County Historical Museum in Cavalier. In Canada and the United States, many of these collections were founded around the federal, provincial, and state centennials in the 1960s and 1970s, including the centennial of the founding of New Iceland in 1975. These anniversaries fuelled the creation of numerous initiatives to identify, collect, and re-disseminate local ethnic histories. See, e.g., provincial projects like Saskatchewan Archives Board, "Icelandic Settlement in the Quill Lakes Area" (oral history collection), Oral History Centre, R-A1871 to R-A1882, University of Winnipeg; and community-history book endeavours like Lundar and District Historical Society, *Wagons to Wings: History of Lundar and Districts, 1872–1980* (Lundar, MB: Lundar Historical Society, 1980); Steinn Thompson, *Riverton and the Icelandic Settlement* (Riverton: Thordis Thompson, 1976).

## 1. Dressing Up

1 Nelson Gerrard, *Icelandic River Saga* (Arborg, MB: Saga Publications, 1985), 230.
2 Sophie Woodward, "Making Fashion Material," *Journal of Material Culture* 7, no. 3 (2002): 345.
3 Peter Boag, *Re-dressing America's Frontier Past* (Berkeley: University of California Press, 2011); Monica J. Miller, *Slaves to Fashion: Black Dandyism and the Styling of Black Diasporic Identity* (Durham, NC: Duke University Press, 2009); Mariana Valverde, "The Love of Finery: Fashion and the Fallen Woman in Nineteenth-Century Social Discourse," *Victorian Studies* 32, no. 2 (1989): 169–88.
4 Cynthia Kuhn and Cindy Carlson, eds., *Styling Texts: Dress and Fashion in Literature* (Amherst, NY: Cambria Press, 2007), 3.
5 Sigurður Guðmundsson, *"Um kvennbúninga á Íslandi: Að fornu og nýju"* (On women's clothing in Iceland: In antiquity and now) (*Ný Félagsrit* 17, 1857), 1–53.
6 Sigríður Mattíasdottír, "The Renovation of Native Pasts: A Comparison between Aspects of Icelandic and Czech Nationalist Ideology," *Slavonic and East European Review* 78, no. 4 (October 2000): 690, 694.
7 Kristín Loftsdóttir, "Shades of Otherness: Representations of Africa in 19th-Century Iceland," *Social Anthropology* 16, no. 2 (2008): 181.
8 Guðmundsson, *"Um kvennbúninga á Íslandi,"* 3.
9 Æsa Sigurjónsdóttir, *Til gagns og til fegurðar: Sjálfsmyndir í ljósmyndum og klæðnaði á Íslandi 1860–1960* (For function and beauty: Identity

in photography and clothing in Iceland, 1860–1960). (Reykjavík: Þjóðminjasafnið Íslands, 2008), 44.

10 Guðmundur Hálfdánarson, "Social Distinctions and National Unity: On Politics of Nationalism in Nineteenth-Century Iceland," *Journal of European Ideas* 21, no. 6 (1995): 772; Sigurður Gylfi Magnússon, *Wasteland with Words: A Social History of Iceland* (London: Reaktion, 2010), 32.

11 Inga Dóra Björnsdóttir, "Nationalism, Gender and the Body in Icelandic Nationalist Discourse," *Nordic Journal of Feminist and Gender Research* 5, no. 1 (1997): 7.

12 Hálfdanarson, "Social Distinctions and National Unity," 772.

13 Magnússon, *Wasteland with Words*, 27.

14 Gísli Ágúst Gunnlaugsson, "'Everyone's Been Nice to Me, Especially the Dogs': Foster-Children and Young Paupers in Nineteenth-Century Southern Iceland," *Journal of Social History* (Winter 1993): 345.

15 Hálfdanarson, "Social Distinctions and National Unity," 770.

16 Magnússon, *Wasteland with Words*, 54–5.

17 Noel Ignatiev, *How the Irish Became White* (New York: Routledge, 2009), 3, 5.

18 Thorstína Walters, *Modern Sagas: The Story of the Icelanders in North America* (Fargo: North Dakota Institute for Regional Studies, 1953), 11.

19 Quoted from an interview in the *New York Star*, 1876, in Wilhelm Kristjanson, *The Icelandic People in Manitoba: A Manitoba Saga* (Winnipeg: Wallingford Press, 1965).

20 Einar Kvaran Hjörleifsson, *Vestur-Íslendingar: Fyrirlestur* (Reykjavík: Prentsmíðja Ísafoldar, 1895), 28–9.

21 Halldór Briem, "Journey of Lord Dufferin, Governor-General of Canada to Manitoba and Keewatin," *Framfari*, 17 November 1877, 29.

22 Lord Dufferin [Frederick Temple Blackwood], *Letters from High Latitudes: Being Some Account of a Voyage in the Schooner Yacht "Foam"* (London: John Murray, 1856), 4.

23 Rev. Friðrik J. Bergmann, *Almanak*, 1908; repr. and trans., W.J. Lindal, *The Icelanders in Canada* (Winnipeg: Viking Press, 1967), 116.

24 Thomas A. Guglielmo, *White on Arrival: Italians, Race, Color, and Power in Chicago, 1890–1945* (Oxford: Oxford University Press, 2003); Ignatiev, *How the Irish Became White*; David R. Roediger, *Working toward Whiteness: How America's Immigrants Became White; The Strange Journey from Ellis Island to the Suburbs* (New York: Basic Books, 2006).

25 *Manitoba Free Press*, "Get Their Pictures Taken," 5 March 1878, 1.

26 See Gudmundur Peterson, letter to the editor, *Lögberg-Heimskringla*, 28 January 2000, 2.

27 Magnús Magnússon, quoted in Kristjana Magnusson, *So Well Remembered* (Winnipeg: A & K Publications, 1978), 19.

28 Vilhjálmur Stefánsson, *Adventures in Error* (New York: Robert M. McBride, 1936), 247.
29 Olof Krarer, *The Esquimaux Lady: A Story of Her Native Home*, ed. Albert S. Post (Ottawa: ILLS, 1887), 6, 9.
30 Krarer, 13.
31 Inga Dóra Björnsdóttir, *Ólöf the Eskimo Lady: Biography of an Icelandic Dwarf in America*, trans. María Helga Guðmundsdóttir (Ann Arbor: University of Michigan Press, 2010); John M. Boyer and John F. Wicks, *Geography by the Brace System or How to Study Geography: Prepared for the Use of Teacher and Pupil* (Chicago: A. Flanagan, 1891), 341–7.
32 Ryan Eyford, "Quarantined within a New Colonial Order: The 1876–77 Lake Winnipeg Smallpox Epidemic," *Journal of the Canadian Historical Association* 17, no. 1 (2006): 74–5.
33 Loftsdóttir, "Shades of Otherness," 181–2.
34 See, e.g., John Taylor and Henry Johnson (Helgi Jónsson) to the Minister of Agriculture John Henry Pope, 3 April 1884, R194-40-3 E, Library and Archives Canada (LAC), Ottawa.
35 Jason E. Box, Edward Hanna, and Trausti Jónsson, "An Analysis of Icelandic Climate since the Nineteenth Century," *International Journal of Climatology* 24 (2004): 1196.
36 Simon Simonson, *Icelandic Pioneers of 1874: From the Reminiscences of Simon Simonson*, trans. Wilhelm Kristjanson (Winnipeg: s.n., 1904), FC 3400 I2 S54, University of Manitoba Archives and Special Collections, Winnipeg.
37 Friðríka Baldvinsdóttir to Baldvin Helgason, in Böðvar Guðmundsson, *Bréf Vestur-Íslendinga* (Letters of Western Icelanders) (Reykjavík: Mál og Menning, 2001–2), 1:60.
38 Björn Andrésson to his father, 6 March 1877; repr. and trans., Gerrard, *Icelandic River Saga*, 32–4.
39 Jóhann Briem, *"Priðji innflytjendahópurinn í Nýja Íslandi, sem kom að heiman 1876: Um slysfarir frá ágúst 1876 til september 1877,"* in *Brot af landnámssögu Nýja Íslands* (Fragments of the settlement history of New Iceland), by Thorleifur Jóakimsson Jackson, trans. courtesy Nelson Gerrard (Winnipeg: Columbia Press, 1919), 19–20.
40 Þorsteinn Þ. Þorsteinsson, *Saga Íslendinga í Vesturheimi* (Saga of Icelanders in North America) (Reykjavík: Þjóðræknisfélag Íslendinga í Vesturheimi, 1940), 2:106.
41 Approximately 200 of the initial group of 1,400 who left in 1876 went to other destinations in Canada and the United States; see Þorsteinsson, 1:102.
42 Augustus Baldwin to Phoebe (Baldwin), 13 March 1877, MG 8 A6-3, 1–2, Provincial Archives of Manitoba (PAM), Winnipeg.

43 Dr. James Spence Lynch, "Clandeboye Agency: District of Keewatin; Report about Trouble with the Icelanders and a Smallpox Epidemic among the Indians of Lake Winnipeg, Especially at Sandy Bar," Indian Affairs, RG 10, vol. 3626, file 8064, 16, LAC, Ottawa.
44 "Saga Magnúsar Stefánssonar frá Fjöllum í Kelduhverfi eftir hans eigin handriti," in *Frá Austri til Vesturs: Framhald af landnámssögu Nýja Íslands* (Fragments of the settlement history of New Iceland), by Thorleifur Jóakimsson Jackson (Winnipeg: Columbia Press, 1921), 82.
45 Elizabeth Fidler et al., "Elizabeth Fidler's Claim for Loss of Houses and Improvements Occasioned by Occupation of Icelandic Settlers," 1877–86, Dominion Land Branch Records, RG 15-D-II-1, vol. 90, file 105883, LAC, Ottawa.
46 For a detailed discussion, see Ryan Eyford, *White Settler Reserve: New Iceland and the Colonization of the Canadian West* (Vancouver: UBC Press, 2016).
47 "Interview/Subject: Alfred Thomas, Grand Marais Beach," transcript of interview by Margaret Stobie, June 1965, Collection of University of Regina, http://ourspace.uregina.ca/bitstream/handle/10294/1862/IH-MS.016A,%20.016B.pdf?sequence=1.
48 "John Ramsey, Indian," Store Accounts, 1881–2, Icelandic Collection, mss. Isl. 11 67, 184–5, University of Manitoba, Winnipeg.
49 Guttormur Guttormson, "John Ramsay the Native Indian," in *Íslendssöguvefurinn: Vesturfaranir* (Icelandic online history: The emigrants), ed. and trans. Viðar Hreinsson and Jón Karl Helgason, 76 (Reykjavík: RUV), 1999–2000; first published 1975 in *Andvari: Nýr flokkur*; accessed 5 January 2010, http://servefir.ruv.is/vesturfarar/SamIndianar.html.
50 Guttormson.
51 Could this early trade in knitwear also be one of the ways in which smallpox moved between the Icelandic and local Cree and Ojibwe communities? Icelanders were responsible for importing the disease to the area; however, the story of John Ramsay's provision of fish for socks in 1877 questions whether this practice may have begun after the epidemic had already reached nearby communities; story attributed to Tómas Björnsson of Geysir, "*Nýlendusögur: Halldór Jónsson og John Ramsay*" (New land saga: Halldór Jónsson and John Ramsay), *Lögberg*, 23 March 1916, 6.
52 Gerrard, *Icelandic River Saga*, 67.
53 Jón Jónsson to unnamed recipient, 25 February 1904, Mary Hill, MB, in "*Vínarbréf til Íslands*" (Friends' letters to Iceland), *Lögberg*, 25 February 1904, 2.
54 Halldór Briem, "My Good Countrymen!," *Framfari*, 24 January 1878, 88.
55 John Taylor, quoted in Kristjanson, *Icelandic People in Manitoba*, 104.
56 Hjörleifsson, *Vestur-Íslendingar*, 29.

57 Pro-British sentiment in Iceland shaped Sigtryggur's decision to choose emigration to Canada over the United States since he "like[d] the British form of governance more than the American"; Sigtryggur Jónasson, quoted in Lindal, *Icelanders in Canada*, 88.
58 Sigtryggur Jónasson, (store account) Jónasson & Fredrickson and Co. Sawmill and Store, store account ledger, Icelandic River (Riverton), MB, Icelandic Collection, mss. Isl. 11, University of Manitoba, Winnipeg, 268.
59 Guðný Sigurðardóttir, wife of Friðjón Friðriksson, spent a winter with her husband in a Milwaukee doctor's household, while Frú Lára lived in Milwaukee, Chicago, and Minneapolis from 1873 to 1877. Rannveig Briem spent time with Torfhildur Holm, her companion, in Toronto en route to Manitoba in 1876.
60 Gerrard, *Icelandic River Saga*, 227.
61 Simonson, *Icelandic Pioneers of 1874*, 10.
62 Rósamunda Guðmundsdóttir, letter to the editor, *Landneminn*, 20 July 1893; repr., Guðjón Arngrímsson, ed. and trans., *Nýja Ísland: Saga of the Journey to New Iceland*, 280–1 (Winnipeg: Turnstone, 1997).
63 Þorsteinsson, *Saga Íslendinga í Vesturheimi*, 4:348.
64 Charles N. Bell, "The Great Winnipeg Boom," *Manitoba History* 23 (October 2006), accessed 19 March 2013, http://www.mhs.mb.ca/docs/mb_history/53/greatwinnipegboom.shtml.
65 Björn Andrésson to his father, 30 July 1877; repr. and trans., Gerrard, *Icelandic River Saga*, 40.
66 Rósamunda Guðmundsdóttir, letter to the editor, *Landneminn*, 3 January 1892, 2.
67 Ingveldur Jónsdóttir to Þorleifur Jónsson, 20 March 1892; repr., Guðmundsson, *Bréf Vestur-Íslendinga*, 2:350.
68 Constance Backhouse, *Petticoats and Prejudice: Women and Law in 19th-Century Canada* (Toronto: Women's Press, 1991), 58–69; Karen Dubinsky, *Improper Advances: Rape and Heterosexual Conflict in Ontario, 1880–1929* (Chicago: University of Chicago Press, 1993), 51–4.
69 See, e.g., "An Alleged Rape Case," *Manitoba Free Press*, 13 August 1888, 4; *Helga Indridator vs. Geo. W. Earl*, City of Winnipeg Police Court Record, 19 October 1894, PAM, Winnipeg.
70 Valverde, "Love of Finery," 169–88.
71 See the description of Ragnheiður in Stephan G. Stephansson's poem *Á ferð og flugi* (En route) (Reykjavík: Jón Ólafsson, 1900); and the depiction of Ninna in Laura Goodman Salverson, *The Viking Heart* (Toronto: McClelland and Stewart, 1975), 265–76.
72 Petition against "persons of bad character flaunting themselves," 4 August 1875, Winnipeg Council Papers, A102, 373, Collection of Winnipeg City Archives; Rhonda Hinther, "The Oldest Profession in

Winnipeg: The Culture of Prostitution in the Point Douglas Segregated District, 1909–1912," *Manitoba History* 41 (2001): 2–13.
73  *Manitoba Free Press*, City and Provincial, 20 November 1879, 1.
74  City and Provincial, 19 November 1879, 1.
75  Kristjanson, *Icelandic People in Manitoba*, 175.
76  Laura Goodman Salverson, *Confessions of an Immigrant's Daughter* (London: Faber, 1939), 330.
77  Hjörleifsson, *Vestur Íslendingar*, 28.
78  "*Nafnabreytingar*," *Lögberg*, 8 August 1888, 2; the name later appeared in Haraldur Bessason, "A Few Specimens of North American Icelandic," *Scandinavian Studies* 39, no. 2 (1967): 115–46.
79  Kristjanson, *Icelandic People in Manitoba*, 171.
80  "*Íslenzkur skraddari*," advertisement in *Lögberg*, 21 September 1888, 1.
81  "Icelanders in Winnipeg," *Framfari*, 22 February 1879, 473.
82  "Carley Bro's," advertisement in *Heimskringla*, 20 August 1892, 1. See also "Icelanders!," advertisement in *Framfari*, 15 February 1879, 470.
83  Hjörleifsson, *Vestur-Íslendingar*, 19–20.
84  Einar Kvaran Hjörleifsson, quoted in Arngrímsson, *Nýja Ísland*, 299.

## 2. The Coffee Pot and King Bacchus

1  "Icelandic Coffee," *Evening Post* (Wellington), 20 March 1937, 27.
2  Séra Kristján Eldjárn, "*Versti farartálminn*" (The biggest obstacle), in *Gríma: Þjóðsögur* (Folk tales) (Akureyri, Iceland: s.n., 1930), 80.
3  See, e.g., Donna Gabaccia's influential *We Are What We Eat: Ethnic Food and the Making of Americans* (Cambridge, MA: Harvard University Press, 1998); the contributions to *Edible Histories, Cultural Politics: Towards a Canadian Food History*, ed. Franca Iacovetta, Valerie J. Korinek, and Marlene Epp (Toronto: University of Toronto Press, 2012); Frances Swyripa, *Wedded to the Cause: Ukrainian-Canadian Women and Ethnic Identity, 1891–1991* (Toronto: University of Toronto Press, 1993), 248–9. See also Marlene Epp, "The Semiotics of Zwieback: Feast and Famine in the Narratives of Mennonite Refugee Women," in *Sisters or Strangers? Immigrant, Ethnic, and Racialized Women in Canadian History*, ed. Marlene Epp, Franca Iacovetta, and Frances Swyripa (Toronto: University of Toronto Press, 2004), 314–40.
4  Craig Heron, *Booze: A Distilled History* (Toronto: Between the Lines, 2003).
5  See, e.g., Linda Kealey, *A Not Unreasonable Claim: Women and Reform in Canada, 1880–1920* (Toronto: Women's Press, 1979); Sharon Anne Cook, "*Through Sunshine and Shadow*": *The Women's Christian Temperance Union, Evangelicalism, and Reform in Ontario, 1874–1930* (Montreal and Kingston: McGill-Queen's University Press, 1995); Jan Noel, *Canada Dry: Temperance*

*Crusades before Confederation* (Toronto: University of Toronto Press, 1995); Mariana Valverde, *Diseases of the Will: Alcohol and the Dilemmas of Freedom* (New York: Cambridge University Press, 1998).

6 Peter DeLottinville, "Joe Beef of Montreal: Working-Class Culture and the Tavern, 1869–1889," *Labour/Le Travail* (1981): 9–40; Heron, *Booze*; Julia Roberts, *In Mixed Company: Taverns and Public Life in Upper Canada* (Vancouver: UBC Press, 2009).

7 Hildigunnur Ólafsdóttir, "The Entrance of Beer into a Persistent Spirits Culture," *Contemporary Drug Problems* 26, no. 4 (1999): 545–75.

8 *"Um kaffi, lit þess, einkenni og notkun"* (On coffee, about its characteristics and uses), *Íslendingur*, 29 June 1860, 49–53, 52.

9 *"Um kaffi,"* 52.

10 *"Um kaffi."*

11 Guðbrandur Erlendsson, *Gudbrandur Erlendsson Autobiography* (draft), trans. Nelson Gerrard (Hnausa, MB: Saga Publications, 2009), 110.

12 Þóra Andrea Nikólína Jónsdóttir, *Ný matreiðslubók ásamt ávísun um litun, þvott o. fl.* (A new cookbook along with advice on dyeing, washing and more) (Akureyri, Iceland: H. Helgasyni, 1858), 183–4.

13 See, e.g., the 1858 recipes for champagne punch and whisky, or "Irish *brennivín*," in Jónsdóttir, 165, 167.

14 Guðbrandur Erlendsson recalled that he first "drank myself to the point of intoxication" at the age of nine after being offered alcohol by a local labourer; see Guðbrandur Erlendsson, *Gudbrandur Erlendsson Autobiography*, 16.

15 Hildigunnur Ólafsdóttir, *Alcoholics Anonymous in Iceland: From Marginality to Mainstream Culture* (Reykjavík: Háskólaútgáfan, 2000), 38.

16 Ólafsdóttir, "The Entrance of Beer," 547.

17 See, e.g., Samuel Edmund Waller, *Six Weeks in the Saddle: A Painter's Journal in Iceland* (London: Macmillan, 1874), 28–9, 135, 147; Frederick Metcalfe, *An Oxonian in Iceland: With Glances at Icelandic Folk-Lore and Sagas* (London: John Camden Hotten, 1867), 153–9.

18 Hildigunnur Ólafsdóttir cautions against taking these reports as representations of all travellers' observations since several also comment on the lack of alcohol use in Iceland. Here these texts are taken instead as representations of Icelandic alcohol consumption circulating in English-language literature in the second half of the nineteenth century; see Hildigunnur Ólafsdóttir, "Drinking in Iceland and Ideas of the North," in *Iceland and Images of the North*, ed. Sumarliði Ísleifsson (Quebec City: Presses de l'Université du Québec, 2011), 337; see also the journal of Hans Frisak, quoted in Gísli Pálsson, *The Man Who Stole Himself: The Slave Odyssey of Hans Jonathan*, trans. Anna Yates (Chicago: University of Chicago Press, 2016), 143–4.

19 Metcalfe, *An Oxonian in Iceland*, 159.

20 Metcalfe, 154.
21 Ólafsdóttir, *Alcoholics Anonymous in Iceland*, 39.
22 Ann Pinson, "Temperance, Prohibition, and Politics in Nineteenth-Century Iceland," *Contemporary Drug Problems* 12 (1985): 250.
23 *"Hallærið og búskapurinn"* (Famine and farming), *Norðri*, 30 May 1859, 51.
24 Sveinn Þórarinsson, "June 6 1869," Daybook of Sveinn Þórarinsson, Nr. 68C, 8vo, 673, Héraðsskjalasafnið á Akureyri (Akureyri Regional Archives), Akureyi, Iceland.
25 Þórarinsson, 679.
26 Þórarinsson, 678.
27 Þórarinsson, "June 20 1869," 679.
28 See, e.g., comparative price lists produced to help immigrants plan for life in North America, such as *"Verðlag veturinn 1873–4"* (Winter prices 1873–4), *Ameríka* (Akureyri), 7 July 1874, 74–5.
29 Einar Ásmundsson, quoted in Gunnar Karlsson, *Iceland's 1100 Years: History of a Marginal Society* (Reykjavík: Mál og Menning, 2000), 235.
30 Jón Jónsson, *"Saga Jóns Jónssonar á Mæri eftir hans eigin handriti,"* in *Frá Austri til Vesturs: Framhald af landnámssögu Nýja-Íslands* (From east to west: Continuation of the settlement history of New Iceland), by Thorleifur Jóakimsson Jackson (Winnipeg: Columbia Press, 1921), 96.
31 Erlendsson, *Gudbrandur Erlendsson Autobiography*, 181.
32 W.J. Lindal, *The Icelanders in Canada* (Winnipeg: Viking Press, 1967), 158.
33 Augustus Baldwin to Phoebe (Baldwin), 13 March 1877, MG 8 A6-3, 3, Provincial Archives of Manitoba (PAM), Winnipeg.
34 Sigríður Jónsdóttir to Þuríður Jónsdóttir, 14 June 1879; repr., Böðvar Guðmundsson, ed., *Bréf Vestur-Íslendinga*, vol. 1 (Reykjavík: Mál og Menning, 2001).
35 Thorstína Walters, *Modern Sagas: The Story of the Icelanders in North America* (Fargo: North Dakota Institute for Regional Studies, 1953), 72.
36 Jón Bjarnason, *"Ferðabréf"* (Letter [about my] journey), *Lögberg*, 4 September 1889, 3.
37 Walters, *Modern Sagas*, 72.
38 *"Frítt fyrir alla"* (Free for all), *Freyja*, 1 February 1898, 10.
39 Magnús Guðlaugson, *Three Times a Pioneer*, ed. Holmfridur Danielson (Winnipeg: s.n., 1958), 49.
40 Guðlaugson.
41 A well-seasoned coffee bag, stained almost black from the grounds, enhanced the flavour of the coffee, so it was not washed with soap after use. These alien drinking practices were a source of amusement, confusion, and occasionally disgust for anglophone onlookers. Kristjana Magnusson recalled a humorous story from the Hnausa district about an Englishwoman named Iris who was unsettled by the sight of a dark,

battered *kaffi póki* in her Icelandic friend's kitchen. According to the story, when her hostess left the kitchen, Iris grabbed the dark coffee sock, declared, "This will never do," and decided to do her friend a favour and scrub it with lye. When she proudly presented the gleaming white sock to her friend, the woman "laughed and laughed as she told her friend that a coffee bag cleaned with lye would have a very strange taste indeed"; see Kristjana Magnusson, *So Well Remembered* (Winnipeg: A & K Publications, 1978), 39–40.

42 For example, before she worked as a Greenlandic impersonator, Ólöf Sölvadóttir reported that some of the first English she learned while working as a domestic in Winnipeg was a request for coffee instead of tea; see Olof Krarer, *The Esquimaux Lady: A Story of Her Native* Home, ed. Albert S. Post (Ottawa: ILLS, 1887), 25.

43 See Kristin Olafson-Jenkyns, *The Culinary Saga of New Iceland: Recipes from the Shores of Lake Winnipeg* (Guelph, ON: Coastline Publishing, 2001), 212–3.

44 Olafson-Jenkyns, 213.

45 Albert Kristjanson, "Afternoon Coffee Not Served!," in *Icelandic-Canadian Oral Narratives*, by Magnús Einarsson (Hull, QC: Canadian Museum of Civilization, 1991), 207.

46 "Heiðruðu landar!" (Honourable countrymen!), *Lögberg*, 25 January 1888, 1.

47 See, e.g., "Mjallhvít," *Nýtt Helgarblað*, 12 December 1988, 16–17; Gene Walz, *Cartoon Charlie: The Life and Art of Animation Pioneer Charles Thorson* (Winnipeg: Great Plains Publications, 1998), 76–8.

48 Frances Swyripa, *Storied Landscapes: Ethno-religious Identity and the Canadian Prairies* (Winnipeg: University of Manitoba Press, 2010), 18.

49 Friðjón Friðriksson to Rev. Jón Bjarnason, 11 August 1881, Correspondence of Friðjón Friðriksson, 1874–5, MG 8 A, 6–7, 1874–85, Letter 23, 2, PAM, Winnipeg.

50 Katherine Harvey, "Amazons and Victims: Resisting Wife-Abuse in Working-Class Montréal, 1869–1879," *Journal of the Canadian Historical Association* 2, no. 1 (1991): 134.

51 In Winnipeg and New Iceland, weather and landscape could pose serious threats to intoxicated men, who could perish from exposure in the winter. See, e.g., Guðrún Þórðarson, *"Vakin um nótt og bjargar manni inn úr kulda"* (Waking up at night and bringing a man in from the cold), in *Sögur úr vesturheimi* (Stories from the New World), by Hallfreður Örn Eiríksson and Olga María Franzdóttir (Reykjavík: Stofnun Árna Magnússonar, 2012), 371–2.

52 Guðmundur Árnason et al., *Minningarrit Stúkunnar Heklu Nr. 33 af Alþjóðareglu Good Templara* (Winnipeg: Ólafs S. Thorgeirssonar Prentsmiðju, 1913), 52.

53 Iceland Parliamentary Documents of the Hearings, vol. B, no. 7 (1934), 2226, quoted in Helgi Gunnlaugsson and John F. Galliher, "Prohibition of Beer in Iceland: An International Test of Symbolic Politics," *Law & Society Review* 20, no. 3 (1986): 341.
54 Bjarni Dalsted, *The Bjarni Dalsted Saga* (Burnsville, MN: Cornerstone Copy Centre, 1988), 9.
55 "To the Shanty Dwellers," *Framfari*, 31 May 1879, 583–4.
56 "Icelanders in Winnipeg," *Framfari*, 22 February 1879, 473.
57 This arrest came several months after Gísli Jónsson's arrest, first reported in *Framfari*; *Manitoba Free Press*, Local and Provincial [News], 20 October 1879, 1.
58 Thorstína Walters, *"Gísli Jónsson frá Saurum"* (Gísli Jónsson from Saura), in *Saga Íslendinga í Northur Dakota* (The history of Icelanders in North Dakota) (Winnipeg: City Printing, 1926), 457.
59 Ólafur Thorgeirsson, "Gísli Jónsson," *Almanak Ólafs S. Thorgeirssonar*, vol. 27 (1921): 34.
60 Clausen cautions that these stories were not verified and are perhaps better understood as indications of the substantial tensions between Dirty Gísli and members of mainstream Icelandic society; see Oscar Clausen, *Saura-Gísla Saga* (Reykjavík: Steindórsprent H.F., 1937), 17–21.
61 "Icelanders in Winnipeg," 473; Wilhelm Kristjanson, *The Icelandic People in Manitoba: A Manitoba Saga* (Winnipeg: Wallingford Press, 1965), 153.
62 "Icelanders in Winnipeg."
63 Jakob Eyfjörd et al., letter to the editor, *Framfari*, 31 May 1879, 584.
64 James H. Gray, *Booze: The Impact of Whisky on the Prairie West* (Toronto: Macmillan, 1972), 6.
65 Magnús Árnason, "A Memoir by Magnus Arnason," trans. Sigurbjörg Stefansson, *Icelandic Canadian* 41, no. 2 (Winter 1982): 15.
66 Nelson Gerrard, *Icelandic River Saga* (Arborg, MB: Sage Publications, 1985), 186.
67 Kristjanson, *Icelandic People in Manitoba*, 198.
68 Gerrard, *Icelandic River Saga*, 155.
69 Kristjanson, *Icelandic People in Manitoba*, 266–7.
70 Gerrard, *Icelandic River Saga*, 153–4.
71 "A Key to Health: Burdock Blood Bitters," *Heimskringla*, 1 August 1889, 4.
72 J.B., *"Frjettablaðið úr byggðum Íslendinga: Frá íslendinga-fljóti, 19 Marz 1891,"* trans. Nelson Gerrard, *Heimskringla*, 1 April 1891, 1.
73 Joe Johnson, interview by author, Arborg, MB, 1 July 2011, tape 2, 3:20 min.
74 Recalled by Lúðvik Kristjánsson, in *Icelandic-Canadian Popular Verse*, by Magnús Einarsson (Hull, QC: Canadian Museum of Civilization, 1994), 122.
75 Gerrard, *Icelandic River Saga*, 156.
76 Johnson, interview, tape 1, 51:50 min.

77 Johnson, interview, tape 1, 47:28 min.
78 George Asgeirson, interview by Laurence Gillespie, 14 August 1989, Icelandic Canadian Fonds, C-1651, PAM, Winnipeg.
79 Metta Johnson, interview by author, Gimli, MB, 22 December 2009.
80 Attributed to Kristján Niels Július by Páll Hallson, in Einarsson, *Icelandic-Canadian Popular Verse*, 138.

### 3. Unsettling Apparitions

1 Nelson Gerrard, *Icelandic River Saga* (Arborg, MB: Sage Publications, 1985), 152.
2 Gunnar Sæmundsson, *"Indjánagrafreitur og tóbak í fararnesti hinna dauða"* (Indian graveyard and tobacco), in *Sögur úr vesturheimi* (Stories from the New World), by Hallfreður Örn Eiríksson and Olga María Franzdóttir (Reykjavík: Stofnun Árna Magnússonar, 1973), 423.
3 Gerrard, *Icelandic River Saga*, 153.
4 The most popular of these is perhaps the story of the restless undead deacon of Myrká, who terrorizes his mistress and must be put to rest by the local practitioner of magic; see "The Deacon of Myrka," in *Icelandic Folktales & Legends*, by Jacqueline Simpson (Berkeley: University of California Press, 1972), 132–6.
5 G. Turville-Petre, "Dreams in Icelandic Tradition," *Folklore* 69, no. 2 (1958): 101.
6 Loftur Reimar Gissurarson and William H. Swatos, Jr., *Icelandic Spiritualism: Mediumship and Modernity in Iceland* (New Brunswick, NJ: Transaction Publishers, 1997), 45.
7 Peter Buse and Andrew Stott, *Ghosts: Deconstruction, Psychoanalysis, History* (London: Palgrave Macmillan, 1999), 10.
8 Buse and Stott, 3.
9 Jacques Derrida, *Spectres of Marx: The State of the Debt, the Work of Mourning and the New International*, trans. Peggy Kamuf (New York: Routledge, 1994), 51.
10 Fredric Jameson, "Marx's Purloined Letter," *New Left Review* 1, no. 209 (January–February 1995): 86.
11 Elizabeth Stern, "Legends of the Dead in Medieval and Modern Iceland" (PhD diss., University of California, Berkeley, 1987), ix.
12 Ruth Leys, *Trauma: A Genealogy* (Chicago: University of Chicago Press, 2000), 7.
13 Gissurarson and Swatos, *Icelandic Spiritualism*, 49.
14 As the broad range of Icelandic Canadian *hjátrú* narratives illustrates, however, narrative components that were borrowed from the North American context were not simply grafted onto older, unchanging

Icelandic narrative structures. Magnús Einarsson, e.g., collected narratives that bore hallmarks of spiritualist symbolism or narratives, including several about a female ghost in white named "Duða," who was eventually contacted and put to rest through a community séance; see Magnús Einarsson, *Icelandic-Canadian Oral Narratives* (Hull, QC: Canadian Museum of Civilization, 1991), 311. Similarly, this collection includes a "vanishing hitchhiker" narrative about an Icelandic Canadian couple en route to visit Expo 67; see Einarsson, 315.

15 Gissurarson and Swatos, *Icelandic Spiritualism*, 49.
16 Kristín Jóhannsdóttir, "The Immigrant Ghost," Margaret and Richard Beck Lecture, University of Victoria, 27 February 2003.
17 Hrund Skulason, interview by Laurence Gillespie, 15 December 1988, Icelandic Canadian Fonds, C-1732, side B, 1:30 min., Provincial Archives of Manitoba, Winnipeg.
18 Jóhannsdóttir, "Immigrant Ghost."
19 Lára M. Daníelsson, *"Um Skottu og borgfjörðsfólkið,"* in *Sögur úr vesturheimi* (Stories from the New World), by Hallfreður Örn Eiríksson and Olga María Franzdóttir (Reykjavík: Stofnun Árna Magnússonar, 1973), 443.
20 Gissurarson and Swatos, *Icelandic Spiritualism*, 62; Ingveldur Jónsdóttir and Soffonías Thorkelson, *Bréf frá Ingu: Héðan og handan* (Winnipeg: Prentsmiðja Ólafs S. Thorgeirssonar, 1931).
21 Jón Karl Helgason, "The Mystery of the Vínarterta: In Search of an Icelandic Canadian Ethnic Identity," *Scandinavian-Canadian Studies* 17 (2007): 42–3.
22 Gissurarson and Swatos, *Icelandic Spiritualism*, 66.
23 Einarsson, *Icelandic-Canadian Oral Narratives*, 7.
24 Einarsson, 3.
25 Although admittedly anecdotal, my field research from 2003 to 2011, which included interviews and conversations with two dozen community members, also gathered recent reports of incidents at "haunted" community places, psychic dreams, and *fylgja* stories (although the *fylgja* tradition had clearly declined in popularity). When I visited community members and "haunted sites," the continuing importance of *hjátrú* belief in community life was conveyed to me.
26 Icelandic anthropologist Tinna Grétarsdóttir recalls that, during her visits to the New Iceland area in 2004, most English-speaking Icelandic Canadians denied believing in the supernatural and declared that most community members were unfamiliar with such narratives. Grétarsdóttir, personal communication with author, 30 June 2008, Winnipeg.
27 Friðjón Friðriksson to Jón Bjarnason, 11 August 1881.
28 Margrét Arngrímsson, "Noises Heard until Body of Drowned Man Is Found," in *Icelandic-Canadian Oral Narratives*, by Magnús Einarsson (Hull, QC: Canadian Museum of Civilization, 1991), 121–2.

29 Bergljót Sigurðsson, *"Reimt í húsi hjá indjánagrafreit á Nesi við Íslendingafljót"* (Hauntings in a house by an Indian graveyard at Nes on the Icelandic River), in *Sögur úr vesturheimi* (Stories from the New World), by Hallfreður Örn Eiríksson and Olga María Franzdóttir (Reykjavík: Stofnun Árna Magnússonar, 1973), 520.
30 Rev. Albert Kristjanson, "Boy Sits in Graveyard to Overcome Fear of the Dark," in *Icelandic-Canadian Oral Narratives*, by Magnús Einarsson (Hull, QC: Canadian Museum of Civilization, 1991), 380–1; "Man Seen in Iceland after Death in Vancouver," in Einarsson, 282–3.
31 See note 14 above.
32 Jón Árnason, "Dead Woman Promoted to Ghost," in *Icelandic-Canadian Oral Narratives*, by Magnús Einarsson (Hull, QC: Canadian Museum of Civilization, 1991), 317.
33 Gissurarson and Swatos, *Icelandic Spiritualism*, 48.
34 See, e.g., Torfhildur Þorsteindóttir Hólm's collection of women's stories from the immigrant generation in *Þjóðsögur og sagnir* (Folk tales and legends) (Reykjavík: Almenna Bókafélagið, 1962), 59, 108, 208.
35 See, e.g., Einarsson, *Icelandic-Canadian Oral Narratives*, 404; Hallgrímur Stadfeldt, "Elf Woman Tries to Lure Young Boy," in *Icelandic-Canadian Oral Narratives*, by Magnús Einarsson (Hull, QC: Canadian Museum of Civilization, 1991), 345.
36 See, e.g., Björn Bjarnason, "Elves Borrow Scabbard," and Þórunn Vigfússon, "Elves Borrow Carpenter's Tool," in *Icelandic-Canadian Oral Narratives*, by Magnús Einarsson (Hull, QC: Canadian Museum of Civilization, 1991), 347–9.
37 Margrét Bjarnason, "Elves Borrow Mittens," in *Icelandic-Canadian Oral Narratives*, by Magnús Einarsson (Hull, QC: Canadian Museum of Civilization, 1991), 346.
38 Bragi Simundsson, interview by author, Geysir, MB, 2 June 2011. Except for their lush forests, British Columbia's and Washington state's proximity to mountain ranges and the ocean made Icelandic settlements some of the most geographically similar to Iceland and the rocky, traditional homes of *huldufólk*. In Point Roberts, WA, some community members retain *huldufólk* belief and respect their affiliated territory. Community members there have avoided disturbing and ploughing too close to a large boulder in a local farm field after an old woman in the community claimed that it was affiliated with hidden people.
39 Thorstína Walters, *Modern Sagas: The Story of the Icelanders in North America* (Fargo: North Dakota Institute for Regional Studies, 1953), 10.
40 Björn Bjarnason, "Ghost of Old Woman Takes Revenge," in *Icelandic-Canadian Oral Narratives*, by Magnús Einarsson (Hull, QC: Canadian Museum of Civilization, 1991), 119–20.

41 Bjarnason, 120.
42 Lára Gudmundsson, "Girl Sees Ghost of Migrant from Iceland," in *Icelandic-Canadian Oral Narratives*, by Magnús Einarsson (Hull, QC: Canadian Museum of Civilization, 1991), 273.
43 Cliff and Lilja Holm, interview by author, Geysir, MB, 2 June 2011.
44 Magnús Elíasson, *"Draumur um blauta og klakaða menn sem frusu á Winnipegvatni"* (Dream of soaking wet men who froze on Lake Winnipeg), in *Sögur úr vesturheimi* (Stories from the New World), by Hallfreður Örn Eiríksson and Olga María Franzdóttir (Reykjavík: Stofnun Árna Magnússonar, 1973), 339.
45 Elíasson.
46 See, e.g., "Dog Ghost Haunts Camp," in *Icelandic-Canadian Oral Narratives*, by Magnús Einarsson (Hull, QC: Canadian Museum of Civilization, 1991), 300.
47 Hjálmur F. Daníelsson, *"Drengur sér afturgenginn hund"* (Boy sees ghost of dog), in *Sögur úr vesturheimi* (Stories from the New World), by Hallfreður Örn Eiríksson and Olga María Franzdóttir (Reykjavík: Stofnun Árna Magnússonar, 1973), 396.
48 Tímoteus Böðvarsson, "Attendant Fetch Heralds Arrival of Guest," in *Icelandic-Canadian Oral Narratives*, by Magnús Einarsson (Hull, QC: Canadian Museum of Civilization, 1991), 259–61.
49 Böðvarsson, 260.
50 Gísli Ágúst Gunnlaugsson, "'Everyone's Been Nice to Me, Especially the Dogs': Foster-Children and Young Paupers in Nineteenth-Century Southern Iceland," *Journal of Social History* (Winter 1993): 345.
51 Lárus Nordal, "Couple Disturbed by Cries of Man's Attendant Fetch," in *Icelandic-Canadian Oral Narratives*, by Magnús Einarsson (Hull, QC: Canadian Museum of Civilization, 1991), 255–8.
52 Nordal, 258.
53 There are several exceptions to this claim as some *hjátrú* narratives were shaped by local First Nations cultural, historical, and/or spiritual components, particularly in more northerly communities. See, e.g., reports from Icelandic fishermen about the apparition of a *lækniskona* (medicine woman) from Hodgson attacking a Cree priest from Jackhead, MB: *"Púkar sem indjánakerling ræður yfir sækja að presti þegar hún deyr,"* in *Sögur úr vesturheimi* (Stories from the New World), by Hallfreður Örn Eiríksson and Olga María Franzdóttir (Reykjavík: Stofnun Árna Magnússonar, 1973), 397–8.
54 Ingólfur Bjarnason, "Man Sees Murdered Indian of Ghost Island," in *Icelandic-Canadian Oral Narratives*, by Magnús Einarsson (Hull, QC: Canadian Museum of Civilization, 1991), 342–3.
55 Bjarnason, 343.

56 For a description of variations on the story, see Anne Brydon's discussion, which includes an interview with Trausti Vigfússon's daughter, in "Dreams and Claims: Icelandic-Saulteaux Interactions in the Manitoba Interlake," *Journal of Canadian Studies* 36, no. 2 (2001): 170, 186–7.
57 The "reminder dream" appears in numerous variations of the story; however, Brydon reports that Trausti's daughter, Tóta, rejected this part of the story as an embellishment. Instead, she recalled that her father "recognized immediately the necessity of obedience" following such a dream and did not need to be reminded; see Brydon, 165. For examples of the reminder dream narrative, see Kristine Kristofferson, "John Ramsay," *Lögberg-Heimskringla*, 4 June 1970, 8.
58 Brydon, "Dreams and Claims," 184.
59 Helga Ögmundardóttir, *"Ímyndir, sjálfsmyndir og vald í samskiptum Indíána og Íslendinga í Vesturheimi 1875–1930"* (Image, identity and power in Indigenous-Icelandic relations in North America 1875–1930) (master's thesis, Háskóli Íslands, 2002).
60 For a larger discussion of this issue, see Laurie K. Bertram, "'Eskimo' Immigrants and Colonial Soldiers: Icelandic Immigrants and the North-West Resistance, 1885," *Canadian Historical Review* 99, no. 1 (2018): 65–8.
61 Björn Bjarnason, "Man Attacked in Haunted Shack," in *Icelandic-Canadian Oral Narratives*, by Magnús Einarsson (Hull, QC: Canadian Museum of Civilization, 1991), 290.
62 Bjarnason, 291.
63 Stefán Stefánsson, *"Indjáni á skógarbraut hverfur"* (Indian on forest road disappears), in *Sögur úr vesturheimi* (Stories from the New World), by Hallfreður Örn Eiríksson and Olga María Franzdóttir (Reykjavík: Stofnun Árna Magnússonar, 1973), 399.
64 Hallgrímur Stadfeldt, "Battling the Giant of Welsh Harbour," in *Icelandic-Canadian Oral Narratives*, by Magnús Einarsson (Hull, QC: Canadian Museum of Civilization, 1991), 291–5.
65 Guttormur J. Guttormsson, quoted in Gerrard, *Icelandic River Saga*, 152.
66 Guttormur J. Guttormsson, "Jón Guttormsson and Pálína Ketilsdóttir," in *My Parents: Memoirs of New World Icelanders*, ed. Birna Bjarnadóttir and Finnbogi Guðmundsson (Winnipeg: University of Manitoba Press, 2007), 86.
67 Gerrard, *Icelandic River Saga*, 317.
68 Hallgrímur Stadfeldt, *"Rauðar eða brúnar kindur steypast út um glugga á húsinu á Nesi"* (Red or brown sheep pour out of a window of the house at Nes), in *Sögur úr vesturheimi* (Stories from the New World), by Hallfreður Örn Eiríksson and Olga María Franzdóttir (Reykjavík: Stofnun Árna Magnússonar, 1973), 516.
69 Sigurðsson, *"Reimt í húsi hjá indjánagrafreit,"* 462.
70 Stadfeldt, *"Rauðar eða brúnar kindur,"* 516.

71 Sigurðsson, *"Reimt í húsi hjá indjánagrafreit,"* 462.
72 Sæmundsson, *"Indjánagrafreitur og tóbak,"* 422–3.
73 Bergljót Sigurðsson, *"Guttormur Guttormsson sér indjánadreng sem hverfur síðan"* (Guttormur Guttormson sees an Indian ghost that then vanishes), in *Sögur úr vesturheimi* (Stories from the New World), by Hallfreður Örn Eiríksson and Olga María Franzdóttir (Reykjavík: Stofnun Árna Magnússonar, 1973), 520.
74 Sigurðsson, *"Reimt í húsi hjá indjánagrafreit,"* 519.
75 Stern, "Legends of the Dead in Medieval and Modern Iceland," ix.

## 4. Main Street Vikings

1 "John David Eaton and Signy Stephenson Wed at Lovely 'Kawandag,'" *Winnipeg Free Press*, 10 August 1933, 10.
2 "Eaton-Stefansson," *Globe* (Toronto), 10 August 1933, 8; "John David Eaton and Signy Stephenson," 10.
3 Franca Iacovetta notes that this type of "celebratory or filiopietistic bent" is typical of many ethnic historiographies published in the 1960s and 1970s; see Franca Iacovetta, "Manly Militants, Cohesive Communities, and Defiant Domestics: Writing about Immigrants in Canadian Historical Scholarship," *Labour/Le Travail* 36 (Fall 1995): 222.
4 *"Íslenzka víkingaskipið vinnur fyrstu verðlaun,"* *Lögberg*, 26 June 1924, 1.
5 See, e.g., David C. Harvey, "The History of Heritage," in *The Ashgate Reader Companion to Heritage and Identity*, ed. Brian J. Graham and Peter Howard (London: Ashgate, 2008), 19; Ian McKay, *Quest of the Folk: Antimodernism and Cultural Selection in Twentieth-Century Nova Scotia* (Montreal and Kingston: McGill-Queen's University Press, 1994), 4.
6 Kirsten Wolf, "Emigration and Mythmaking: The Case of the Icelanders in Canada," *Canadian Ethnic Studies Journal* 33, no. 2 (2001): 2–3.
7 A.R. Ford, "Icelanders," in *Strangers at Our Gates: Or, Coming Canadians*, by J.S. Woodsworth (Toronto: Missionary Society of the Methodist Church, 1909), 92.
8 Ford, 92, 89.
9 Elisabeth I. Ward, "Reflections on an Icon: Vikings in American Culture," in *Vikings: The North Atlantic Saga*, ed. William W. Fitzhugh and Elisabeth I. Ward (Washington, DC: Smithsonian Institution Press, 2000), 370–1; Andrew Wawn, *The Vikings and the Victorians: Inventing the Old North in Nineteenth-Century Britain* (Cambridge: D.S. Brewer, 2000), 3–6.
10 Geraldine Barnes, *Viking America: The First Millennium* (Cambridge: D.S. Brewer, 2001), 44.
11 Marie A. Brown, *The Icelandic Discoverers of America: Honour to Whom Honour Is Due* (London: Trubner, 1887), 14.

12 Mark Paul Richard, "'This Is Not a Catholic Nation': The Ku Klux Klan Confronts Franco-Americans in Maine," *New England Quarterly* 82, no. 2 (2009): 289.
13 Ward, "Reflections on an Icon," 366.
14 Ward, 2, 367.
15 Salome Halldorson, "Speech of Miss Salome Halldorson Member for St. George, Delivered in the Manitoba Legislative Assembly, 26 February 1937," booklet, MG 14. B3, 1, Provincial Archives of Manitoba (PAM), Winnipeg.
16 "Nationalist Propaganda in Manitoba," *Manitoba Free Press*, 14 February 1916, 9.
17 Wilhelm Kristjanson, *The Icelandic People in Manitoba: A Manitoba Saga* (Winnipeg: Wallingford Press, 1965), 505–6.
18 Jonina Britton, interview by author, Winnipeg, 4 February 2003; Carol Hryhorchuk, interview by author, Riverton, MB, 21 May 2009.
19 Guðrún H. Finnsdóttir, "Lost Tracks," in *Writings by Western Icelandic Women*, ed. and trans. Kirsten Wolf (Winnipeg: University of Manitoba Press, 1997): 88–108, 109.
20 Haraldur Bessason, "A Few Specimens of North American Icelandic," *Scandinavian Studies* 39, no. 2 (1967): 118–19.
21 Birna Arnbjörnsdóttir, *North American Icelandic: The Life of a Language* (Winnipeg: University of Manitoba Press, 2006), 46.
22 Arnbjörndóttir, 47.
23 Þorsteinn Þ. Þorsteinsson, *Saga Íslendinga í Vesturheimi* (Saga of Icelanders in North America) (Winnipeg: Columbia Press), 234, quoted in Arnbjörnsdóttir, 30.
24 Kristjanson, *Icelandic People in Manitoba*, 361.
25 Rev. Albert Kristjansson, "Boy Beats Brits in Spelling Bee," in *Icelandic-Canadian Oral Narratives*, by Magnús Einarsson (Hull, QC: Canadian Museum of Civilization, 1991), 390–1.
26 Ryan Eyford, "From Prairie Goolies to Canadian Cyclones: The Transformation of the 1920 Winnipeg Falcons," *Sport History Review* 37 (2006): 6.
27 Gísli Pálsson, *Travelling Passions: The Hidden Life of Vilhjalmur Stefansson*, trans. Keneva Kunz (Winnipeg: University of Manitoba Press, 2003), 151.
28 Eyford, "From Prairie Goolies to Canadian Cyclones," 8.
29 Sarah Michaelson recalled getting an angry call after using the term *goolie* on her Winnipeg radio show in 2006; personal communication with author, 22 October 2008.
30 Helga Gerrard, interview by author, 9 June 2011.
31 Gerrard, interview.
32 "Jóhanna Guðrún Skaptason," *Lögberg-Heimskringla*, 3 November 1960, 2.

33 Jón Sigurðsson Chapter IODE, *Minningarrit Íslenzkra Hermanna 1914–1918* (Winnipeg: Félagið Jón Sigurðsson, 1923); Jón Sigurðsson Chapter IODE, *Veterans of Icelandic Descent, World War II, 1939–1945* (Winnipeg: Jón Sigurðsson Chapter IODE, 1990); Jón Sigurðsson Chapter IODE, *A Supplement to Veterans of Icelandic Descent* (Winnipeg: Jón Sigurðsson IODE, 1993).

34 This number represents those identified by the Jón Sigurðsson Chapter IODE in its book on Icelandic soldiers, although not all Icelandic enlistees could be identified. Wilhelm Kristjanson contends that this is "probably well below the true figure"; see Jón Sigurðsson Chapter IODE, *Minningarrit Íslenzkra Hermanna 1914–1918*, 44; Kristjanson, *Icelandic People in Manitoba*, 380.

35 Frances Swyripa, *Storied Landscapes: Ethno-religious Identity and the Canadian Prairies* (Winnipeg: University of Manitoba Press, 2010), 166.

36 "197th Making Rapid Strides in Recruiting," *Winnipeg Evening Tribune*, 6 May 1916, 26.

37 Laura Goodman Salverson, *The Viking Heart* (Toronto: McClelland and Stewart, 1975), 297.

38 See, e.g., "Icelandic Newspapers and Periodicals – Voröld," Chief Press Censor files 1918–19, RG 6-E, file 352-1, Library and Archives Canada (LAC), Ottawa.

39 Royden Loewen and Gerald Friesen, *Immigrants in Prairie Cities: Ethnic Diversity in Twentieth-Century Canada* (Toronto: University of Toronto Press, 2009), 47.

40 Loewen and Friesen, 48.

41 Frances Swyripa, *Wedded to the Cause: Ukrainian-Canadian Women and Ethnic Identity, 1891–1991* (Toronto: University of Toronto Press, 1993), 52.

42 Howard H. Palmer, "Reluctant Hosts: Anglo-Canadian Views of Multiculturalism in the Twentieth Century," *Cultural Diversity and Canadian Education: Issues and Innovations* 130 (1984): 25.

43 Kristjanson, *Icelandic People in Manitoba*, 250–1.

44 Einar Arnason, interview by Laurence Gillespie, 20 July 1988, Icelandic Canadian Frón, C-1646, side B, 25:55–27:00 min, PAM, Winnipeg.

45 For a discussion of community conflicts over loyalty and commemoration in the wake of the Great War, see Víðar Hreinsson, *Wakeful Nights: Stephan G. Stephansson, Icelandic-Canadian Poet* (Calgary: Benson Ranch, 2012), 490–5.

46 Hrund Skulason, interview by Laurence Gillespie, 15 December 1988, Icelandic Canadian Frón, C-1733, side B, 18:20 min, PAM, Winnipeg.

47 "Court Satisfied with Johannesson's Denial: Editor of *Voröld* May Bring Action for Perjury," *Manitoba Free Press*, 13 March 1920, 4.

48 Hreinsson, *Wakeful Nights*, 409.

49 Hreinsson, 493.

50 Gregory S. Kealy and Reg Whitaker, eds., *RCMP Security Bulletins: The Early Years, 1919–1929* (St. John's: Canadian Committee on Labour History, 1996), 267.
51 See, e.g., Laurie K. Bertram, "'Fight like Auður': Gender, Ethnicity and Dissent in the Career of Salome Halldorson, Social Credit MLA, 1936–41," *Icelandic Connections* 62, no. 3 (Fall 2010): 41–57.
52 Annette Kolodny, *In Search of First Contact: The Vikings of Vinland, the Peoples of the Dawnland, and the Anglo-American Anxiety of Discovery* (Durham, NC: Duke University Press, 2012), 209.
53 "Eirik the Red," in *Eirik the Red and Other Icelandic Sagas*, ed. Gwyn Jones (Oxford: Oxford University Press, 2008), 152–3.
54 Tinna Grétarsdóttir argues that immigrants also occasionally launched tributes to Freydís and Leifur's Christian sister-in-law, Guðríður Þorbjarnardóttir, whom they referred to as "the first white mother in America"; see Tinna Grétarsdóttir, "'Art Is in Our Heart': Transnational Complexities of Art Projects and Neoliberal Governmentality" (PhD diss., Department of Anthropology, Temple University, 2010), 148–58.
55 Jónas Thor, *Íslendingadagurinn: An Illustrated History* (Gimli, MB: Icelandic Festival of Manitoba, 1988), 38.
56 Jón Bildfell, *"Sköllóttar konur"* (Bald women), *Lögberg*, 10 July 1924, 4.
57 *"Íslendingadagsnefndarfundur að Árborg"* (Icelandic Day planning meeting in Arborg), *Heimskringla*, 11 June 1924, 1.
58 Bildfell, *"Sköllóttar konur,"* 4.
59 *"Fróðleikur og forvitni"* (Knowledge and curiosity), *Heimskringla*, 22 October 1924, 1.
60 Bertram, "'Fight like Auður,'" 41–57.
61 Carrin Orrling, "The Old Norse Dream," in *Vikings: The North Atlantic Saga*, ed. William W. Fitzhugh and Elisabeth I. Ward (Washington, DC: Smithsonian Institution Press, 2000), 362–3.
62 Julia Zernack, "Old Norse-Icelandic Literature and German Culture," in *Iceland and Images of the North*, ed. Sumarliði R. Ísleifsson (Quebec City: Presses de l'Université du Québec), 2011, 175.
63 Jón Karl Helgason, *The Rewriting of Njáls's Saga: Translation, Ideology and Icelandic Sagas* (Toronto: Multilingual Matters, 1999), 36.
64 H.W. Koch, *Hitler Youth: Origins and Developments, 1922–1945* (Lanham, MD: Rowman and Littlefield, 2000), 144.
65 Laura Goodman Salverson, editorial, *Icelandic Canadian* 1, no. 1 (October 1942): 2.
66 Gunnar Karlsson, *Iceland's 1100 Years: History of a Marginal Society* (Reykjavík: Mál og Menning, 2000), 313. For North American examples, see the references to Norse blood and war in Salverson, 1–3.
67 Although discussions of the Norse past endured in the *Icelandic Canadian* for the course of the war, its content turned increasingly to immigrant

memoirs, political histories of Iceland, and contemporary concerns, including news about enlistees and scholarship programs. Other English-language content produced throughout the war, including *Iceland on the Prairies* by the National Film Board (NFB), almost completely omitted references to the Viking past.

68 For a detailed discussion of these themes in the Icelandic context, see Daisy Neijmann, "'A Fabulous Potency': Masculinity in Icelandic Occupation Literature," in *Men after War*, ed. Stephen McVeigh and Nicola Cooper (New York: Routledge, 2013), 152–69.
69 "Threat in Air Seen by Drew," *Globe and Mail*, 26 January 1939, 1.
70 Donald F. Bittner, *The Lion and the White Falcon: Britain and Iceland in the World War II Era* (Hamden, CT: Archon Books, 1983), 16.
71 Karlsson, *Iceland's 1100 Years*, 314, 319.
72 Neijmann, "'A Fabulous Potency,'" 155.
73 John McLure, interview by author, London, ON, 21 July 2010, tape 1, 7:50 min., 28:45 min. For additional references to heckling and spitting in retaliation for sexual harassment and livestock theft, see Bittner, *Lion and the White Falcon*, 95.
74 Bittner, 103–5.
75 High Commissioner for Canada in Great Britain to the Secretary of State for External Affairs (ENG), London, 28 June 1940, telegraph, RG 25, vol. 2749, file 501-1-40C, LAC, Ottawa.
76 For example, "Resentment and scorn by the Icelanders was evident, and coldness and disdain facially expressed ... [they] had for generations known no soldiers, seen no weapons of war, [and] wanted neither"; see Singleton Gates, "Breaking the Ice in Iceland," *Icelandic Canadian*, March 1944, 14.
77 "Iceland: A Hard Life," *Time*, 13 January 1941, 23.
78 "Iceland."
79 Stuart Legg, *Food, Weapon of Conquest*, NFB, Ottawa, 1941.
80 "Iceland," *Time*, 23.
81 V.J. Eylands, letter to *Time*; repr., *Lögberg*, 16 January 1941, 4.
82 "Iceland," *Time*, 23.
83 Karlsson, *Iceland's 1100 Years*, 316.
84 Neijmann, "'A Fabulous Potency,'" 155–6, 162.
85 Neijmann, 158.
86 Herdís Helgadóttir, *Úr fjötrum: Íslenskar konur og erlendur her* (Icelandic women and the foreign army) (Reykjavík: Mál og Menning, 2001), 185–6; trans. and repr., Minjasafn Reykjavíkur, 2005.
87 Kenneth Campbell, *Keeping the Boats Afloat: Boatbuilding Communities of the North West* (Victoria: Royal Museum of British Columbia, 2006).
88 Frances Hanson, *Memories of Osland* (Prince Rupert, BC: Excel Printing, 1997), 83.

89 J.B. Skaptason to G.H. Lash, Director of Public Information, 30 July 1940, RG 25, vol. 3022, file 385-A-40, LAC, Ottawa.
90 Ivana Caccia, *Managing the Canadian Mosaic in Wartime: Shaping Citizenship Policy, 1939–45* (Montreal and Kingston: McGill-Queen's University Press, 2010), 38–9.
91 J.T. Thorson to O.D. Skelton, 10 September 1940, RG 25, vol. 3022, file 385-A-40, LAC, Ottawa.
92 J.T. Thorson to Mackenzie King, 18 March 1941, MG 31 E38, vol. 25, file 8, LAC, Ottawa.
93 Radford Crawley, *Iceland on the Prairies* (Ottawa: NFB, 1941).
94 Caccia, *Managing the Canadian Mosaic*, 51.
95 Einar Jónsson and S.J. Jóhannesson, *Icelandic for Soldiers* (Winnipeg: Columbia Press / Canadian Legion War Services, n.d.), 5.
96 Jónsson and Jóhannesson, 5–6.
97 H. Bruce Humberstone, *Iceland* (Los Angeles: Twentieth Century Fox, 1942).
98 *"Fáránleg kvikmynd, sem er látin gerast í Reykjavík"* (Ridiculous film that is supposed to take place in Reykjavík), *Morgunblaðið*, 19 September 1942.
99 Guðmundur Jónsson, "Iceland, OEEC and the Trade Liberalisation of the 1950s," *Scandinavian Economic History Review* 52, no. 2–3 (2004): 69; and Helge Danielsen, "Making Friends at Court: Slow and Indirect Media in US Public Diplomacy in Norway, 1950–1965," *Contemporary European History* 18, no. 2 (2009): 179–80.
100 Danielsen, 186.
101 Thorstína Walters to Milton Young, 8 January 1954, box 1, folder 9, MSS 630, "Correspondence, 1954," Thorstína Walters Papers, Institute for Regional and Ethnic Studies, Fargo, ND; Thorstína Walters, *Modern Sagas: The Story of the Icelanders in North America* (Fargo: North Dakota Institute for Regional Studies, 1953).
102 "Viking Spirits Sparkle at Gimli Celebration," *Winnipeg Free Press*, 1 August 1967, 1.
103 "Viking Spirits Sparkle."

### 5. Icelandic Cake Fight

1 Bill Holm, *The Heart Can Be Filled Anywhere on Earth* (Minneapolis, MN: Milkweed Press, 2000), 217.
2 W.D. Valgardson, "Vínarterta by M," *wdvalgardsonkaffihus.com Blog*, 6 August 2012, http://wdvalgardsonkaffihus.com/blog/2012/08/06/vinarterta-by-m/.
3 See, e.g., Geir H. Gunnarsson, "How Many Prunes Are in One *Vínarterta*?," *Lögberg-Heimskringla*, 13 January 1978, 2; Jón Karl Helgason, "The Mystery of *Vínarterta*: In Search of an Icelandic Ethnic Identity,"

*Scandinavian-Canadian Studies* 17 (2007): 36–52; Alison Gillmor, "Towering Torte," *Winnipeg Free Press*, 24 November 2012.

4 Elisabet Polson, interviewed in Helen Gougeon, "Icelandic Dishes," *Times Colonist* (Victoria), 16 May 1953, 35.

5 Sigurður Gylfi Magnússon, *Wasteland with Words: A Social History of Iceland* (London: Reaktion, 2010), 32.

6 Carol Gold, *Danish Cookbooks: Domesticity & National Identity, 1616–1901* (Copenhagen: Museum Tusculanum Press / University of Copenhagen Press, 2007), 20.

7 See, e.g., the *Wienertærte* recipes in the following cookbooks: Line Eibe, *Kogebog for smaae og store huusholdninger, indeholdende anviisning til en mængde: Forskjellige retters og kagers tillavning, samt syltning og slagtning* (Copenhagen: s.n., 1849); Clara Margrethe Fristrup, ed., *Fuldstændig kogebog, samt anviisning til at bage og sylte, saavel for smaa som store huusholdninge: Efter mange aars egen erfaring*, trans. Emily Albertsen and Martin Albertsen (Copenhagen: s.n., 1840), Collection of Landsbókasafn Íslands; Mathilde Roedsted Schmidt, *Huusholdningsbog, en anviisning for unge koner og piger til selv i enhver henseende at kunne bestyre deres huus: Forfattet af en huusmoder* (Velje, Denmark: N.O., 1843); Christine Rostrup, *Fem hundrede recepter i kogekunsten, eller veiledning for bestyrere af herskabskjøkkener, som og til huusholdningsbrug* (Copenhagen, s.n., 1844).

8 Darra Goldstein, ed., with a foreword by Sidney Mintz, *The Oxford Companion to Sugar and Sweets* (Oxford University Press, 2015), s.v.v. "Vienna," 770.

9 Although stories abound about the Turkish origin of Viennese foods, the actual influence of Turkey is a matter of some debate; see Goldstein.

10 Lovise Beate Augustine Friedel, "Wienertærte," *Nye og fuldstændige confecture* (New and complete confectionery) (Copenhagen, s.n., 1795), 6; repr., Bi Skaarup et al., "*Madhistorie: Kager*," trans. Emily Albertsen and Martin Albertsen, 2006, http://madhistorie.dk/opskrifter/wienertarte1795.html.

11 Klaus Nielsen, "Learning to Do Things with Things: Apprenticeship in Bakery as Economy and Practice," in *Doing Things with Things*, ed. Alan Costall and Ole Dreier (London: Ashgate, 2012), 212–3.

12 Friedel, "*Wienertærte*," 6.

13 Fristrup, "*Wienertærte.*"

14 Þóra Andrea Jónsdóttir, *Ný matreiðslubók ásamt ávísun um litun, þvott o. fl.* (A new cookbook along with advice on dyeing, washing and more) (Akureyri, Iceland: H. Helgasyni, 1858), 62, 128.

15 Jeannette Allis Bastian, *Owning Memory: How a Caribbean Community Lost Its Archives and Found Its History* (London: Libraries Unlimited, 2003), 58–9.

16 Nanna Rögnvaldardóttir and Michael R. Leaman, "Þorrablót – Icelandic Feasting," in *Celebration: Proceedings of the Oxford Symposium on Food and Cookery 2011* (Oxford: Oxford Symposium, 2012), 277–83, 278.
17 The number of Icelandic newspaper advertisements for prunes increased dramatically between 1889 and 1899; see, e.g., "*Í verzlun Sigfúsar Jónssonar,*" *Norðurljósið*, 28 October 1889, 72; "M. Johannessen," *Ísafold*, 3 August 1889, 248; "Verzlun Sigurður Waage," *Fjallkona*, 23 December 1897, 205.
18 Trine Hahnemann, "Scandinavia," in *The Oxford Companion to Sugar and Sweets*, ed. Darra Goldstein, with a foreword by Sidney Mintz (Oxford: Oxford University Press, 2015), 598.
19 See, e.g., Fristrup, "*Wienertærte.*"
20 I draw here from the twentieth- and twenty-first-century collections of intergenerational nineteenth-century objects and traditions found in the homes of oral history contributors as well as the New Iceland Heritage Museum, Manitoba Museum, Hecla Island Historic Village, Icelandic State Park, Pembina County Historical Museum, and Canadian Museum of History. For a more detailed discussion of the endurance of nineteenth-century material traditions and cultures, see Laurie K. Bertram, "Public Spectacles, Private Narratives: Canadian Heritage Campaigns, Maternal Trauma and the Rise of the Koffort (Trunk) in Icelandic-Canadian Popular Memory," *Material Culture Review* 71 (2010): 39–53.
21 "*Þorrablót,*" *Lögberg*, 22 January 1903, 1.
22 Carol (Thorarinson) Hryhorchuk, interview by author, Riverton, MB, 21 May 2009; Agnes (Bardal) Comack, interview by author, Winnipeg, 10 May 2009.
23 "*Um jólin,*" *Lögberg*, 17 December 1903, 8.
24 "Geysir Bakery," *Lögberg*, 19 December 1939, 10; "Geysir Bakery," *Lögberg*, 21 December 1939, 11.
25 Madeleine Day, "Danish and Icelandic Women Come to F.P. Kitchen," *Winnipeg Free Press*, 1 December 1936, 7.
26 Early precursors of these festivals existed during the 1920s and early 1930s, in both the United States and Canada, although Manitoba events tended to focus more on folk traditions, including music, textile production, and costumes, rather than food. *Vínarterta* may have also not become popular as a symbol of Icelandic culture in the 1920s because of the number of those from the immigrant generation who were still living and understood the torte as Viennese, not Icelandic. For more on interwar events, see Stuart Henderson, "'While There Is Still Time ...': J. Murray Gibbon and the Spectacle of Difference in Three CPR Folk Festivals, 1928–1931," *Journal of Canadian Studies* 39, no. 1 (2004): 139–74;

Diana Selig, *Americans All: The Cultural Gifts Movement* (Cambridge, MA: Harvard University Press, 2008).

27 Marcus Lee Hansen, "The Problem of the Third Generation Immigrant," lecture delivered to the Augustana Historical Society (Rock Island, IL: Augustana Historical Society, 1938), 6.
28 Hansen, 9.
29 Hansen, 10.
30 See, e.g., the following wartime films, all directed by Laura Boulton for the National Film Board: *Polish Dance*, 1941; *New Scotland*, 1941; *Ukrainian Winter Holidays*, 1942.
31 US Department of State, *The American Scene: Swedes in America*, ca. 1941–5, National Archives, National Archives Identifier 11940.
32 Kathleen B. Gilbert, "Iceland," *Grade Teacher* 59 (February 1942): 58.
33 Clare Marcus, "Tasty Icelandic Dishes," *Winnipeg Free Press*, 4 August 1962, 18.
34 Franca Iacovetta and Valerie J. Korinek. "Jell-O Salads, One-Stop Shopping, and Maria the Homemaker: The Gender Politics of Food," in *Sisters or Strangers? Immigrant, Ethnic, and Racialized Women in Canadian History*, ed. Marlene Epp, Franca Iacovetta, and Frances Swyripa (Toronto: University of Toronto Press, 2004), 192–3.
35 Valur Ingimundarson writes that resistance to a continued occupation reflected the public's resentment of the stationing of so many troops in Iceland during the Second World War as well as elevated nationalism in the wake of the 1944 establishment of the Republic of Iceland; see Valur Ingimundarson, "Immunizing against the American Other: Racism, Nationalism and Gender in U.S.-Icelandic Military Relations during the Cold War," *Journal of Cold War Studies* 6, no. 4 (Fall 2004): 65.
36 See, e.g., "Atlantic Bloc," *Winnipeg Free Press*, 31 March 1949, 1, 6.
37 US Department of State, "Program to Decrease the Vulnerability of the Icelandic Government to Communist Seizure of Power," 24 November 1949, *Foreign Relations 1950*, vol. 3 (S/S-NSC Files: Lot 63 D 351: NSC 40 Series), 1458, 1459.
38 Kenneth Osgoode, *Total Cold War: Eisenhower's Secret Propaganda Battle at Home and Abroad* (Lawrence: University Press of Kansas, 2006); Helge Danielsen, "Making Friends at Court: Slow and Indirect Media in US Public Diplomacy in Norway, 1950–1965," *Contemporary European History* 18, no. 2 (2009): 181.
39 For reactions to the story, see the energetic report on the honour by *Lögberg*'s women's interests columnist: Ingibjörg Jónsson, *Áhúgamál kvenna* (Women's interests), *Lögberg*, 15 December 1949, 12.
40 Helen McCully, "The Best Cook in Our Town," *McCall's*, December 1949, 72.

41 Jónsson, *Áhugmál kvenna*.
42 Margaret Sigvaldason, "Address of Miss Canada," *Lögberg*, 5 July 1951, 5.
43 Helgason, "Mystery of *Vínarterta*," 44.
44 Nanna Rögnvaldardóttir, communication with EJM and TPH, repr. with permission, on "About Vínarterta," *Recipes from OUR Kitchen* (blog), accessed 20 July 2019, http://etherwork.net/recipes/vinartertainfo.html.
45 See, e.g., Gillmor, "Towering Torte."
46 Gunnarsson, "How Many Prunes?"
47 Gunnarsson.
48 Helgason, "Mystery of *Vínarterta*," 48.
49 Matt Kwong, "Don't Ask Icelanders How to Make Their Traditional Christmas Cake," *Maclean's*, 24 December 2012, https://www.macleans.ca/society/life/dont-ask-icelanders-how-to-make-their-traditional-christmas-cake/.
50 Louise Kahler, comment on W.D. Valgardson, "Vínarterta by M," 8 August 2012, repr. with permission.
51 Ben MacFee-Sigurdson, written communication with author, 30 November 2011.
52 Valgardson, "Vínarterta by M."
53 Sarah Arnason, written communication with author, 10 February 2010, Atlanta and Toronto.
54 Jennifer Miller, interview by author (written communication), Ottawa and Toronto, 15 February 2010.
55 Brett Lamoureux, interview by author (written communication), Winnipeg and Toronto, 12 February 2010.
56 Maxine Ingalls, interview by author, Hecla Island, MB, 30 June 2011.
57 Colleen Simmard, "Band Election of the Year," *Winnipeg Free Press*, 21 March 2009, A17.
58 Elizabeth and Tom Dorey, personal communication with author, 17 December 2017.
59 Ladies Aid of the First Lutheran Church, *Cook Book* (Winnipeg: s.n., ca. 1938), private collection.
60 "Kristín Gunnlaugson," *Lögberg-Heimskringla*, 15 January 1983, 7.
61 Donna Gabaccia, *We Are What We Eat: Ethnic Food and the Making of Americans* (Cambridge, MA: Harvard University Press, 1998), 176.
62 S. Holyk Hunchuk, "Feeding the Dead: The Ukrainian Food Colossi of the Canadian Prairies," in *Edible Histories, Cultural Politics: Towards a Canadian Food History*, ed. Franca Iacovetta, Valerie J. Korinek, and Marlene Epp (Toronto: University of Toronto Press, 2012), 142; Marlene Epp, "The Semiotics of Zwieback: Feast and Famine in the Narratives of Mennonite Refugee Women," in *Sisters or Strangers? Immigrant, Ethnic, and Racialized Women in Canadian History*, ed. Marlene Epp, Franca

Iacovetta, and Frances Swyripa (Toronto: University of Toronto Press, 2016), 421–3.

63 See, e.g., Eygló Svala Arnarsdóttir, "The Iceland Family Tree," *Iceland Review*, February 2007, accessed 29 July 2019, http://efeyvua.icelandtourist.is/stuff/views/2007/02/08/iceland-family-tree.

64 Richard M. Rice, "Mothers, Daughters and Granddaughters: An Examination of the Matrilineal Bias and Related Variables in Jews and Icelanders in Canada" (master's thesis, Department of Anthropology, University of Manitoba, 1971), 61, 67.

65 "Sunna" Pam Furstenau, written communication with author, 4 November 2011, Mountain, ND, and Toronto.

66 See, e.g., Agnes Bardal Comack, *"This, Too, Will Happen to You": The Stories of an Icelander* (Winnipeg: printed by the Bardal family, n.d.); Evelyn K. Thorvaldson, *My Amma and Me* (Winnipeg: Watson & Dwyer, 1993); Katrina Anderson, *Blessed: The Story of Asdis Sigrun Anderson* (Winnipeg: Peanut Butter Press, 2007).

67 Steinþór Guðbjartsson, "Promoting the Culture of the Community," *Lögberg Heimskringla*, 2 July 2004, 8–9.

68 Marjorie Gillies, "Traditional Yule Baking Recalls Holidays of Past," *Winnipeg Tribune*, 27 December 1978, 34.

69 Hunchuk, "Feeding the Dead," 142.

70 Holm, *The Heart Can Be Filled Anywhere on Earth*, 208–9.

71 Epp, "The Semiotics of Zwieback," 418.

72 For a more detailed discussion, see Bertram, "Public Spectacles, Private Narratives."

73 Ken Melsted, interview by author (written response), Winnipeg and Wynyard, SK, 4 February 2003.

74 The rock has since become the focus of an annual pilgrimage for Icelandic Canadians during the "Walk to the Rock," an event put on by the Gimli Icelandic Canadian Society. It is an occasion to reflect on "the hardships that the first pioneers overcame in establishing the community of Gimli and how they persevered to ensure the New Iceland settlement would survive and flourish"; see "Gimli Icelandic Canadian Society," accessed 29 July 2019, http://www.inlofna.org/Gimli-Icelandic-Canadian-Society.

75 S.J. Björnsson, *"Skýrsla yfir dána árið 1876"* [Report of deaths for the year 1876], Skipalækur, New Iceland, 1 February 1877, courtesy Eyrarbakki Icelandic Heritage Centre.

76 David E. Sutton, *Remembrance of Repasts: An Anthropology of Food and Memory* (Oxford: Berg, 2001), 28.

77 Sutton.

78 Gillmor, "Towering Torte."

79 Miller, written communication with author.
80 Daisy Neijmann, *The Icelandic Voice in Canadian Letters* (Montreal and Kingston: McGill-Queen's University Press, 1997), 373.

## Conclusion

1 Stephansson's work is notoriously difficult to translate into English, and I have borrowed from the 1967 translation offered by noted Icelandic linguist Haraldur Bessason in his work on linguistic phenomena in the immigrant community; see Haraldur Bessason, "A Few Specimens of North American Icelandic," *Scandinavian Studies* 39, no. 2 (1967): 146. A more precise version of the verse in Icelandic is as follows: *Þó að spör á eld og örk Yrðu kjörin ferða, Axarmörk á bjarka björk Benda á örugg leiðamörk.* Nelson Gerrard offers this direct translation: "Though shortages of fire and paper / Would be the journey's consequence, / Axe marks in the tree bark / Blaze a certain trail." See Stephan G. Stephansson, *Kolbeinslag* (Winnipeg: Viking Press, 1914), 29.
2 Bessason; Daisy Neijmann, *The Icelandic Voice in Canadian Letters* (Montreal and Kingston: McGill-Queen's University Press, 1997), 129; Víðar Hreinsson, *Wakeful Nights: Stephan G. Stephansson, Icelandic-Canadian Poet* (Calgary: Benson Ranch, 2012), 129.

## Appendix

1 Lovise Beate Augustine Friedel, *"Wienertærte," Nye og fuldstændige confecture bog* (New and complete confectionery book) (Copenhagen, s.n., 1795), 6; repr., *"Madhistorie: Kager,"* by Bi Skaarup et al., trans. Emily Albertsen and Martin Albertsen, 2006, accessed 13 August 2019, http://madhistorie.dk/opskrifter/wienertarte1795.html.
2 Clara Margrethe Fristrup, ed., *"Wienertærte," Fuldstændig kogebog, samt anviisning til at bage og sylte, saavel for smaa som store huusholdninge: Efter mange aars egen erfaring,* trans. Emily Albertsen and Martin Albertsen (Copenhagen: s.n., 1840), Collection of Landsbókasafn Íslands.
3 Fristrup. Note from the translators: "This is a translation of the text as it stands in the original nineteenth-century Danish, not in clear, modern Danish. The translators have taken a few liberties to make the translation understandable. It is a close translation but is not word for word in order to clarify a few things and make it read nicely in English."
4 Aðalbjörg Benediktsdottir Brandson, "Icelandic Cake"; repr., with text by Madeleine Day, "Danish and Icelandic Women Come to F.P. Kitchen," *Winnipeg Free Press*, 1 December 1936, 7.

5 F.J. Bergmann, "Cook Book" (Winnipeg: Ladies' Aid, First Lutheran Church, ca. 1938), private collection.
6 "The Best Cook in Our Town," *McCall's*, December 1949, 73.
7 Helen Josephson, "Icelandic Vínarterta"; repr., Clare Marcus, "Tasty Icelandic Dishes," *Winnipeg Free Press*, 4 August 1962, 18.
8 Janis Ólöf Magnusson, personal communication with author, 6 December 2018.
9 "Sorry – We Goofed," *Winnipeg Free Press*, n.d. Newspaper cutting of filling recipe provided by Janis Ólöf Magnusson.

# Bibliography

### Primary Sources

#### Newspapers

*Ameríka* (Akureyri)
*Fálkinn* (Reykjavík)
*Framfari* (New Iceland)
*Freyja* (Winnipeg)
*Globe* (Toronto)
*Globe and Mail* (Toronto)
*Heimskringla* (Winnipeg)
*Ingólfur* (Reykjavík)
*Íslendingur* (Reykjavík)
*Lögberg* (Winnipeg)
*Lögberg-Heimskringla* (Winnipeg)
*Manitoba Free Press* (Winnipeg)
*Morgunblaðið* (Reykjavík)
*Winnipeg Evening Tribune*
*Winnipeg Free Press*

#### Periodicals and Magazines

*Almanak Ólafs S. Thorgeirssonar*
*Maclean's*
*McCall's*
*Icelandic Canadian*
*Time*

*Other*

Anderson, Katrina. *Blessed: The Story of Asdis Sigrun Anderson.* Winnipeg: Peanut Butter Press, 2007.
Arnason, Einar. Oral history interview. Icelandic Canadian Frón. C-1646, Side B, 27:00 min, Provincial Archives of Manitoba (PAM), Winnipeg.
Árnason, Guðmundur et al. *Minningarit Stúkunnar Heklu Nr. 33 af Alþjóðareglu Good Templara.* Winnipeg: Ólafs S. Thorgeirssonar Prentsmiðju, 1913.
Árnason, Magnús. "A Memoir by Magnus Arnason." Translated by Sigurbjörg Stefansson. *Icelandic Canadian* 41, no. 2 (Winter 1982): 14–27.
Asgeirson, George. Oral history interview. Icelandic Canadian Frón. C-1651, recorded 14 August 1989. PAM, Winnipeg.
Baldwin, Augustus to Phoebe (Baldwin). 13 March 1877. MG 8 A6-3. PAM, Winnipeg.
Bardal Comack, Agnes. Interview by author. Winnipeg, 10 May 2009.
– "'This, Too, Will Happen to You': The Stories of an Icelander." Winnipeg: printed by the Bardal family, n.d.
Bazilewich, Lynne. Interview by author. Víðir, MB, 18 January 2003.
Bell, Charles N. "The Great Winnipeg Boom." *Manitoba History* 23 (October 2006). Accessed 19 March 2013. http://www.mhs.mb.ca/docs/mb_history/53/greatwinnipegboom.shtml.
Benedictson, Rose, and Lily Benedictson. "In Memory of Three Prominent Pioneers of the Mountain: North Dakota Icelandic Pioneers." Cavalier, ND: Homemade book, n.d. Collection of Pembina Country Historical Museum, Cavalier.
Bjarnadóttir, Birna, and Finnbogi Guðmundsson, eds. *My Parents: Memoirs of New World Icelanders.* Winnipeg: University of Manitoba Press, 2007.
Bjornson, Sig II, ed. "The Bjornson Saga: The Story of an Icelandic-American Family." Cedar Falls, ND: printed by the Bjornson family, n.d.
Björnsson, S.J. *"Skýrsla yfir dána árið 1876"* [Report of deaths for the year 1876]. 1 February 1877. Collection of Eyrarbakki Icelandic Heritage Centre, Hnausa, MB.
Boyer, John M., and John F. Wicks. *Geography by the Brace System or How to Study Geography: Prepared for the Use of Teacher and Pupil.* Chicago: A. Flanagan, 1891.
Crawley, Radford. *Iceland on the Prairies.* Ottawa: National Film Board of Canada (NFB), 1941.
Dalsted, Bjarni. *The Bjarni Dalsted Saga.* Burnsville, MN: Cornerstone Copy Centre, 1988.
Dufferin, Lord [Frederick Temple Blackwood]. *Letters from High Latitudes: Being Some Account of a Voyage in the Schooner Yacht "Foam."* London: John Murray, 1856.

– Speech to Winnipeg City Hall. "Speeches of the Earl of Dufferin, Governor-General of Canada, 1872–1878: Complete." Microform. Accessed 10 March 2010. http://www.archive.org/stream/cihm_02788/cihm_02788_djvu.txt.
Einarsson, Helgi. *Helgi Einarsson: A Manitoba Fisherman*. Translated by George Houser. Winnipeg: Queenston House, 1982.
Einarsson, Magnús, ed. *Icelandic-Canadian Memory Lore*. Hull, QC: Canadian Museum of Civilization, 1992.
– *Icelandic-Canadian Oral Narratives*. Hull, QC: Canadian Museum of Civilization, 1991.
– *Icelandic-Canadian Popular Verse*. Hull, QC: Canadian Museum of Civilization, 1994.
Eiríksson, Hallfreður Örn, and Olga María Franzdóttir. *Sögur úr vesturheimi* (Stories from the New World). Reykjavík: Stofnun Árna Magnússonar, 2012.
Eldjárn, Séra Kristján. *Gríma: Þjóðsögur*. Akureyri, Iceland: s.n., 1930.
Erlendsson, Guðbrandur. *Gudbrandur Erlendsson Autobiography*. Draft. Translated by Nelson Gerrard. Hnausa, MB: Saga Publications, 2009.
Executive Committee of the National Committee for the Celebration of the Diamond Jubilee of Confederation. *Diamond Jubilee of Confederation: General Suggestions for the Guidance of Committees in Charge of Local Celebrations*. Ottawa: National Committee for the Celebration of the Diamond Jubilee of Confederation, 1927.
Fidler, Elizabeth, et al. "Elizabeth Fidler's Claim for Loss of Houses and Improvements Occasioned by Occupation of Icelandic Settlers," 1877–86. Dominion Land Branch Records, RG15-D-II-1, vol. 90, file no. 105883. Library and Archives Canada (LAC), Ottawa.
Friðriksson, Friðjón. *Correspondence of Fridjon Fridricksson*, 1874–85. MG 8 A, 6-7, PAM, Winnipeg.
Friedel, Lovise Beate Augustine. *Nye og fuldstændige confecture*. Copenhagen: s.n., 1795.
Fristrup, Clara Margrethe, ed. *Fuldstændig kogebog, samt anviisning til at bage og sylte, saavel for smaa som store huusholdninge: Efter mange aars egen erfaring*. Translated by Emily Albertsen and Martin Albertsen. Copenhagen: s.n., 1840. Collection of Landsbókasafn Íslands.
Gerrard, Helga. Interview by author. 9 June 2011.
Gerrard, Nelson. *Silent Flashes*. Museum exhibit. Hofsós, Iceland: Icelandic Emigration Centre; Hnausa, MB: Eyrarbakki Icelandic Heritage Centre.
Gimli Women's Institute. *Gimli Saga: The History of Gimli Manitoba*. Gimli: s.n., 1975.
Gránufélag. *Gránufélag Verslunarbók* [Gránufélag record of accounts], 1875. V-3, 11, Héraðsskjalasafnið á Akureyri (Akureyri Regional Archives), Iceland.
Grønfedlt, Þóra Þ. *Stutt Matreiðslubók fyrir Sveitaheimili* (A short cookbook for the country home). Reykjavík: Prentsmiðjan Gutenberg, 1906.

Guðlaugson, Magnús. *Three Times a Pioneer*. Edited by Holmfridur Danielson. Winnipeg: s.n., 1958.
Guðmundsson, Böðvar, ed. *Bréf Vestur-Íslendinga* (Letters of Western Icelanders). 2 vols. Reykjavík: Mál og Menning, 2001–2.
Guðmundsson, Sigurður. "Um kvennbúninga á Íslandi: Að fornu og nýju" (On women's clothing in Iceland: In antiquity and now). *Ný Félagsrit* 17 (1857): 1–53.
Gunnars, Kristjana. *Wake Pick Poems*. Toronto: Anansi, 1981.
Guttormsson, Guttormur. *Bóndadóttir*. Winnipeg: Thorgerisons Company, 1920.
– "John Ramsay the Native Indian." In *Íslendssöguvefurinn: Vesturfaranir*, edited and translated by Viðar Hreinsson and Jón Karl Helgason, 75–83. Reykjavík: RUV, 1999–2000. First published 1975 in *Andvari: Nýr flokkur*. Accessed 5 January 2010. http://servefir.ruv.is/vesturfarar/SamIndianar.html.
Guttormsson, Guttormur J. "Jón Guttormsson and Pálína Ketilsdóttir," in *My Parents: Memoirs of New World Icelanders*, edited by Birna Bjarnadóttir and Finnbogi Guðmundsson, 73–90. Winnipeg: University of Manitoba Press, 2007.
Halldorson, Salome. "Speech of Miss Salome Halldorson Member for St. George, Delivered in the Manitoba Legislative Assembly, 26 February 1937." Booklet. MG 14, B3, PAM, Winnipeg.
– Untitled speech, n.d., MG 14, B3, PAM, Winnipeg.
Hannesson, Magnea. Icelandic Oral History Frón, C-1684–1686, PAM, Winnipeg.
Hanson, Frances. *Memories of Osland*. Prince Rupert, BC: Excel Printing, 1997.
High Commissioner for Canada in Great Britain to the Secretary of State for External Affairs, (ENG). *London Telegraph*, 28 June 1940. RG 25, file no. 501-1-40C, LAC, Ottawa.
Hjörleifsson, Einar Kvaran. *Vestur-Íslendingar: Fyrirlestur*. Reykjavík: Prentsmiðja Ísafoldar, 1895.
Holm, Bill. *The Heart Can Be Filled Anywhere on Earth*. Minneapolis, MN: Milkweed Press, 2000.
Holm, Cliff, and Lilja Holm. Interview by author. Geysir, MB, 2 July 2011.
Hryhorchuk, Carol. Interview by author. Riverton, MB, 21 May 2009.
Humberstone, H. Bruce, dir. *Iceland*. Los Angeles: Twentieth Century Fox, 1942.
Ingalls, Maxine. Interview by author. Hecla Island, MB, 30 June 2011.
Jackson, Thorleifur Jóakimsson. *Brot af landnámssögu Nýja Íslands* (Fragments of the settlement history of New Iceland). Winnipeg: Columbia Press, 1919.
– *Frá Austri til Vesturs: Framhald af landnamssögu Nýja Íslands* (From east to west: Continuation of the settlement history of New Iceland). Winnipeg: Columbia Press, 1921.
Johnson, Metta. Interview by author. Gimli, MB, 21 December 2009.
Jónasson & Fredrickson and Co. Sawmill and Store. Store account ledger, Icelandic River (Riverton), MB. Mss. Isl 11, Icelandic Collection, University of Manitoba, Winnipeg.

Jones, Gwyn, ed. *Eirik the Red and Other Icelandic Sagas*. Oxford: Oxford University Press, 2008.
Jónsdóttir, Þóra Andrea Nikólína. *Ný matreiðslubók ásamt ávísun um litun, þvott o. fl.* (A new cookbook along with advice on dyeing, washing and more). Akureyri, Iceland: H. Helgasyni, 1858.
Jón Sigurðsson Chapter IODE. *Minningarrit Íslenzkra Hermanna 1914–1918.* Winnipeg: Félagið Jón Sigurðsson, 1923.
– *A Supplement to Veterans of Icelandic Descent* (Winnipeg: Jón Sigurðsson Chapter IODE, 1993.
– *Veterans of Icelandic Descent, World War II, 1939–1945*. Winnipeg: Jón Sigurðsson Chapter IODE, 1990.
Jónsson, Einar, and S.J. Jóhannesson. *Icelandic for Soldiers*. Winnipeg: Columbia Press; Canadian Legion War Services, n.d.
Jónsson, Jón (frá Vogum við Mývatn). "*Útflutnings-undirbúningur.*" Handwritten booklet, 1865. Collection of *Landsbókasafn Íslands*, Lbs. 2415 8, vol. 25.
Kealy, Gregory S., and Reg Whitaker, eds. *RCMP Security Bulletins: The Early Years, 1919–1929*. St. John's: Canadian Committee on Labour History, 1996.
King, Mackenzie. *William Lyon Mackenzie King Diaries*. 23 March 1939. LAC, Ottawa. Accessed September 27, 2009. http://king.archives.ca/EN/PageView.asp.
Krarer, Olof. *The Esquimaux Lady: A Story of Her Native Home*. Edited by Albert S. Post. Ottawa: ILLS, 1887.
Krug, Thomas K. Thomas K. Krug, assistant to the publisher of *Time*, to J.T. Thorson, 17 February 1941. MG 31, E38, vol. 25, file 8. LAC, Ottawa.
Ladies' Aid, First Lutheran Church. *Cook Book*. Winnipeg: s.n., ca. 1938. Private collection.
Larrington, Carolyne, trans. *The Prose Edda*. Oxford: Oxford University Press, 2006.
Laxness, Halldór Kiljan. "New Iceland." Translated by Axel Eyberg and John Watkins. In *Seven Icelandic Short Stories*, edited by Ásgeir Pétursson and Steingrímur J. Þorsteinsson, 151–66. New York: American-Scandinavian Foundation, 1961.
Legg, Stuart. *Food, Weapon of Conquest*. Ottawa: National Film Board, 1941.
Loreen, Lola. Interview by author. Point Roberts, WA, 21 May 2009.
Lynch, Dr. James Spencer. "Clandeboye Agency: District of Keewatin; Report about Trouble with the Icelanders and a Smallpox Epidemic among the Indians of Lake Winnipeg, Especially at Sandy Bar." Indian Affairs, RG 10, vol. 3626, file 8064, 1–25, LAC, Ottawa.
Magnusson, Kristjana. *So Well Remembered*. Winnipeg: A & K Publications, 1978.
McLure, John. Interview by author. London, ON, 21 July 2010.
Melsted, Ken. Interview by author (written response). Winnipeg and Wynyard, SK, 4 February 2003.

Metcalfe, Frederick. *An Oxonian in Iceland: With Glances at Icelandic Folk-Lore and Sagas*. London: John Camden Hotten, 1867.
Miller, Jennifer. Interview by author (written communication). Ottawa and Toronto, 15 February 2010.
Ostertag, Charlie. Interview by author. Riverton, MB, 18 January 2003.
Paulson, Olive. *My Memoir of North Dakota*. Hand-produced booklet sold at Pembina County Historical Museum, ND, n.d.
Rafn, Carl Christian. *Antiquitates Americanae: sive scriptores septentrionales rerum ante-columbianarum in America*. Hafniæ [Copenhagen]: Typis Officinæ Schultzianæ, 1837.
Salverson, Laura Goodman. *Confessions of an Immigrant's Daughter*. London: Faber, 1939.
– *The Dark Weaver*. Toronto: Ryerson Press, 1937.
– *The Viking Heart*. Toronto: McClelland and Stewart, 1975.
Sigurdson, Glenn. *Vikings on a Prairie Ocean: The Saga of a Lake, a People, a Family and a Man*. Winnipeg: Great Plains Publications, 2014.
Sigurðsson, Sigurður frá Fagranesi. "Brasilíuferðir Íslendinga" (Icelandic emigration to Brazil), edited by Júlíana Guðmundsdóttir, *Ingólfur*, 31 December 1914, 202–03.
Simonson, Simon. *Icelandic Pioneers of 1874: From the Reminiscences of Simon Simonson*. Translated by Wilhelm Kristjanson. Winnipeg: s.n., 1904. FC 3400 I2 S54, University of Manitoba Archives and Special Collections, Winnipeg.
Skaptason, J.B. J.B. Skaptason to G.H. Lash, Director of Public Information, 30 July 1940. RG 25, vol. 3022, file 385-A-40, LAC, Ottawa.
Skelton, O.D. O.D. Skelton to Mackenzie King. RC 30, MG 501-1-40, LAC, Ottawa.
– O.D. Skelton to Joseph Thorson, 5 August 1940. RG 25, vol. 3022, file 385-A-40, LAC, Ottawa.
Skulason, Hrund. Untitled audio tape. Icelandic Oral History Fonds. C-1733, 9:45 min., PAM, Winnipeg.
Stefansson, Vilhjálmur. *Adventures in Error*. New York: Robert M. McBride, 1936.
Steinn, Thompson. *Riverton and the Icelandic Settlement*. Riverton, MB: Thordis Thompson, 1976.
Stephansson, Stephan G. *Á ferð og flugi* (En route). Reykjavík: Jón Ólafsson, 1900.
– *Kolbeinslag*. Winnipeg: Viking Press, 1914.
Thomas, Alfred. "Transcript of Interview Conducted by Margaret Stobie, June 1965." Collection of University of Regina. http://ourspace.uregina.ca/bitstream/handle/10294/1862/IH-MS.016A,%20.016B.pdf?sequence=1.
Thors, Thor. Thor Thors to the editor of *Time*, *Lögberg*, 30 January 1941, 3. First published 14 January 1941 in *Time*.
Thorson, J.T. J.T. Thorson to Dr. S.J. Jóhannesson, 7 March 1941. MG 31 E38, vol. 25, file 8, LAC, Ottawa.

- J.T. Thorson to Mackenzie King, 31 January 1941. MG 31 E38, vol. 25, file 8, LAC, Ottawa.
- J.T. Thorson to Mackenzie King, 12 February 1941. MG 31 E38, vol. 25, file 8, LAC, Ottawa.
- J.T. Thorson to Mackenzie King, 18 March 1941. MG 31 E38, vol. 25, file 8, LAC, Ottawa.
- J.T. Thorson to O.D. Skelton, 8 August 1940. MG 31 E38, vol. 25, file 8, LAC, Ottawa.
- J.T. Thorson to O.D. Skelton, 10 September 1940. RG 25, vol. 3022, file 385-A-40, LAC, Ottawa.

Thorvaldson, Evelyn K. *My Amma and Me*. Winnipeg: Watson & Dwyer, 1993.

Waller, Samuel Edmund. *Six Weeks in the Saddle: A Painter's Journal in Iceland*. London: Macmillan, 1874.

Walters, Thorstína. *Modern Sagas: The Story of the Icelanders in North America*. Fargo: North Dakota Institute for Regional Studies, 1953.

- *Saga Íslendinga í North Dakota* (The history of Icelanders in North Dakota). Winnipeg: City Printing and Publishing, 1926.

Wishnowski, Margret. Interview by author. Lundi (Riverton), MB, 8 February 2003.

Woodsworth, J.S. *Strangers at Our Gates: Or, Coming Canadians*. Toronto: Missionary Society of the Methodist Church, 1909.

Young, Milton R. Milton R. Young to Thorstína Walters, 8 January 1954. Folder 9, box 1, MSS 630, "Correspondence, 1954." Thorstína and Emile Walters Fonds, Institute for Regional Studies Archive, North Dakota State University, Fargo.

Þorsteinsdóttir Hólm, Torfhildur. *Þjóðsögur og Sagnir* (Folk stories and tales). Reykjavík: Almenna Bókafélagið, 1962.

Þórarinsson, Sveinn. Daybook of Sveinn Þórarinsson. Nr. 68C, 8vo, *Héraðsskjalasafnið á Akureyri* (Akureyri Regional Archives), Akureyi, Iceland.

Þorsteinsson, Þorsteinn Þ. *Saga Íslendinga í Vesturheimi* (History of Icelanders in North America). 4 vols. Reykjavík: Þjóðræknisfélag Íslendinga Í Vesturheimi, 1940.

- *Vestmenn: Landnám Íslendinga í Vesturheimi* (Western men: Icelandic settlement in North America). Reykjavík: Ísafoldarprentsmiðju, 1935.

**Secondary Sources**

Anderson, Erla Louise Colvil. "Tolerance, Intolerance, and Fanaticism: W. D. Valgardson's Reaction to the Religious Debate in New Iceland." Master's thesis, University of Manitoba, 2000.

Appadurai, Arjun. *Modernity at Large: Cultural Dimensions of Globalization*. Minneapolis: University of Minnesota Press, 1996.

Arnbjörnsdóttir, Birna. *North American Icelandic: The Life of a Language.* Winnipeg: University of Manitoba Press, 2006.
Arngrímsson, Guðjón. *Annað Ísland: Gullöld Vestur-Íslendinga í máli og myndum* (Another Iceland: Golden age of Icelandic North Americans in words and pictures). Reykjavík: Mál og Menning, 1998.
– ed. and trans. *Nýja Ísland: Saga of the Journey to New Iceland.* Winnipeg: Turnstone, 1997.
Attfield, Judy. *Wild Things: The Material Culture of Everyday Life.* New York: Berg, 2000.
Backhouse, Constance. *Petticoats and Prejudice: Women and Law in 19th-Century Canada.* Toronto: Women's Press, 1991.
Barnes, Geraldine. *Viking America: The First Millennium.* Cambridge: D.S. Brewer, 2001.
Bastian, Jeannette Allis. *Owning Memory: How a Caribbean Community Lost Its Archives and Found Its History.* London: Libraries Unlimited, 2003.
Bertram, Laurie K. "'Eskimo' Immigrants and Colonial Soldiers: Icelandic Immigrants and the North-West Resistance, 1885." *Canadian Historical Review* 99, no. 1 (2018): 63–97.
– "'Fight like Auður': Gender, Ethnicity and Dissent in the Career of Salome Halldorson, Social Credit MLA, 1936–41." *Icelandic Connections* 62, no. 3 (Fall 2010): 41–57.
– "Public Spectacles, Private Narratives: Canadian Heritage Campaigns, Maternal Trauma and the Rise of the Koffort (Trunk) in Icelandic-Canadian Popular Memory." *Material Culture Review* 71 (2010): 39–53.
Bessason, Haraldur. "A Few Specimens of North American Icelandic." *Scandinavian Studies* 39, no. 2 (1967): 115–46.
Biggs, Leslie. "In Search of Gudrun Goodman: Reflections on Gender, 'Doing History' and Memory." *Canadian Historical Review* 87, no. 2 (2006): 293–316.
Bittner, Donald F. *The Lion and the White Falcon: Britain and Iceland in the World War II Era.* Hamden, CT: Archon Books, 1983.
Bjarnadóttir, Birna, and Finnbogi Guðmundsson, eds. *My Parents: Memoirs of New World Icelanders.* Winnipeg: University of Manitoba Press, 2007.
Björnsdóttir, Inga Dóra. "Nationalism, Gender and the Body in Icelandic Nationalist Discourse." *Nordic Journal of Feminist and Gender Research* 5, no. 1 (1997): 3–13.
– *Ólöf the Eskimo Lady: Biography of an Icelandic Dwarf in America.* Translated by María Helga Guðmundsdóttir. Ann Arbor: University of Michigan Press, 2010.
Boag, Peter. *Re-dressing America's Frontier Past.* Berkeley: University of California Press, 2011.
Box, Jason E., Edward Hanna, and Trausti Jónsson. "An Analysis of Icelandic Climate since the Nineteenth Century." *International Journal of Climatology* 24 (2004): 1193–210.

Brayshay, Mark, and John Grattan. "An Amazing and Portentous Summer: Environmental and Social Responses in Britain to the 1783 Eruption of an Iceland Volcano." *Geographical Journal* (1995): 125–34.

Brown, Marie A. *The Icelandic Discoverers of America: Honour to Whom Honour Is Due.* London: Trubner, 1887.

Brydon, Anne. "Dreams and Claims: Icelandic-Saulteaux Interactions in the Manitoba Interlake." *Journal of Canadian Studies* 36, no. 2 (2001): 164–90.

– "Mother to Her Distant Children: The Icelandic Fjallkona in Canada." In *Undisciplined Women: Tradition and Culture in Canada,* edited by Pauline Greenhill and Diane Tye. Montreal and Kingston: McGill-Queen's University Press, 1997, 87–100.

Buse, Peter, and Andrew Stott. *Ghosts: Deconstruction, Psychoanalysis, History.* London: Palgrave Macmillan, 1999.

Butler, Judith. *Precarious Life: The Powers of Mourning and Violence.* New York: Verso, 2004.

Caccia, Ivana. *Managing the Canadian Mosaic in Wartime: Shaping Citizenship Policy, 1939–45.* Montreal and Kingston: McGill-Queen's University Press, 2010.

Campbell, Kenneth. *Keeping the Boats Afloat: Boatbuilding Communities of the North West.* Victoria: Royal Museum of British Columbia, 2006.

Chauncey, George. *Gay New York: Gender, Urban Culture, and the Making of the Gay Male World, 1890–1940.* London: Hachette, 2008.

Churchill, Winston. *The Grand Alliance.* New York: Houghton Mifflin, 1985.

Clausen, Oscar. *Saura-Gísla Saga.* Reykjavík: Steindórsprent H.F., 1937.

Cook, Sharon Anne. *"Through Sunshine and Shadow": The Women's Christian Temperance Union, Evangelicalism, and Reform in Ontario, 1874–1930.* Montreal and Kingston: McGill-Queen's University Press, 1995.

Cooke, Nathalie, ed. *What's to Eat? Entrées in Canadian History.* Montreal and Kingston: McGill-Queen's University Press, 2009.

Cupido, Robert. "Appropriating the Past: Pageants, Politics, and the Diamond Jubilee of Confederation." *Journal of the Canadian Historical Association* 9, no. 1 (1998): 155–86.

Danielsen, Helge. "Making Friends at Court: Slow and Indirect Media in US Public Diplomacy in Norway, 1950–1965." *Contemporary European History* 18, no. 2 (2009): 179–98.

DeLottinville, Peter. "Joe Beef of Montreal: Working-Class Culture and the Tavern, 1869–1889." *Labour/Le Travail* (1981): 9–40.

Derrida, Jacques. *Spectres of Marx: The State of the Debt, the Work of Mourning and the New International.* Translated by Peggy Kamuf. New York: Routledge, 1994.

Deutsch, Jonathan, and Annie Hauck-Lawson, eds. *Gastropolis: Food and New York City.* New York: Columbia University Press, 2009.

Diner, Hasia R. *Hungering for America: Italian, Irish, and Jewish Foodways in the Age of Migration.* Cambridge, MA: Harvard University Press, 2003.

Dubinsky, Karen. *Improper Advances: Rape and Heterosexual Conflict in Ontario, 1880–1929*. Chicago: University of Chicago Press, 1993.

Edwards, Elizabeth, Chris Gosden, and Ruth Phillips, eds. *Sensible Objects: Colonialism, Museums and Material Culture*. New York: Berg, 2006.

Epp, Marlene. *Mennonite Women in Canada: A History*. Winnipeg: University of Manitoba Press, 2008.

– "More than 'Just' Recipes: Mennonite Cookbooks in Mid-twentieth Century North America." In *Edible Histories, Cultural Politics: Towards a Canadian Food History*, edited by Franca Iacovetta, Valerie J. Korinek, and Marlene Epp, 173–88. Toronto: University of Toronto Press, 2012.

– "The Semiotics of Zwieback: Feast and Famine in the Narratives of Mennonite Refugee Women." In *Sisters or Strangers? Immigrant, Ethnic, and Racialized Women in Canadian History*, edited by Marlene Epp, Franca Iacovetta, and Frances Swyripa, 314–40. Toronto: University of Toronto Press, 2004.

– *Women without Men: Mennonite Refugees of the Second World War*. Toronto: University of Toronto Press, 2000.

Eyford, Ryan. "An Experiment in Immigrant Colonization: Canada and the Icelandic Reserve, 1875–1897." PhD diss., University of Manitoba, 2010.

– "From Prairie Goolies to Canadian Cyclones: The Transformation of the 1920 Winnipeg Falcons." *Sport History Review* 37 (2006): 5–18.

– "Lucifer Comes to New Iceland: Margret Benedictsson's Radical Critique of Marriage and the Family." Paper presented at the Canadian Historical Association Annual Meeting, Saskatoon, 30 May 2007.

– "Quarantined within a New Colonial Order: The 1876–77 Lake Winnipeg Smallpox Epidemic." *Journal of the Canadian Historical Association* 17, no. 1 (2006): 55–78.

– *White Settler Reserve: New Iceland and the Colonization of the Canadian West*. Vancouver: UBC Press, 2016.

Frager, Ruth. *Sweatshop Strife: Class, Ethnicity and Gender in the Jewish Labour Movement of Toronto, 1900–39*. Toronto: University of Toronto Press, 1992.

Frye Jacobson, Matthew. *Roots Too: White Ethnic Revival in Post–Civil Rights America*. Cambridge, MA: Harvard University Press, 2008.

– *Special Sorrows: The Diasporic Imagination of Irish, Polish, and Jewish Immigrants in the United States*. Berkeley: University of California Press, 2002.

Gabaccia, Donna. *We Are What We Eat: Ethnic Food and the Making of Americans*. Cambridge, MA: Harvard University Press, 1998.

Gerrard, Nelson. "Gimlunga Saga." Unpublished manuscript. 2015.

– *Icelandic River Saga*. Arborg, MB: Saga Publications, 1985.

Giesbrecht, Donovan. "Metis, Mennonites and the 'Unsettled Prairie,' 1874–1896." *Journal of Mennonite Studies* 19 (2001): 103–11.

Gissurarson, Loftur Reimar, and William H. Swatos, Jr. *Icelandic Spiritualism: Mediumship and Modernity in Iceland*. New Brunswick, NJ: Transaction Publishers, 1997.

Gold, Carol. *Danish Cookbooks: Domesticity & National Identity, 1616–1901.* Copenhagen: Museum Tusculanum Press; University of Copenhagen Press, 2007.
Goldie, Terry. *Fear and Temptation: The Image of the Indigene in Canadian, Australian, and New Zealand Literatures.* Montreal and Kingston: McGill-Queen's University Press, 1989.
Goldstein, Darra, ed., with a foreword by Sidney Mintz. *The Oxford Companion to Sugar and Sweets.* Oxford: Oxford University Press, 2015.
Gordon, Alan. *Making Public Pasts: The Contested Terrain of Montreal's Public Memories.* Montreal and Kingston: McGill-Queen's University Press, 2001.
Gray, James H. *Booze: The Impact of Whisky on the Prairie West.* Toronto: Macmillan, 1972.
Grétarsdóttir, Tinna. "'Art Is in Our Heart': Transnational Complexities of Art Projects and Neoliberal Governmentality." PhD diss., Department of Anthropology, Temple University, 2010.
Guglielmo, Thomas A. *White on Arrival: Italians, Race, Color, and Power in Chicago, 1890–1945.* Oxford: Oxford University Press, 2003.
Gunnlaugsson, Gísli Ágúst. "'Everyone's Been Nice to Me, Especially the Dogs': Foster-Children and Young Paupers in Nineteenth-Century Southern Iceland." *Journal of Social History* (Winter 1993): 341–58.
Gunnlaugsson, Helgi, and John F. Galliher. "Prohibition of Beer in Iceland: An International Test of Symbolic Politics." *Law & Society Review* 20, no. 3 (1986): 335–53.
Hálfdánarson, Guðmundur. "Social Distinctions and National Unity: On Politics of Nationalism in Nineteenth-Century Iceland." *Journal of European Ideas* 21, no. 6 (1995): 763–79.
Handlin, Oscar. *The Uprooted: The Epic Story of the Great Migrations That Made the American People.* Philadelphia: University of Pennsylvania Press, 2002.
Hansen, Marcus Lee. "The Problem of the Third Generation Immigrant." Lecture delivered to the Augustana Historical Society. Rock Island, IL: Augustana Historical Society, 1938.
Hansson, Heidi. "The Gentleman's North: Lord Dufferin and the Beginnings of Arctic Tourism." *Studies in Travel Writing* 13, no. 1 (2009): 61–73.
Harvey, David C. "The History of Heritage." In *The Ashgate Reader Companion to Heritage and Identity*, edited by Brian J. Graham and Peter Howard, 19–37. London: Ashgate, 2008.
Harvey, Katherine, "Amazons and Victims: Resisting Wife-Abuse in Working-Class Montréal, 1869–1879." *Journal of the Canadian Historical Association* 2, no. 1 (1991): 131–48.
Helgason, Jón Karl. "The Mystery of Vínarterta: In Search of an Icelandic Canadian Ethnic Identity." *Scandinavian-Canadian Studies* 17 (2007): 36–52.
– *The Rewriting of Njáls's Saga: Translation, Ideology and Icelandic Sagas.* Toronto: Multilingual Matters, 1999.

Henderson, Stuart. "'While There Is Still Time ...': J. Murray Gibbon and the Spectacle of Difference in Three CPR Folk Festivals, 1928–1931." *Journal of Canadian Studies* 39, no. 1 (2004): 139–74.

Heron, Craig. *Booze: A Distilled History*. Toronto: Between the Lines, 2003.

Hinther, Rhonda. "The Oldest Profession in Winnipeg: The Culture of Prostitution in the Point Douglas Segregated District, 1909–1912." *Manitoba History* 41 (2001): 2–13.

Hobsbawm, Eric, and Terence Ranger, eds. *The Invention of Tradition*. Cambridge: Cambridge University Press, 1983.

Hoerder, Dirk. *Creating Societies: Immigrant Lives in Canada*. Montreal and Kingston: McGill-Queen's University Press, 1999.

Holyk Hunchuk, S. "Feeding the Dead: The Ukrainian Food Colossi of the Canadian Prairies." In *Edible Histories, Cultural Politics: Towards a Canadian Food History*, edited by Franca Iacovetta, Valerie J. Korinek, and Marlene Epp, 140–55. Toronto: University of Toronto Press, 2012.

Houser, George J. *Pioneer Icelandic Pastor: The Life of the Reverend Paul Thorlaksson*, edited by Paul A. Sigurdson. Winnipeg: Manitoba Historical Society, 1990.

Hreinsson, Víðar. *Wakeful Nights: Stephan G. Stephansson, Icelandic-Canadian Poet*. Calgary: Benson Ranch, 2012.

Iacovetta, Franca. *Gatekeepers: Reshaping Immigrant Lives in Cold War Canada*. Toronto: Between the Lines, 2006.

– "Immigrant Gifts, Canadian Treasures and Spectacles of Pluralism." Unpublished manuscript. 2010.

– "Manly Militants, Cohesive Communities, and Defiant Domestics: Writing about Immigrants in Canadian Historical Scholarship." *Labour/Le Travail* 36 (Fall 1995): 217–52.

– *Such Hardworking People: Italian Immigrants in Postwar Toronto*. Montreal and Kingston: McGill-Queen's University Press, 1993.

Iacovetta, Franca, and Valerie J. Korinek. "Jell-O Salads, One-Stop Shopping, and Maria the Homemaker: The Gender Politics of Food." In *Sisters or Strangers? Immigrant, Ethnic, and Racialized Women in Canadian History*, edited by Marlene Epp, Franca Iacovetta, and Frances Swyripa, 190–230. Toronto: University of Toronto Press, 2004.

Iacovetta, Franca, Valerie J. Korinek, and Marlene Epp. *Edible Histories, Cultural Politics: Towards a Canadian Food History*. Toronto: University of Toronto Press, 2012.

Ignatiev, Noel. *How the Irish Became White*. New York: Routledge, 2009.

Ingimundarson, Valur. "Immunizing against the American Other: Racism, Nationalism and Gender in U.S.-Icelandic Military Relations during the Cold War." *Journal of Cold War Studies* 6, no. 4 (Fall 2004): 65–88.

Jakobsson, Sverrir. *Images of the North: Histories, Identities, Ideas*. Amsterdam: Rodopi, 2009.

Jameson, Fredric. "Marx's Purloined Letter." *New Left Review* 1, no. 209 (January–February 1995): 75–109.
Jóhannesdóttir, Kristín. "The Immigrant Ghost." Margaret and Richard Beck Lecture, University of Victoria, 27 February 2003.
Jónsdóttir, Ingveldur, and Soffanías Thorkelson. *Bréf frá Ingu: Héðan og handan*. Winnipeg: Prentsmiðja Ólafs S. Thorgeirssonar, 1931.
Jónsson, Guðmundur. "Iceland, OEEC and the Trade Liberalisation of the 1950s." *Scandinavian Economic History Review* 52, no. 2–3 (2004): 62–84.
Kansteiner, Wulf. "Finding Meaning in Memory: A Methodological Critique of Collective Memory Studies." *History and Theory* 41, no. 2 (2002): 179–97.
Karlsson, Gunnar. *Iceland's 1100 Years: History of a Marginal Society*. Reykjavík: Mál og Menning, 2000.
– "Plague without Rats: The Case of Fifteenth-Century Iceland." *Journal of Medieval History* 22, no. 3 (1996): 263–84.
Kealey, Linda. *A Not Unreasonable Claim: Women and Reform in Canada, 1880–1920*. Toronto: Women's Press, 1979.
Kirschenblatt-Gimblett, Barbara. *Destination Culture: Tourism, Museums, and Heritage*. Berkeley: University of California Press, 1998.
Koch, H.W. *Hitler Youth: Origins and Developments, 1922–1945*. Lanham, MD: Rowman and Littlefield, 2000.
Kolodny, Annette. *In Search of First Contact: The Vikings of Vinland, the Peoples of the Dawnland, and the Anglo-American Anxiety of Discovery*. Durham, NC: Duke University Press, 2012.
Kristinsson, Júníus H. *Vesturfaraskrá 1870–1914* (Index of Icelandic emigrants 1870–1914). Reykjavík: Sagnfræðistofnun Háskóla Íslands, 1983.
Kristjanson, Wilhelm. *The Icelandic People in Manitoba: A Manitoba Saga*. Winnipeg: Wallingford Press, 1965.
Kuhn, Cynthia, and Cindy Carlson, eds. *Styling Texts: Dress and Fashion in Literature*. Amherst, NY: Cambria Press, 2007.
Latour, Bruno. "The Berlin Key or How to Do Words with Things." In *Matter, Materiality and Modern Culture*, edited by P.M. Graves-Brown, 10–21. London: Routledge, 2000.
Leys, Ruth. *Trauma: A Genealogy*. Chicago: University of Chicago Press, 2000.
Lindal, W.J. *The Icelanders in Canada*. Winnipeg: Viking Press, 1967.
Loewen, Royden. *Family, Church and Market: A Mennonite Community in the Old and New Worlds*. Chicago: University of Illinois Press, 1993.
Loewen, Royden, and Gerald Friesen. *Immigrants in Prairie Cities: Ethnic Diversity in Twentieth-Century Canada*. Toronto: University of Toronto Press, 2009.
Loftsdóttir, Kristín. "Shades of Otherness: Representations of Africa in 19th-Century Iceland." *Social Anthropology* 16, no. 2 (2008): 172–86.
Lux, Maureen Katherine. *Medicine That Walks: Disease, Medicine, and Canadian Plains Native People, 1880–1940*. Toronto: University of Toronto Press, 2001.

Mackey, Eva. *The House of Difference: Cultural Politics and National Identity in Canada*. Toronto: University of Toronto Press, 2002.

Magnússon, Sigurður Gylfi. *Wasteland with Words: A Social History of Iceland*. London: Reaktion, 2010.

Matthíasdottír, Sigríður. "The Renovation of Native Pasts: A Comparison between Aspects of Icelandic and Czech Nationalist Ideology." *Slavonic and East European Review* 78, no. 4 (October 2000): 688–709.

Matthiasson, John. "The Icelandic Canadians: The Paradox of an Assimilated Ethnic Group." In *Two Nations, Many Cultures: Ethnic Groups in Canada*, edited by Jean L. Elliott, 195–205. Scarborough, ON: Prentice Hall, 1979.

McKay, Ian. *Quest of the Folk: Antimodernism and Cultural Selection in Twentieth-Century Nova Scotia*. Montreal and Kingston: McGill-Queen's University Press, 1994.

Miller, Monica J. *Slaves to Fashion: Black Dandyism and the Styling of Black Diasporic Identity*. Durham, NC: Duke University Press, 2009.

Neijmann, Daisy. "'A Fabulous Potency': Masculinity in Icelandic Occupation Literature." In *Men after War*, edited by Stephen McVeigh and Nicola Cooper, 152–69. New York: Routledge, 2013.

- *A History of Icelandic Literature*. Lincoln: University of Nebraska Press, 2007.
- *The Icelandic Voice in Canadian Letters*. Montreal and Kingston: McGill-Queen's University Press, 1997.

Nielsen, Klaus. "Learning to Do Things with Things: Apprenticeship in Bakery as Economy and Practice." In *Doing Things with Things*, edited by Alan Costall and Ole Dreier, 209–24. London: Ashgate, 2012.

Noel, Jan. *Canada Dry: Temperance Crusades before Confederation*. Toronto: University of Toronto Press, 1995.

Odess, Daniel, William Loring, and William W. Fitzhugh, "First Peoples of Helluland, Markland and Vinland." In *Vikings: The North Atlantic Saga*, edited by William W. Fitzhugh and Elisabeth I. Ward, 193–205. Washington, DC: Smithsonian Institution Press, 2000.

Ögmundardóttir, Helga. "Ímyndir, sjálfsmyndir og vald í samskiptum Indíána og Íslendinga í Vesturheimi 1875–1930" (Image, identity and power in Indigenous- Icelandic relations in North America 1875–1930). Master's thesis, Háskóli Íslands, 2002.

Ólafsdóttir, Hildigunnur. *Alcoholics Anonymous in Iceland: From Marginality to Mainstream Culture*. Reykjavík: Háskólaútgáfan, 2000.

- "Drinking in Iceland and Ideas of the North." In *Iceland and Images of the North*, edited by Sumaliði Ísleifsson, 329–50. Quebec City: Presses de l'Université du Québec, 2011.
- "The Entrance of Beer into a Persistent Spirits Culture." *Contemporary Drug Problems* 26, no. 4 (1999): 545–75.

Olafson-Jenkyns, Kristin. *The Culinary Saga of New Iceland: Recipes from the Shores of Lake Winnipeg*. Guelph, ON: Coastline Publishing, 2001.
Osborne, Brian. "Landscapes, Memory, Monuments and Commemoration: Putting Identity in its Place." *Canadian Ethnic Studies* 33, no. 3: 1–39.
Osgoode, Kenneth. *Total Cold War: Eisenhower's Secret Propaganda Battle at Home and Abroad*. Lawrence: University Press of Kansas, 2006.
Oslund, Karen. *Iceland Imagined: Nature, Culture, and Storytelling in the North Atlantic*. Seattle: University of Washington Press, 2011.
Palmer, Alexandra, ed. *Fashion: A Canadian Perspective*. Toronto: University of Toronto Press, 2004.
Palmer, Howard H. "Reluctant Hosts: Anglo-Canadian Views of Multiculturalism in the Twentieth Century." *Cultural Diversity and Canadian Education: Issues and Innovations* 130 (1984): 21–40.
Pálsson, Gísli. *The Man Who Stole Himself: The Slave Odyssey of Hans Jonathan*. Translated by Anna Yates. Chicago: University of Chicago Press, 2016.
– *Travelling Passions: The Hidden Life of Vilhjalmur Stefansson*. Translated by Keneva Kunz. Winnipeg: University of Manitoba Press, 2003.
Patrias, Carmella. *Patriots and Proletarians: Politicizing Hungarian Immigrants in Interwar Canada*. Montreal and Kingston: McGill-Queen's University Press, 1994.
Perin, Roberto. "Clio as Ethnic: The Third Force in Canadian Historiography." *Canadian Historical Review* 64, no. 4 (1983): 441–67.
Phillips, Ruth B. *Trading Identities: The Souvenir in Native North American Art from the Northeast, 1700–1900*. Montreal and Kingston: McGill-Queen's University Press, 1999.
Pinson, Ann. "Temperance, Prohibition, and Politics in Nineteenth-Century Iceland." *Contemporary Drug Problems* 12 (1985): 249–66.
Ponzi, Frank. *Ísland fyrir aldamót / Iceland: The Dire Years 1882–1888*. Reykjavík: Brennholt, 1995.
Rand, Erica. *The Ellis Island Snow Globe*. Durham, NC: Duke University Press, 2005.
Rice, Richard M. "Mothers, Daughters and Granddaughters: An Examination of the Matrilineal Bias and Related Variables in Jews and Icelanders in Canada." Master's thesis, Department of Anthropology, University of Manitoba, 1971.
Richard, Mark Paul. "'This Is Not a Catholic Nation': The Ku Klux Klan Confronts Franco-Americans in Maine." *New England Quarterly* 82, no. 2 (2009): 285–303.
Roberts, Julia. *In Mixed Company: Taverns and Public Life in Upper Canada*. Vancouver: UBC Press, 2009.
Roediger, David R. *Working toward Whiteness: How America's Immigrants Became White; The Strange Journey from Ellis Island to the Suburbs*. New York: Basic Books, 2006.

Selig, Diana. *Americans All: The Cultural Gifts Movement*. Cambridge, MA: Harvard University Press, 2008.

Sigurjónsdóttir, Æsa. *Til gagns og til fegurðar: Sjálfsmyndir í ljósmyndum og klæðnaði á Íslandi 1860–1960* (For function and beauty: Identity in photography and clothing in Iceland 1860–1960). Reykjavík: Þjóðminjasafnið Íslands, 2008.

Simpson, Jacqueline. *Icelandic Folktales & Legends*. Berkeley: University of California Press, 1972.

Simundsson, Elva. *Fjallkonas of Íslendingadagurinn 1924–1989*. Gimli, MB: s.n., 1990.

Stern, Elizabeth. *Legends of the Dead in Medieval and Modern Iceland*. PhD diss. University of California, Berkeley, 1987.

Sutton, David E. *Remembrance of Repasts: An Anthropology of Food and Memory*. Oxford: Berg, 2001.

Swyripa, Frances. "The Mother of God Wears a Maple Leaf: History, Gender, and Ethnic Identity in Sacred Space." In *Sisters or Strangers: Immigrant, Ethnic and Racialized Women in Canadian History*, edited by Marlene Epp, Franca Iacovetta, and Frances Swyripa, 341–60. Toronto: University of Toronto Press, 2004.

– *Storied Landscapes: Ethno-religious Identity and the Canadian Prairies*. Winnipeg: University of Manitoba Press, 2010.

– *Wedded to the Cause: Ukrainian-Canadian Women and Ethnic Identity, 1891–1991*. Toronto: University of Toronto Press, 1993.

Thatcher Ulrich, Laurel. *The Age of Homespun: Objects and Stories in the Creation of an American Myth*. New York: Vintage, 2009.

Thisted, Kirsten. "On Narrative Expectations: Greenlandic Oral Traditions about the Cultural Encounter between Inuit and Norsemen." *Scandinavian Studies* 73, no. 3 (2001): 253–96.

Thor, Jónas. *Icelanders in North America: The First Settlers*. Winnipeg: University of Manitoba Press, 2002.

– *Íslendingadagurinn: An Illustrated History*. Gimli, MB: Icelandic Festival of Manitoba, 1988.

– *A Monument in Manitoba*. Translated by Daniel Teague. Winnipeg: Heartland Associates, 2011.

– "A Religious Controversy among Icelandic Immigrants in North America, 1874–1880." Master's thesis, University of Manitoba, 1980.

Turville-Petre, G. "Dreams in Icelandic Tradition." *Folklore* 69, no. 2 (1958): 93–111.

Valverde, Mariana. *Diseases of the Will: Alcohol and the Dilemmas of Freedom*. New York: Cambridge University Press, 1998.

– "The Love of Finery: Fashion and the Fallen Woman in Nineteenth-Century Social Discourse." *Victorian Studies* 32, no. 2 (1989): 169–88.

Walz, Gene. *Cartoon Charlie: The Life and Art of Animation Pioneer Charles Thorson*. Winnipeg: Great Plains Publications, 1998.

Ward, Elisabeth I. "Reflections on an Icon: Vikings in American Culture." In *Vikings: The North Atlantic Saga*, edited by William W. Fitzhugh and Elisabeth I. Ward, 365–73. Washington, DC: Smithsonian Institution Press, 2000.

Wawn, Andrew. *The Vikings and the Victorians: Inventing the Old North in Nineteenth-Century Britain*. Cambridge: D.S. Brewer, 2000.

Wolf, Kirsten. "Emigration and Mythmaking: The Case of the Icelanders in Canada." *Canadian Ethnic Studies Journal* 33, no. 2 (2001): 1–15.

– ed. *Western-Icelandic Short Stories*. Winnipeg: University of Manitoba Press, 1992.

– ed. and trans. *Writings by Western Icelandic Women*. Winnipeg: University of Manitoba Press, 1997.

Woods, Fred E. *Fire on Ice: The Story of Icelandic Latter-day Saints at Home and Abroad*. Provo, UT: Brigham Young University, 2005.

Woodward, Sophie. "Making Fashion Material." *Journal of Material Culture* 7, no. 3 (2002): 345–53.

Zernack, Julia. "Old Norse-Icelandic Literature and German Culture." In *Iceland and Images of the North*, edited by Sumarliði R. Ísleifsson, 157–86. Quebec City: Presses de l'Université du Québec, 2011.

# Index

Note: Page numbers in italics refer to figures.

*Áhugamál kvenna* (Women's interests; column in *Lögberg* newspaper), 147
Alaska/Alaskan Territory, settlements in, 11, 14
alcohol consumption among Icelanders: and availability of alcohol, 60–4; excessive, 59, 66–8; gendered nature of, 57–9; and home-brew production, 72–3; overview, 74–5; significance of, 55, 163; as source of comfort, 60; travellers' observations of, 189n18. *See also* temperance movement
Allied occupation of Iceland, 103–4, 121–30, 145
almonds and almond extract in food, 135, 138, 139, 141, 151–3
American military interest in and programs involving Iceland. *See* Allied occupation of Iceland; Cold War
American settlements. *See* Alaska/Alaskan Territory, settlements in; Dakota Territory/North Dakota; Minnesota; Utah, settlements in; Washington state; Wisconsin
*amma* (grandmother), 86, 154, 155, 158, 160
Amma's Kitchen, Gimli, 155

Amma's Teahouse, Gimli, 155
Andrésson, Björn, 36, 48
anglicization: and anti-immigrant sentiment, 22, 103, 109, 113–14; and assimilation, 6–7, 42–3, 108, 114; and "cohesive community" model explanations, 19; and language decline, 108–13; of names, 50–2; and Viking-themed parades, 22, 164–5; and *vínarterta*, 142, 159; xenophobic sentiment encouraging, 144–5, 164. *See also* assimilation; bilingualism; language, Icelandic
anglophone society: and appearance, 27, 42; and class issues, 27; elite, 101; and English-language employment, 50–2, 109; gender roles in, 49; and North American nationalisms, 115; and taboos against non-Christian superstitious beliefs, 77, 82
Anishinaabe (Ojibwe) people, 14, 15, 17, 39, 40, 89, 90, 153
Appadurai, Arjun, 3–4
Arborg, Manitoba, 5, 84, 85, 87, 142
Argyle (Baldur-Glenboro), Manitoba, 18, 46
Arnason, Einar, 116

Árnason, Magnús, 69
Arnbjörnsdóttir, Birna, 109
Arngrímsson, Margrét, 83, 86–7
Asgeirson, George, 73
Askja volcano, Iceland, 8, 13, 37
Ásmundsson, Einar, 61
assimilation: and anglicization, 6–7, 42–3, 108, 114, 144–5; and clothing fashions, 42–3, 53, 162–3; and "cohesive community" model, 19; and *einstaklingur* (individual) attitude, 151; and material-cultural traditions, 142, 143; Simundsson on, 151; and Viking branding of Icelandic immigrants, 101–29
Austro-Hungarian Empire, 138
autobiographical tradition, Icelandic, 20, 116, 181n54, 182n55
*Ástandið* crisis ("the Situation"), 124–31, 132–4

Backhouse, Constance, 49
baking, 137–40. *See also vínarterta; specific foods and ingredients*
*Bakkús Konungur* (King Bacchus), 65, 163
Baldvinsdóttir, Friðríka, 36
Baldwin, Augustus, 37, 38, 62
"bald women epidemic," 118–21, 162
Bardal, Agnes, xii, 205n22, 208n66
Barnes, Geraldine, 106–7
Battle of Little Big Horn, 17
Bell, Charles Napier, 47
Benedictsson, Margrét, 115, 117, 162
Beothuk people, 14
*berdreymi* (prophetic dreaming), 80. *See also* dreams and dream interpretation
Bergmann, Friðrik J., 32
Bessason, Haraldur, 209n1
"big group," 13
Bildfell, Jón, 116, 119

bilingualism, 108, 109, 114. *See also* anglicization; language, Icelandic
Bjarnason, Björn, 85, 93
Bjarnason, Ingólfur, 89
Bjarnason, Jón, 11, 83, 157
Bjarnason, Lára, 44
Bjarnason, Margrét, 84
Björn of Víðimýri, 76
Björnsdóttir, Inga Dóra, 30
Boag, Peter, 26
bobbed hair, 118–20
Böðvarsson, Tímoteus, 87–8
body, the, and migrant culture, 27, 103, 162, 166
*bóluveturinn* ("smallpox winter"), 13, 15, 17, 27, 37–9, 62, 76, 101, 144, 157; and ghost stories about, 89–92. *See also* Nes smallpox cemetery; smallpox epidemic
bootlegging, 71–3
Bottineau, North Dakota, 147. *See also* Dakota Territory/North Dakota
Brandson, Aðalbjörg Benediktsdóttir, 154
Brazil, Icelandic migration to, 10, 54, 61
*brennivín*, 57–8, 60, 65
Briem, Rannveig, 44, 45, 187n59
British Columbia: Indigenous communities in, 14; and Japanese internment, 126; landscape in, 195n38; settlements in, 18, 126–7
brothels, 49–50
Brown, Marie A., 107
Brydon, Anne, 7, 90–1, 197n57
Búason, Guðrún, 66, 67
Burdock Blood Bitters, 71–2
Burial Point. *See* Nes smallpox cemetery
Buse, Peter, 78

Canada: colonial expansion into northwest, 14–17; Departments of Public Information and External Affairs, 128; early migration to, 10–12; eugenics movement in, 107; Indian Act (1876), 16; Japanese internment camps in, 126; Manitoba Act (1870), 15–16; and nationalism among Icelandic immigrants, 18; North-West Resistance in, 15; pro-pluralism campaigns in, 146; public ethnic-revival campaigns, 205n26. *See also specific locations and provinces*
Canadian Museum of History, 20
cardamom in baking, 135, 151–3
Carley Brothers' Clothing Company, Winnipeg, 52
Catholicism and anti-Catholic sentiment, 32, 106–7, 114, 152–3
Chicago: during Second World War, 122; World's Columbian Exposition (1893), 107
children: and child mortality, 22, 36, 88, 97, 156–7, 164; foster, 88; as ghosts, 76–7, 80–1, 84, 87–8, 97, 99; as labourers, 77, 87–8
Chinese immigrants, 33
Christmas cake. *See vínarterta*
class. *See* elite classes; merchants and merchant class; poverty and class issues
Clausen, Oscar, 192n60
clothing practices: and class, 47–9; climate-appropriate, 19, 27, 36, 40, 42; and clothing markets, Icelandic-language, 52; and dress-reform fashions, 28–32; and Icelandic independence movement, 27–30; Indigenous, 38–40; moral and sexual corruption associated with, 49; North American reception of Icelandic, 31–2; overview, 53, 162–3; and racial identity, 32–5; role of 24–7; and xenophobia, 26, 53, 163. *See also* knitting and knitwear
coffee (*kaffi*) culture among Icelanders: among new immigrants, 60–4; and coffee-cup readings, 86; in daily working and social life, 57, 63, 63–4; and *kaffihús* (coffeehouses), 64; history of, 56; overview, 54–5, 73–5; in private sphere, 143; and quality assessments, 57, 163; roasting and brewing methods, 62–3; in rural areas, 142; significance of, 163; as source of comfort, 60; symbolic associations with, 150. *See also kaffi poki*
"cohesive community" model, 19
Cold War, 131–2, 145–50, 154, 157, 165
colonialism and colonial encounters, 11, 13, 14–17, 19, 22, 37–42, 89–90, 92; and ghost stories discussing, 77–80, 90, 92, 97, 99–100, 164
Columbia Press, 116
Columbus, Christopher, 106–7
communism. *See* Cold War
cooking, 137–8. *See also vínarterta*
*coolie* (as term), 33
Copenhagen: baking trends and recipes in, 138–40; political climate in, 27
Cree people (Nehiyawak), 14, 15, 17, 39–40, 89–90, 153, 186n51
critical ethnic-community historiography, 176n5
"cultural death" narrative, 7, 23, 166
Custer, General George A., 17

Dakota Territory/North Dakota, 3, 13, 17, 18, 33, 46, 62, 66, 69, 105, 116, 145, 147, 150, 155, 157, 161. *See also specific towns and settlements*

Danielsen, Helge, 132, 147
Danish Empire and connections to Iceland, 10, 11, 21, 27–30, 35, 43, 55–60, 115, 124, 137–41
Danish migrants to North America, 10, 139–40. *See also* Denmark
Danish West Indies, 29, 140
Danish pastry, 138–9
Day, Madeleine, 143
deacon of Myrká, story of, 193n4
Denmark: and alcohol consumption among Icelandic people, 55–6, 59–60, 138; clothing fashions from, 28–30; coffee and confections as signs of status in, 138; cookbook publication in, 138–9; culinary trends from, 137–41, 159; emigration from, 6; Icelandic independence from, 8, 13, 26, 27; Manitoban Icelanders' perceptions of, 115; migrants from, 10, 139–40; Nazi occupation of, 122–4; racialized systems of power within empire of, 35; and Viennese baking, 137–41
Derrida, Jacques: *The Spectres of Marx*, 79
Deuce of August festival, 105
Diamond Jubilee parade, Winnipeg, 104–5, *105*
Dirty Gísli (Gísli Jónsson), 66–8, 192n60
dogs and dogsleds, 33, 87, 93; dog ghost story, 87
domestic violence, 65
domestic work, 23, 47, 49, 50, 53
Dorey, Elizabeth, 154
Dorset people, 14
dreams and dream interpretation, 78, 80, 82, 86–7; and John Ramsay, 90, 92, 197n57
drownings and disappearances on Lake Winnipeg, 36, 86–7

*drykkjuvísa* (drinking poem), 73
Dubinsky, Karen, 49
"Duða" ghost story, 194n14
Dufferin, Lord, 12, 31–2, 179n36

Eaton, John David, 101, *102*
Eaton, Signy, 101, *102*, 108, 132–3, *133*
Einarsson, Helgi, 14, *15*
Einarsson, Henry, *15*
Einarsson, John, *15*
Einarsson, Magnús, 82–4, 87, 194n14
Einarsson, Sigríður, 126, *127*
Einarsson, William, *15*
Eiríksdóttir, Freydís (sister of Leifur Eiríksson), 118
Eiríksdóttir, Þóra, 81
Eiríksson, Hallfreður Örn, 83, 86; *Sögur úr vesturheimi* (Stories from the New World), 82
Eiríksson, Leifur, 10, 104, 106, 132
Eliasson, Magnús, 14, 86–7
elite classes: and alcohol imports, 60; clothing fashion of, 44; coffee consumption among, 56; and "cohesive community" model, 19; and continental-style baking, 138, 139; and Icelandic Women's Society, 50; and inequality in Iceland, 30; urban labourers' resentment towards, 68. *See also* poverty and class issues
elves. *See huldufólk*
Engimýri, Manitoba, 96
English-language employment, 50–2, 109. *See also* anglicization; anglophone society
English-only education, 114, 115
Epp, Marlene, 154–6
Erlendsson, Guðbrandur, 61, 189n14
"Eskimo Lady." *See* Sölvadóttir, Ólöf
"Eskimos," Icelanders labelled as, 32–5, 104, 106, 130. *See also* ethnic

and racial identities; race and racialization; xenophobia
ethnic foods, depictions of, 145–6. *See also specific foods*
ethnic and racial identities: clothing as sign of, 27, 53; of Icelanders in Canada, 35; and labour, 32–3; during world wars, 22, 108–9, 114, 126, 130, 144; and xenophobia, 22, 26, 109–11, 133. *See also* "Eskimos," Icelanders labelled as; race and racialization; Viking imagery; whiteness
eugenics movement, 107
Europe. *See* Austro-Hungarian Empire; Denmark; First World War; Norway; Second World War; Sweden, migrants from
European immigrants in North America, land rights for, 10–16. *See also* Catholicism and anti-Catholic sentiment; Denmark; Norway; Scandinavians and Scandinavian culture; Sweden
exoticism, 26, 101. *See also* Sölvadóttir, Ólöf
Eyford, Ryan, 16, 90–1, 110, 180n47
Eyrarbakki Icelandic Heritage Centre, Hnausa, Manitoba, 20

farms and farming: and autobiographical writing by farmers, 181n54; and coffee breaks, 64; and colonial project, 92–3; difficulties in establishing, 13; ghost stories connected to, 85, 87, 89, 90, 96–7, 195n38; in Iceland, 8, 178n4; in *Iceland on the Prairies*, 129; Norwegian, 11; outside New Iceland, 43; and priority of "luxury items" over produce from, 60, 74; subsistence versus wealthier, 59; urban wages supporting, 44, 46. *See also specific farmers and settlements*
*feigð* (pending death), premonitions of, 85–6
feminism, 66, 103, 115, 117–18
*fépúki* (ghost), 80
festivals and parades, 4, 103–5, 117–18, 129, 132–4, 165. *See also specific festivals and parades*
Fidler, Elizabeth, 38
Finkelstein, Moses, 62
Finnsdóttir, Guðrún H.: "Lost Tracks," 108
*fínum tízkufötum* (fashionable clothing), 52
First Nations communities. *See* Indigenous communities; *specific nations and communities*
First World War: and diverse political culture of Icelandic immigrants, 134; and English-only education law, 114; and ethnic difference, fear and concealment of, 22, 108, 114, 126, 144; and fitness of soldiers, 107; and support and dissent within Icelandic immigrant community, 111, 115, 117, 121; and Viking spirit narrative, 122, 134
Fisher River Cree Nation, 14
fishing and ice fishing: and alcohol consumption and production, 60, 72–3, 164; and apparitions of fishermen, 86; and autobiographical writing by fishermen, 20, 181n54; clothing worn for, 21, 39, 40; dangers of, 156; and dreams, beliefs around, 86, 90; and economic and social structure in Iceland, 8; among First Nations, 16; and

First Nations spirits, 89, 186n53; in Iceland, 8, 60, 178n14; and Indigenous fishermen, 14, 38; in New Iceland, 44; on Pacific Coast, 18; pack ice affecting, 178n14. *See also specific settlements and fishing communities*

*Fjallkona* (Mountain Woman), 118–21, *119*, 132–3, *133*

folk costumes, 26. *See also* clothing practices

food: depictions of Icelandic immigrant, 146; and food culture from Iceland in North America, 137; and food security, 10; and hospitality, 125, 129–30, 145, 147; in *Iceland on the Prairies*, 129–30, 145; imported, 138; and "luxury items," 60, 62, 74; as medium of immigrant histories, 154–6, 158, 160; merchant suppliers of, 39; and private Icelandic material culture, 142; propaganda campaigns promoting immigrant, 145, 146; Turkish and Viennese, 204n9; in wintertime, 36–7. *See also amma*; hunger and food shortages; recipes; *specific foods and desserts*

Ford, A.R., 106

foster children, 88

Framfarafélagið (Progressive Society), 71

*Framfari* newspaper, 52, 67, 68

Franzdóttir, Olga María, 86; *Sögur úr vesturheimi* (Stories from the New World), 82

freezing temperatures and deaths, 36, 87, 88

French Canadians, 114

*Freyja* (publication), 115, 117

Friðriksson, Friðjón, 24, *25*; business pursuits of, 39, 43–4; employment agency established by, 46; migrant journey of, 24; on purging the old "sins," 65; and Ramsay, John, 180n42; on superstitious belief, 83

Friedel, Lovise Beate Augustine: *Nye og fuldstændige confecture*, 138–9, 141

Friesen, Gerald, 114

Fristrup, Clara Margrethe, 138, 139

Furstenau, "Sunna" Pam, 155

*fylgjur*. *See* spirit followers

Gabaccia, Donna, 154

gender, 19, 21, 26, 30, 44–52, 55, 57, 64–70, 73, 74–5, 99, 101, 104, 111, 117–31, 132, 140–2, 146–50, 153–60, 162–6. *See also* men; Viking imagery; women

Gerrard, Helga, xiv, 110–11

Gerrard, Nelson, 31, 84, 157; *Icelandic River Saga*, 177n9

Geysir, Manitoba, 81, 84

Geysir Bakery, Winnipeg, 143

ghosts and *hjátrú* (superstition, or folk belief): Christian religious figures in, 78, 193n4; and First Nations, 89–99, 100, 164, 196n53; and "ghost settlement," Manitoba, 81; and *hjátrú* and hauntology, 77–80, 82–3, 86–7, 92–3, 97, 99, 164, 193n14, 194n25, 196n53; and *huldufólk*, 83–8; justice understood through, 89–100; language of, 77; migration themes within, 81, 84; oral collections of, 82; overview, 76–7, 164; and physical reality and seriousness of, 76–7, 85; and power dynamics, 77, 80, 87, 88, 99

Gilbert, Kathleen B., 145

Gimli, Manitoba: arrival in, 12; coffee culture in, 142; Good Templar lodges in, 71; Icelandic Canadian Society in, 208n74; Icelandic Day

festivals in, 129, 132–3; parades in, 3, 105; symbolic status of, 17–18; Viking statue in, 132–3
Gíslason, Erlendur, 52
Gissurarson, Loftur Reimar, 78
Glyndon, Minnesota, 31
Goebbels, Joseph, 125
Gold, Carol, 138
Goodman, Elizabeth, 50
Goodman (Peterson), Jóna S., 147–9, *148*, 171
Good Templar movement, 55, 65, 71. *See also* temperance movement
*goolie* (as term) and associations, 5, 33, 71, 110, 161–2, 175n3, 199n29
"Goolie Hall" (Icelandic Good Templars Hall), Winnipeg, 71
Graftarnes. *See* Nes smallpox cemetery
Great Depression, 22, 103
Greenland: Icelandic colony in, 10, 179n25; communities in, 14, 29
Grétarsdóttir, Tinna, 7, 194n26, 201n54
Guðlaugson, Magnús, 62
Guðmundsdóttir, Anna Sigríður, 36
Guðmundsdóttir, Rósamunda, 47, 48
Gudmundson, Alice, 156
Gudmundsson, Lára, 85–6, 187n59
Guðmundsson, Sigurður "Málari" (the Painter), 28
Guglielmo, Thomas, 32
Gunnarsson, Geir H., 150
Gunnlaugsson, Gísli Ágúst, 88
Gunnlaugson, Kristín, 154
Guttormsson, Guttormur, 39–40, *91*, 96, 97, 109

Hahnemann, Trine, 141
hair, 31, 32, 35, 69, *70*, 113, 118–21, *120*, 125, 155
Hálfdánarson, Guðmundur, 8, 30
Halldór Briem, 31–2, 43
Halldorson, Salome, 107, 121–2
Hallgrímsson, Magnús, 96, 97
Hamilton, Alice, 50
Hansen, Marcus Lee, 144
*harðfiskur* (dried fish eaten with butter), 137, 142
Harvey, Katherine, 65
hauntings. *See* ghosts and *hjátrú*; Nes smallpox cemetery
Hecla Island, Manitoba, 153
Hecla Press, 116
*Heimskringla* newspaper, 71, 115, 119–20, 128. *See also Lögberg-Heimskringla* newspaper
Hekla IOGT lodge, 66, 71
Helgadóttir, Herdís, 126
Helgason, Jón Karl, 150
Henie, Sonja, 130, *131*
Heron, Craig, 56
hidden people. *See huldufólk*
Hjálmarsson, Hjálmur, 36
*hjátrú* (superstition, or folk belief). *See* ghosts and *hjátrú*
Hjörleifsson, Einar (Kvaran), 31, 43, 52, 82
Hnausa, Manitoba, 20, 150, 190n41
Hoffman's Drops, 72
Holm, Bill, 135, 151, 156, 160
Holm, Cliff and Lilja, 86
Holm, Torfhildur, 44, 187n59
hospitality and wartime campaigns, 103, 121–6, 129–31, 137, 145–50
Hreinsson, Viðar, 117
Hudson's Bay Company, 11, 15
*huldufólk* (hidden people, or land spirits), 80, 83–8, 92, 195n38
Hunchuk, S. Holyk, 154–6
hunger and food shortages, 12, 55, 60, 140, 156; during Cold War, 146; and desserts as status symbols, 140; in Iceland, 60, 156; and sacred nature of food, 156. *See also* food

Iacovetta, Franca, 19, 146, 198n3
ice fishing. *See* fishing and ice fishing
Iceland: Allied occupation of, 103–4, 121–9, 145; American forces in, 131–2; anti-emigration sentiment in, 6, 105–6; Christianity in, 78; climate and geography of, 7–8, 13, 35–6, 177n14; coffee and desserts as signs of status in, 140; cultural gaps and exchange with, 6; Danish and continental baking in, 137–9; food culture shifts in, 150–1; "gentleman travellers" to, 12; and hospitality of Icelanders, 125, 129–31, 145; and international markets, access to, 137; modernization and urbanization of, 5; nationalism and independence movement in, 8, 13, 26–9, 35, 53, 124, 128, 176n6; NATO forces in, 146–7, 165, 206n35; poverty and class issues in, 8, 178n18; pro-British sentiment in, 187n57; superstition in, 78; temperance and feminist sentiment in, 65–6; US propaganda campaign in, 146. *See also* coffee (*kaffi*) culture among Icelanders; *specific foods and desserts*
*Iceland* (film), 130–1, *131*
*Icelandic Canadian* magazine, 121, 201n67
Icelandic Collection, University of Manitoba, 20
Icelandic Day festivals, 105, 118, 129, 132–3
Icelandic Good Templars Hall ("Goolie Hall"), Winnipeg, 71
"Icelandic House," Winnipeg, 67
Icelandic immigrant culture and communities: and Allied occupation of Iceland, 103–4, 121–9, 145; beverage culture among, 164; *einstaklingur* (individual) attitude in, 151; *goolie* component of, 161–2; identity among, 32, 35, 134, 160, 166; literary output of, 6, 20, 49, 103, 104, 115–18, 181n54; material-cultural traditions of, 142, 143, 159; and NATO forces in Iceland, 146–7, 165, 206n35; and propaganda about hospitality of, 129–31; second-, third-, and fourth-generation, 144–5; status and acceptance of, 165; urbanization of, 52, 68. *See also* alcohol consumption among Icelanders; coffee (*kaffi*) culture among Icelanders; identity and identity formation; private and public natures of Icelandic immigrant culture; *specific locations*
Icelandic-language forums, 77, 80, 101–34
Icelandic Main Street, Winnipeg, 18
Icelandic National League, 128
Icelandic River settlement, Riverton, 44, 71, 72, 89
Icelandic sagas, 10, 14, 28–9, 66, 78, 82, 106–7, 117–18, 122. *See also* Viking imagery; *specific names from the sagas*
Icelandic State Park, North Dakota, 183n57. *See also* Dakota Territory/North Dakota
Icelandic Student Society, 71
Icelandic Women's Society, 50, *51*
identity and identity formation: and the *amma*, importance of, 155; and anglicization, 109; through clothing practices, 26, 30; coffee as part of, 55; endurance of, 3, 7, 134, 151; masculine gender identities, 69; and three-dimensional texture of immigrant cultures, 3–4; Viking, 6; and *vínarterta*, 135, 152, 160, 165; and whiteness, 32; world wars

affecting, 104. *See also* ethnic and racial identities
Ignatiev, Noel, 32
immigration, overview of Icelandic, 3–14. *See also* Icelandic immigrant culture and communities; *specific communities and groups*
Imperial Order Daughters of the Empire, Jón Sigurðsson Chapter, 71, 111, 128, 200n34
Independent Order of Good Templars, 71. *See also* Good Templar movement
Indian Act (1876), 16
Indigenous communities: clothing of, 27, 38–40, *41*, 163; and Icelandic immigrants, relations with, 13–17, 90–2, 100; resistance, 14–17, 38; smallpox epidemic and, 13, 15, 37–9, 93, 97, 186n51. *See also* Fidler, Elizabeth; marriage and intermarriage; Métis communities; Monkman, Joseph; Ramsay, John; Riel, Louis; Thomas, Rev. Edward; *specific communities and nations*
infant mortality. *See* children
Ingalls, Maxine, 153
Ingimundarson, Valur, 206n35
Innu people, 14
intergenerational ghosts, 89
Interlake First Nations, 153
Inuit people, 14, 29
Irish Catholic immigrants, 32
Ísleifsson, Sumarliði, 28
*Íslendingadagurinn* (Icelandic Festival), 105
*Íslendingur* newspaper, 56
Italian immigrants, 32, 106

Jacobson, Matthew Frye, 3–4
Jameson, Fredric, 79
Japanese Canadians, 126–7
Jóakimsdóttir, Aðalbjörg and Sigríður, 47, *48*
Johannesson, Conrad ("Air Ace"), 129
Jóhannesson, Sigurður Júlíus (Siggi Júl), 115–17, 121, 130
Jóhannsdóttir, Kristín M., 81
Jóhannsdóttir, Ólafía, 66
Jóhannsson, Jón Ólafur (Willow Point baby), 157
Johnson, Helga, 61–2
Johnson, Joe, 72–3
Johnson, Metta, 73
Johnson, Skúli, 129
Johnson, Thomas H., 110, 115, 117
Jónasson, Sigtryggur, 11, 12, 43–4, *45*, 187n57
Jónasson, Tómas, 96
Jónasson and Fredrickson Sawmill and Store, Icelandic River, 44
Jón Bjarnason Academy, Winnipeg, 109
Jónsdóttir, "Fabulous Sigga," 44, 62
Jónsdóttir, Guðrún, 47
Jónsdóttir, Ingveldur, 49
Jónsdóttir, Sigríður, 44, *46*
Jónsdóttir, Þóra Andrea Nikólína, 139
Jónsson, Gísli (Dirty Gísli), 66–8, 192n60
Jónsson, Jón, 40, 61
Jónsson, Jónína, 126, *127*
Josephson, Helen, 141
Júlíus, Kristján Niels (Káinn), 73

*kaffi poki* (coffee bag), 62–3, 142, 163, 190n41. *See also* coffee (*kaffi*) culture among Icelanders
Kahler, Louise, 152
Káinn (Júlíus, Kristján Niels), 73
*Kelduskóga-skotta* ghosts, 84–5
King, Mackenzie, 128
Kinmount, Ontario, 11–12, 24, 36
*kleinur* (knotted donuts), 137

knitting and knitwear, 28, 31, 40, 111, 142–3, 186n51. *See also* wool
Kolodny, Annette, 117
Kópavogur, Reykjavík, 84
Korinek, Valerie, 146
Krarer, Olof. *See* Sölvadóttir, Ólöf
Kristinsson, Júníus H., 177n13
Kristjanson, Albert, 64, 83
Kristjanson, Wilhelm, 19, *133*, 200n34
Kristjánsson, Albert, 109, 110
Ku Klux Klan, 107
Kvaran. *See* Hjörleifsson, Einar
Kwong, Matt, 152

Ladies' Aid of the Icelandic First Lutheran Church, Winnipeg, 154
*lækniskona* (medicine woman) ghost story, 196n53
Lake Winnipeg settlements: clothing worn in, 19, 38–40, 163; First Nations spirits inhabiting, 89; ghost stories from, 77, 81–100; homebrew production and consumption in, 71–3. *See also* fishing and ice fishing; immigration, overview of Icelandic; New Iceland settlement; smallpox epidemic; *specific communities*
Laki volcano, Iceland, 177n14
Lamoureux, Brett, 153
*Landneminn* publication, 47
land rights of Métis and First Nations peoples, 15–16, 180n47
Landsbókasafn Íslands (National Library of Iceland), 20
land spirits. *See huldufólk*
language, Icelandic, 6–7, 101–3, 108–15, 134, 159. *See also* anglicization; bilingualism; Icelandic-language forums
Lash, G.H., 128
Latour, Bruno, 19

laundry work, 18, 33, 50, 84, 126
"Leif the Lucky" Eiríksson, 10, 104, 106, 132
*Leirár-skotta*, 81
Leslie, Saskatchewan, 88
Library and Archives Canada, 20
Lindal, Sigrún, 118–21, *120*, 162
Lindal, Walter J., 19
Loewen, Royden, 114
Loftsdóttir, Kristín, 28, 35
Lögberg area, Saskatchewan, 61
*Lögberg-Heimskringla* newspaper, 150, 154. *See also Heimskringla* newspaper
*Lögberg* newspaper, 52, 71, 114–16, 147
lumber industry, 69, 93

Magnússon, Eiríkur, 118
Magnusson, Kristjana, 190n41
Magnússon, Magnús, 33, 35
Magnússon, Sigurður Gylfi, 137
Magnússon, Stefanía, 121
Maliseet people, 14
Manitoba: English-only education in, 114, 115; Jóhannsdóttir, Ólafía in, 66; public ethnic-revival campaigns, 205n26; *vínarterta* in, 153. *See also specific settlements and locations*
Manitoba Act (1870), 15–16
*Manitoba Free Press*, 108, 114
Manitoba Museum, 20
Marcus, Clare, 145
Markerville, Alberta, 18, 116
Markland, Nova Scotia, 12, 14
marriage and intermarriage, 14–15, 47, 108, 109, 144
Marshall Plan, 132
masculinity and drinking culture, 66–74. *See also* alcohol consumption among Icelanders; men; Viking imagery

material culture, 4, 19, 20, 142–3, 159.
    *See also specific objects*
Matheson Island, Manitoba, 14
"matrilineal bias," 155
Mattíasdóttir, Sigríður, 28
*McCall's* magazine, 147, *149*, 153–4
McCully, Helen, 147
Melsteð, Jón, 87, 89
Melsted, Ken, 156–7
men: alcohol consumption among, 55, 57, 65, 69, 74, 163–4; as urban labourers, 68–9
Mennonite communities, 13, 16, 153, 156
merchants and merchant class, 52, 59–60, 137–8. *See also specific individuals*
Metcalfe, Frederick, 59
Métis communities, 14–16, 39–40, 89–90, 153. *See also* Indigenous communities; Monkman, Joseph; Riel, Louis; *specific communities*
Michaelson, Sarah, 199n29
migrant (as term), 179n29
Mi'kmaq people, 14
Miller, Jennifer, 153, 158
Miller, Monica J., 26
Milwaukee, Icelandic community in, 24, *48*, 187n59
Minnesota: reception of Icelandic immigrants in, 31; settlements in, 18; *vínarterta* recipes in, 151
"Mist Famine" *(Móðuharðindi)*, 177n14
mixed-race children, 14. *See also* marriage and intermarriage
moccasins, 39–40
*moccasintreyjur* (moccasin jackets), 40, *41*
Möðruvellir, Manitoba, 44
Monkman, Joseph, 37
Mormon missionaries and migration, 10, 18

Morris, Alexander, 16
Mountain, North Dakota, 3, 105, 155, 157. *See also* Dakota Territory/ North Dakota
Mulligan, Dave, 38
Muskoka, Ontario, 36

names, anglicization of, 17, 50–2, 144. *See also* assimilation
Náströnd (Corpse Beach), Riverton, 76. *See also* Nes smallpox cemetery
National Film Board: *Food: Weapon of Conquest*, 125; *Iceland on the Prairies*, 129–30, 134, 145, 147, 202n67
NATO forces in Iceland, 146–7
Nazi propaganda, 103, 122, *123*. *See also* Second World War
Nehiyawak (Cree) language, 14
Neijmann, Daisy, 124, 159, 182n55
Nes smallpox cemetery, 76, 89, 93–9, *94–5*
New Iceland Heritage Museum, Gimli, 20
New Iceland settlement: child mortality at, 157; conditions and climate at, 13, 36–7, 191n51; early migration to, 11–12; exodus from, 17–18, 43; food traditions at, 142; governance in, 13–14; and Indigenous communities, relations with, 13–17; infant mortality at, 157; parades in, 3; reputation of immigrants in, 68; tea in, 61; temperance and conflict in, 71–3. *See also* Icelandic immigrant culture and communities; immigration, overview of Icelandic; smallpox epidemic; *specific communities*
*New York Star*, 31
*New York Times*, 110
Nordal, Lárus, 88

Norse mythology and pre-Christian belief, 12, 78. *See also* Viking imagery
North Dakota. *See* Dakota Territory/ North Dakota; *specific towns and locations*
northern peoples, perceptions of, 33–5. *See also* "Eskimos," Icelanders labelled as; xenophobia
North-West Resistance (Canada), 15
Norway: coffee consumption among migrants from, 61; ghost story involving man from, 83, 87; Icelanders' connection to, 28–9, 35; migrants from, 6, 10, 11; Nazi propaganda in, 122, *123*
Norway House Cree Nation, 16
Norwegian Lutheran Synod, 11
Núnanow festival, 4

Oddsdóttir Vigfússon, Rósa, 84
Ögmundardóttir, Helga, 92
Ojibwe (Anishinaabe) people, 15, 39, 40, 89–90, 186n51
Ólafsdóttir, Hildigunnur, 56, 59, 189n18
Ólafsson, Jón, 11
Ólafsson, Ólafur, 16–17
"old Icelandic Adam" metaphor, 64–5, 75
"old Indian trails," 93
197th (Vikings of Canada) Battalion, 111–13, *112–13*
Ontario, settlements in, 11–12, 24, 36
Osgoode, Kenneth, 147
Ósland, British Columbia, 18, 126, *127*
overview of chapters, 20–3

Pacific Coast settlements, 18. *See also* Alaska/Alaskan Territory, settlements in; British Columbia; Washington state
pacifism, 116–17, 121, 122, 129, 134

Palmer, Howard, 114
Pálsdóttir, Steinvör Wilhelmína, 157
Payne, John, 130, *131*
Peguis First Nation, 38, 153
Pembina County, Dakota Territory, 18. *See also* Dakota Territory/ North Dakota
Pembina County Historical Museum, North Dakota, 183n57
Peterson, Mrs. Svein (Jóna Goodman), 147–9, *148*, 171
*peysuföt* (outfit), 28, *29*, 30–1
Point Roberts, Washington, 18, 195n38
Polish immigrants, 145
political radicalism, 19, 103, 113–17, 121–2
"politicized culturalism," 131–2
*pönnukökur* (pancakes), 137, 142
popular historical scholarship, 181n54
poverty and class issues: and alcohol consumption, 59–60, 69; clothing styles reflecting, 42–3, 47–50; and "cohesive community" model explanations, 19; in Iceland, 8, 137–8; in Möðruvellir, Manitoba, 44; among women, 30, 47–50. *See also* elite classes; merchants and merchant class
"principle of third generation interest," 144
private and public natures of Icelandic immigrant culture: alcohol consumption, 55, 72, 74; assimilation discussions, 166; *hjátrú* narratives, 76–101; material-cultural traditions, 142, 143; pre-Christian faith in Iceland, 78; superstition, 76–101; *vínarterta*, 137, 151, 156, 157, 159. *See also* anglicization; Icelandic immigrant culture and communities
prophetic dreaming *(berdreymi)*, 80

Index                                                                 241

pro-pluralism campaigns, 146, 154
*Prose Edda*, 12, 122
Provincial Archives of Manitoba, 20
prunes in Icelandic baking, 140–1, 152, 205n17
psychic ability *(skyggni)*, 80, 194n25
public ethnic-revival campaigns, 144, 205n26
publishing industry, Icelandic, 103, 115–18

quarantine (smallpox epidemic), 37, 48, 62
Quebec City, immigration sheds in, 13, 37

race and racialization: ambiguity, 32–5, 166; anglicization, 144–5; *hjátrú* narratives, 99, 164; Icelandic–Indigenous relationships, racism affecting, 14–15; mixed-race children, 14; power in Denmark, 35; Viking heritage, politics of, 6, 104–7, 122, 165. *See also* "Eskimos," Icelanders labelled as; ethnic and racial identities; whiteness; xenophobia
Rafnsson, Sveinbjörn, 177
*ragnarök* (end of the world), 12
Ramsay, Betsey, 38, 90, 91
Ramsay, John: and confrontations with Icelandic immigrants, 16; dream story featuring, 90–2, 197n57; economic activities of, 39–40, 180n46; grave of, *91*; language abilities of, 14, 180n42; smallpox epidemic affecting, 37–8, 186n51
*randalín* (dessert), 137, 151, 153
recipes for *vínarterta*, 137–59, 167–74. *See also vínarterta; specific foods*
Red River Resistance (1869–70), 15–16

"Republic of New Iceland," 13. *See also* New Iceland settlement
Reykjavík, 4, 48; Allied forces in, 124–6; Icelandic Parliament riot (1949) in, 146; women and soldiers in, 126, 131
Rice, Richard M., 155
Riel, Louis, 14–15
Riverton, Manitoba: alcohol production in, 72; coffee culture in, 142; fishermen in, *42*; ghost stories from, 76, 81, 86; Icelandic sites in, 5; knitwear production in, 143; Ramsay graves in, *91*; smallpox epidemic near, 90; supernatural figures in, 76–99. *See also* Icelandic River settlement; Möðruvellir, Manitoba; New Iceland settlement
Roberts, Julia, 56
Roediger, David, 32
Roedsted Schmidt, Mathilde, 138
Rögnvaldardóttir, Nanna, 150
Roman Catholic Church, 107. *See also* Catholicism and anti-Catholic sentiment
Rosseau, Ontario, 11–12
Rostrup, Christine, 138
Royal Canadian Mounted Police, 126
Royal North-West Mounted Police, 117
*rúllupylsa* (rolled spiced lamb), 137, 142, 147–8, 151
Rupert's Land, 15

sagas, Icelandic, 10, 14, 28–9, 66, 78, 82, 106–7, 117–18, 122. *See also* Viking imagery; *specific names from the sagas*
Sainte Rose du Lac, Manitoba, 14
Sakamoto, Hatsue, 126, *127*
Salverson, Laura Goodman, 50, 113, 121, 122, 182n55

Sandy Bar Band, 37, 180n47. *See also* Ramsay, Betsey; Ramsay, John
Sandy River, Manitoba, 38
Saskatchewan: farms in, 46; Leslie, 88; Lögberg area, 61; and Rupert's Land, 15; Vatnabyggð district, 18; Wynyard, 156
Scandinavians and Scandinavian culture, 6, 35, 103, 104, 106, 117, 132, 134; Icelanders identifying themselves as, 5–6, 110–13
Scottish Burns Supper, 142
Seattle, 18
Second World War, 22, 103, 108, 109, 111, 121–31, 145, 150–1; celebrations of Icelandic immigrant food during, 145; and ethnic difference, fear of, 22, 109; and Icelandic independence movement, 128; and Nazi appropriation of Viking past, 103; occupation of Iceland during, 121–4, 128, 130–1, 206n35; and political views of Icelandic immigrants, 134. *See also* Nazi propaganda
sewing, 44
sex trade, 27, 49–50
Shanty Town, Winnipeg, 18, 68
Shawano County, Wisconsin, 18
Siggi Júl. *See* Jóhannesson, Sigurður Júlíus
Sigurðardóttir (Friðriksson), Guðný, 24, *25*, 39, 44, 187n59
Sigurdson, Halldora, 152
Sigurdsson, Bergljót, 83, 97, *98*
Sigurðsson, Jón, 71, 111, 128, 200n34
Sigvaldason, Margaret (Miss Canada), 150
Simonson, Simon, 36, 44
Simundsson, Erla, 151
Sioux people, 17
*sjómannavettlingar* (fishermen's mittens), 40

Skallagrímsson, Egill, 65–6
Skaptason, J.B., 128
Skaptason, Jóhanna Guðrún, 111
*skinnskór* (Icelandic shoes), 39–40
*skotta* or *móri* (female or male ghosts), 81, 84–5, 99
*skotthúfa*, 28, *29*, 30–1, 53, 142, 163
Skrámur (ghost story about), 76
Skúlason, Hrund, 81, 116
Skuld Temperance Lodge, 71
*skyr* (Icelandic yogurt), 147–8
smallpox epidemic (1876–7), 13, 15, 17, 27, 37–9, 62, 76, 90, 101, 144, 157, 186n51; and ghost stories about, 89–92. *See also* Nes smallpox cemetery
Sölvadóttir, Kristín, as influence for Snow White, 64
Sölvadóttir, Ólöf, 26–7, 33–5, *34*, 191n42
South Asian immigrants, 33
Spanish Fork, Utah, 10, 18
spirit followers (*fylgjur*), 80, 81, 87–8, 164, 194n25
spiritualist movement, 81–2
*staðardraugar* (place ghosts), 81
Stadfeldt, Hallgrímur, 93, 97
Stefánsdóttir, Guðleif, 8, *9*
Stefansdóttir, Stefanía Friðrika, 86
Stefánsson, Jóhannes ("long-haired Joe"), 69, *70*
Stefánsson, Kristján, 8, *9*, 178n19
Stefánsson, Magnús, 38
Stefansson, Sigurbjörg "Bogga": *Gimli Saga*, 182n55
Stefánsson, Vilhjálmur, 69, 110
Stefansson, Canadian political family, 178n19
Steinsson, Friðbjörn, 60
Stephansson, Stephan G., 18, 116, 121, 161, 209n1; *Vígslóði*, 117
Stephenson, Friðrik, 101, 116

Stephenson, Signy. *See* Eaton, Signy
Stern, Elizabeth, 79, 99–100
Stobie, Margaret, 38
stone hearths, 137
Stony Mountain Prison, 33
Stott, Andrew, 78
St. Thomas, St. Croix, and St. John islands, 29, 140
Sutton, David, 158
Swatos, William H., Jr., 78
Sweden, migrants from, 6, 61, 69, 106, 145
Swyripa, Frances, 7, 65, 114

Taylor, John, 12, 43
tea, 54, 57, 61
T. Eaton Company, 101
temperance movement: in Iceland, 59–60; overview, 73–5, 164–5; popularity of, 55, 73; scholarly focus on, 56; and social progress, notions of, 64–6. *See also* Good Templar movement
*teppi* (quilt), 143
Thingvellir district, Saskatchewan, 18
Thomas, Alfred, 38
Thomas, Edward, 38
Thor, Jónas, 7
Thórarinsson, Thorvaldur, 69
Thorláksson, Reverend Páll, 11, 13
Thorson, Charlie, 64
Thorson, Joseph T., 128–9
three-dimensional nature of immigrant cultures, 3–4, 23, 162
time, cultural conceptions of, 79
*Time* magazine, 124–5
Tómasdóttir, Rannveig, 14
Trach, Doreen-Dawne, 158
transport and mail infrastructure, 71
trauma and colonialism, 164; ghost stories reflecting, 77–80, 92, 97, 99–100, 164; and Icelandic immigrant culture, 19, 90; and immigrants' role in the colonial project, 90, 92. *See also* smallpox epidemic
Turkish origin of Viennese foods, 204n9
Turville-Petre, G., 78
Twentieth Century Fox: *Iceland*, 130–1, *131*
223rd Battalion (Canadian Scandinavians), 111–13, *112–13*

Ukrainian immigrants, 72, 87, 110, 114, 145, 155, 156
Unitarians, 81, 115
United States: and Allied occupation of Iceland, 103–4, 121–30, 145; early immigration to, 10–11; eugenics movement in, 107; Information Services, 147; and nationalism among Icelandic immigrants, 18; Program to Decrease the Vulnerability of the Icelandic Government to Communist Seizure of Power, 146; pro-pluralism campaigns in, 146; public ethnic-revival campaigns in, 205n26; treatment of immigrants in, 160. *See also* Alaska/Alaskan Territory, settlements in; Dakota Territory/North Dakota; Minnesota; Utah, settlements in; Washington state; Wisconsin; *specific locations*
University of Manitoba, 109
Utah, settlements in, 10, 18

Valgardson, W.D., 135, 152–3
Valverde, Mariana, 26, 49
Vatnabyggð district, Saskatchewan, 18
*Vestur Íslendingar* (Western Icelanders; as term), 7. *See also* Icelandic immigrant culture

and communities; immigration, overview of Icelandic; New Iceland settlement
Victoria, British Columbia, 18
Víðir, Manitoba, 72, 81
Vienna bakeries, 138–9
Vienna Cake, 140
Viennese baking, 138–40, 204n9, 205n26
Viennese bread (Danish pastry), 138–9
Vigfússon, Trausti, 90, 197n57
Viking Age, 5–6, 10, 117, 201n67. *See also* Viking imagery
"Viking" gene and alcoholism myth, 66
Viking imagery, 10, 14, 28–9, 66, 78, 82, 106–7, 117–18, 122; and anti-immigrant sentiment, 101–3, 105–7; and Cold War propaganda, 132; and *Fjallkona* (Mountain Woman) parade, 118–21, *119*, 132–3, *133*; and heritage, politics of, 104–7; and Nazism, associations with, 122; overview, 164–5; strategic use of, 133, 164–5; and Viking immigrant soldier, 111–13; and Viking statue in Gimli, 132, *133*; and whiteness, 103, 106–7, 165. *See also* Viking-themed parades
Viking Press, 116
Viking-themed parades, 3, 22, 104, 164–5. *See also specific parades and festivals*
*vínarterta* (fruit torte), 135–60, 167–74; and Cold War, 145–50, 154, 157, 165; in First Nations and Métis communities, 14; in *Iceland on the Prairies*, 145; memory and generational bonds through tradition of, 153–8, 160, 165–6; and nineteenth-century Icelandic society, 139–41; in North America, 141–3, 150–1; overview, 136–7, 158–60, 165–6; popularity of, 150–1; and public ethnic-revival campaigns, 144, 205n26; recipes for, 135, 151–4, 159, 165, 167–74; symbolic associations with, 135, 144, 147, 150–2, 154–60, 162, 165–6
Vinland voyages, 10, 104, *105*, 106–7, 132
*vinnumenn* and *vinnukonur* (male and female farm servants), 178n18
Virgin Islands, 140
*Voröld* newspaper, 114

Walt Disney Company, 64
Walters, Thorstína, 31, 62, 84–5, 150; *Modern Sagas*, 132, 182n55
Ward, Elisabeth, 107
Washington Island, Lake Michigan, 10
Washington state, 18; landscape in, 195n38
West Indies, 29, 140
Wevel Café, Winnipeg, 64
Whatcom County, Washington, 18
wheat flour, 138, 167, 168
wheat sheaves, 156
whiteness, 28–9, 32–3, 35, 103, 106–7, 165. *See also* "Eskimos," Icelanders labelled as; race and racialization; Viking imagery; xenophobia
White Rock monument, Gimli, 157, 208n74
Wickmann, William, 10
*Wienerbrød* (Viennese bread), 138–9
*Wienertærte* (Vienna Torte), 138–9, 141, 167–8. *See also vínarterta*
Willow Point, Manitoba, 12, 157, 208n74
Willow Point baby, 157, 160
Winnipeg: climate in, 191n51; coffee culture in, 142; coffee quality in,

62; construction boom (1880s) in, 46–7, 69; *Fjallkona* pageant (1924), 118–21; Icelandic immigrants in, 18, 68; *kaffihús* (coffeehouses) in, 64; labourers and employment in, 43–7, 68–9; reputation of Icelandic community in, 68; sex trade in, 49–50; tailors in, 52; West End, 5, 116; working Icelandic women in, 27, 44–5
Winnipeg Falcons, 110
*Winnipeg Free Press*, 132, 154
Winnipeg General Strike, 103, 114, 116
"Winnipeg Icelandic," 109
*Winnipeg Tribune*, 111–13
winter climates, 35–6
Wisconsin: economic opportunities in, 30; Icelandic immigrants in, 11, 12, 18; Norwegian communities in, 11; Sigurðardóttir, Guðný, and Friðriksson, Friðjón, in, 24. *See also* Milwaukee, Icelandic community in
Wolf, Kirsten, 105, 182n55
women: and Allied occupation in Iceland, 104, 124–31; and "bald women epidemic," 118–21, 162; clothing fashion of, 28–32, 47–9, 53; and coffee preparation, 57, 58; and femininity, 118; and food production, 137–9, 154; in heritage festivals and parades, 103, 118; hospitality of Icelandic, 124–6, 129–31; and immigrant motherhood, 157; and immigrant press, 117–18; and marriage, 47; political participation of, 121; and soldiers, dating, 125–6, 130; as symbolic embodiment of Icelandic nation, 134; in temperance movement, 65, 73; and *vínarterta* traditions, 154–5, 158; violence against, 49; working conditions for, 46–7, 49–50, 52–3; and written record, underrepresentation in, 20, 182n55
Woodward, Sophie, 26
wool, 19, 28–9, 31, 36, 40, 142–3. *See also* knitting and knitwear
World's Columbian Exposition, Chicago (1893), 107
world wars. *See* First World War; Second World War
Wynyard, Saskatchewan, 156

xenophobia: and anglicization, 109–10, 133, 144–5; and clothing practices, 26, 32–5, 53, 163; and nationalist fashions, 26; and Viking branding of Icelandic immigrant community, 101–3, 105–7; during world wars and Great Depression, 22, 111, 133–4. *See also* "Eskimos," Icelanders labelled as; race and racialization; Viking imagery

Zernack, Julia, 122
Zwecker, J.B.: *The Fjallkona*, 118, *119*

Þjóðminjasafn Íslands (National Museum of Iceland), 20; "Story of a Nation" permanent exhibit, 176n6
*Þjóðviljinn* (Icelandic Communist Party newspaper), 124
Þórarinsson, Sveinn, 60
Þorbjarnardóttir, Guðríður, 201n54
*Þorgeirsboli* (Thorgeir's bull), 81
Þórgilsson, Halldór, 66
Þorláksson, Páll, 11, 13
*Þorrablót* feast, 142

# Studies in Gender and History

General Editors: Franca Iacovetta and Karen Dubinsky

1 Suzanne Morton, *Ideal Surroundings: Domestic Life in a Working-Class Suburb in the 1920s*
2 Joan Sangster, *Earning Respect: The Lives of Working Women in Small-Town Ontario, 1920–1960*
3 Carolyn Strange, *Toronto's Girl Problem: The Perils and Pleasures of the City, 1880–1930*
4 Sara Z. Burke, *Seeking the Highest Good: Social Service and Gender at the University of Toronto, 1888–1937*
5 Lynne Marks, *Revivals and Roller Rinks: Religion, Leisure, and Identity in Late-Nineteenth-Century Small-Town Ontario*
6 Cecilia Morgan, *Public Men and Virtuous Women: The Gendered Languages of Religion and Politics in Upper Canada, 1791–1850*
7 Mary Louise Adams, *The Trouble with Normal: Postwar Youth and the Making of Heterosexuality*
8 Linda Kealey, *Enlisting Women for the Cause: Women, Labour, and the Left in Canada, 1890–1920*
9 Christina Burr, *Spreading the Light: Work and Labour Reform in Late-Nineteenth-Century Toronto*
10 Mona Gleason, *Normalizing the Ideal: Psychology, Schooling, and the Family in Postwar Canada*
11 Deborah Gorham, *Vera Brittain: A Feminist Life*
12 Marlene Epp, *Women without Men: Mennonite Refugees of the Second World War*
13 Shirley Tillotson, *The Public at Play: Gender and the Politics of Recreation in Postwar Ontario*
14 Veronica Strong-Boag and Carole Gerson, *Paddling Her Own Canoe: The Times and Texts of E. Pauline Johnson (Tekahionwake)*

15 Stephen Heathorn, *For Home, Country, and Race: Constructing Gender, Class, and Englishness in the Elementary School, 1880–1914*
16 Valerie J. Korinek, *Roughing It in the Suburbs: Reading* Chatelaine *Magazine in the Fifties and Sixties*
17 Adele Perry, *On the Edge of Empire: Gender, Race, and the Making of British Columbia, 1849–1871*
18 Robert A. Campbell, *Sit Down and Drink Your Beer: Regulating Vancouver's Beer Parlours, 1925–1954*
19 Wendy Mitchinson, *Giving Birth in Canada, 1900–1950*
20 Roberta Hamilton, *Setting the Agenda: Jean Royce and the Shaping of Queen's University*
21 Donna Gabaccia and Franca Iacovetta, eds, *Women, Gender, and Transnational Lives: Italian Workers of the World*
22 Linda Reeder, *Widows in White: Migration and the Transformation of Rural Women, Sicily, 1880–1920*
23 Terry Crowley, *Marriage of Minds: Isabel and Oscar Skelton Reinventing Canada*
24 Marlene Epp, Franca Iacovetta, and Frances Swyripa, eds, *Sisters or Strangers? Immigrant, Ethnic, and Racialized Women in Canadian History*
25 John G. Reid, *Viola Florence Barnes, 1885–1979: A Historian's Biography*
26 Catherine Carstairs, *Jailed for Possession: Illegal Drug Use, Regulation, and Power in Canada, 1920–1961*
27 Magda Fahrni, *Household Politics: Montreal Families and Postwar Reconstruction*
28 Tamara Myers, *Caught: Montreal's Modern Girls and the Law, 1869–1945*
29 Jennifer A. Stephen, *Pick One Intelligent Girl: Employability, Domesticity, and the Gendering of Canada's Welfare State, 1939–1947*
30 Lisa Chilton, *Agents of Empire: British Female Migration to Canada and Australia, 1860–1930*
31 Esyllt W. Jones, *Influenza 1918: Disease, Death, and Struggle in Winnipeg*
32 Elise Chenier, *Strangers in Our Midst: Sexual Deviancy in Postwar Ontario*
33 Lara Campbell, *Respectable Citizens: Gender, Family, and Unemployment in Ontario's Great Depression*
34 Katrina Srigley, *Breadwinning Daughters: Young Working Women in a Depression-Era City, 1929–1939*
35 Maureen Moynagh with Nancy Forestell, eds, *Documenting First Wave Feminisms, Volume I: Transnational Collaborations and Crosscurrents*

36 Mona Oikawa, *Cartographies of Violence: Japanese Canadian Women, Memory, and the Subjects of the Internment*
37 Karen Flynn, *Moving beyond Borders: A History of Black Canadian and Caribbean Women in the Diaspora*
38 Karen Balcom, *The Traffic in Babies: Cross-Border Adoption and Baby-Selling between the United States and Canada, 1930–1972*
39 Nancy M. Forestell with Maureen Moynagh, eds, *Documenting First Wave Feminisms, Volume II: Canada – National and Transnational Contexts*
40 Patrizia Gentile and Jane Nicholas, eds, *Contesting Bodies and Nation in Canadian History*
41 Suzanne Morton, *Wisdom, Justice, and Charity: Canadian Social Welfare through the Life of Jane B. Wisdom, 1884–1975*
42 Jane Nicholas, *The Modern Girl: Feminine Modernities, the Body, and Commodities in the 1920s*
43 Pauline A. Phipps, *Constance Maynard's Passions: Religion, Sexuality, and an English Educational Pioneer, 1849–1935*
44 Marlene Epp and Franca Iacovetta, eds, *Sisters or Strangers? Immigrant, Ethnic, and Racialized Women in Canadian History*, Second Edition
45 Rhonda L. Hinther, *Perogies and Politics: Canada's Ukrainian Left, 1891–1991*
46 Valerie J. Korinek, *Prairie Fairies: A History of Queer Communities and People in Western Canada, 1930–1985*
47 Julie Guard, *Radical Housewives: Price Wars and Food Politics in Mid-Twentieth-Century Canada*
48 Nancy Janovicek and Carmen Nielson, *Reading Canadian Women's and Gender History*
49 L.K. Bertram, *The Viking Immigrants: Icelandic North Americans*

www.ingramcontent.com/pod-product-compliance
Lightning Source LLC
Chambersburg PA
CBHW030312080526
44584CB00012B/534